Education and the Law
A Dictionary

CONTEMPORARY LEGAL ISSUES

Education and the Law
A Dictionary

Bonnie B. Taylor

ABC-CLIO
Santa Barbara, California
Denver, Colorado
Oxford, England

Library of Congress Cataloging-in-Publication Data

Taylor, Bonnie B., 1967–
Education and the law : a dictionary / Bonnie B. Taylor
p. cm. — (Contemporary legal issues)
Includes bibliographical references and index.
1. Educational law and legislation—United States—Dictionaries.
I. Title. II. Series
KF 4117.T39 1996 344.73'07'03—dc21 96-45171

ISBN 0-87436-813-0(alk. paper)

02 01 00 99 98 97 96 10 9 8 7 6 5 4 3 2 1 (cloth)

ABC-CLIO, Inc.
130 Cremona Drive, P.O. Box 1911
Santa Barbara, California 93116-1911

This book is printed on acid-free paper ∞.
Manufactured in the United States of America

For Fred, Michael, and Annabelle

Contents

Preface

My first experience with the relationship between education and the law was not an especially positive one. At the age of six, I decided that school was not for me. When I told my parents of my decision, they replied, "Tough. The law says that you must go to school until you are 16." Every day for several weeks, they hauled me, kicking and screaming, to my classroom until finally I gave up and went in willingly. And thus I received my initiation to the concept of "compulsory education."

During the rest of my years of public education, I (like most other students, I imagine) was unaware of the many ways in which the U.S. educational system involves the legal system. Not until I took a law school seminar on education law did I realize that there was more to it than a stone tablet etched with the commandment: "Thou shalt go to school."

Education law is about much more than compulsory education. It is also about the constitutional rights of students and teachers and how those rights—such as freedom of speech and religion—fit into the school environment. It also concerns the rights of parents to control what their children learn and where—whether in a public school, private school, or even a home school—they learn it.

The purpose of this book is to shed some light on these issues and many others. While the book is intended for laypeople in general, I hope that the subject matter will be of particular interest to U.S. students and their teachers, since the book is largely about them in the first place.

The book opens with an introductory chapter in which I have provided an overview of the history and sources of education law. The rest of the text is an encyclopedia of issues and ideas that are currently affecting education law. These entries are arranged alphabetically by key word; words that appear in bold face direct the reader to related sections that provide more information. Readers may access desired information either by going directly to the pertinent key words or by using the index in the back.

This book is intended to be a starting point for people interested in learning something about the face of education law today. It is not an exhaustive account of the topic, and some issues are not discussed at all. For readers who wish to learn more, I have provided a table of cases and a list of additional sources. In addition, a number of sections in the book cover organizations whose work is related in some respect to education law and that approach the topic from a wide variety of perspectives, from the far left to the far right. For readers who wish to contact any of these organizations to learn more about their work, I have included mailing addresses, as well as Internet addresses where applicable.

This book is the result of patience on the part of many people. I would like to thank my editor, Mr. Henry Rasof, for his unwavering support and frequent pep talks. I would also like to thank my husband, Fred Taylor, for being my sounding board, and my children, Michael and Annabelle, who—I'm sure—have wondered what their mother has been doing in the basement for the past two years. Finally, I would like to thank my parents, Mike and Jean Boyd, for dragging me to school those first few weeks and for seeing me through 17 more years of education.

Education and the Law

Who should go to school? What should students learn? Who should run the schools and do the teaching?

At first glance, these basic questions appear to be more closely related to the theories of education than to theories of law. They become legal issues, however, when society attempts to answer them and enforce these answers by means of legislation and judicial opinions.

Take the first question, for example. Philosophers may hold differing opinions on how educational resources should be allocated. Some may believe that limited resources should be reserved for the most capable students. Others may favor full inclusion of disabled students regardless of the financial cost to the system or the educational costs to other students. Still others fall somewhere between these two extremes.

Before the 1970s, each school system decided—or ignored—the issue of education for the disabled on its own. In 1972, however, two federal district courts were appalled at the number of disabled children in Pennsylvania and Washington, D.C., who were languishing without public education services. The courts ordered the boards of education in Pennsylvania and the District of Columbia to establish procedures to protect the rights of these children to education in spite of the financial burden involved. [*P.A.R.C. v. Commonwealth of Pennsylvania,* 334 F. Supp. 1257 (E.D. Pa. 1971) and *Mills v. Board of Education of the District of Columbia,* 318 F. Supp. 866 (D.D.C. 1972)] Three years later, Congress adopted many of these procedural safeguards in the Education for All Handicapped Children Act (later renamed the Individuals with Disabilities Education Act), which applies to all the nation's school systems and disabled children.

Most legislation (at both the state and federal levels) involving education deals with the operation of public schools. Education law is not restricted to the public arena, however. Some states have laws that affect the operation of both public and private schools. The state of Michigan, for example, has a law requiring all students, regardless of whether they attend public or private schools or even if they are educated in their homes, to be taught by a state-certified teacher. Other state laws are directed at only private or home schools. For example, while all states now allow the practice of home schooling, many have specific laws addressing the issue in order to guarantee some standard of educational quality.

Education law is about much more than just the nuts-and-bolts operation of schools. It also pertains to the civil liability faced by schools in their operation. Suppose, for example, that a student is run over by a car while waiting for her school bus and that her parents sue the school district. Under what conditions would the school district be responsible? Such issues also come under the umbrella of education law.

Or suppose that students in a public high school decide to wear black armbands to school in silent protest against a war. The administration gets wind of the plan and tells the students to forget it or face punishment, but some of the students carry out the plan and are suspended. This actually happened in an Iowa school in 1965, and the suspended students pursued their case against the school district all the way to the U.S. Supreme Court, which held in favor of the students and declared that students do not "shed their constitutional rights to freedom of speech or expression at the schoolhouse gate."

This case, *Tinker v. Des Moines Independent School District* [393 U.S. 503 (1969)], was not an isolated example of students and the state fighting over their rights on the playing field of the legal system. Indeed, education law cases abound that deal with a balancing of the rights of students, teachers, parents, and the state.

The field of education law is not one finite set of rules, laws, and court cases. Instead, legal directives concerning the administration of schools, cases involving school liability for actions or inactions, and dramatic battles over constitutional issues, as well as other miscellaneous topics that creep in over time, comprise the body of knowledge known collectively as "education law."

THE SOURCES OF EDUCATION LAW

Faced with the question of where education law comes from, many people think first of the laws that are passed by federal and state legislatures. These laws are usually called statutes or acts, and they are compiled into codes.

Constitutions, which provide a framework for how a government is to be run, are also sources of education law, since they set out, either explicitly or implicitly, the role the government should play in the area of education.

FEDERAL CONSTITUTION AND STATUTES

It is interesting to note that education is not mentioned in the U.S. Constitution. Since the Constitution does not specifically give the federal government control over education, it is an issue that is reserved for the states to control. Even so, Congress still finds a number of justifications within the Constitution for adding education-related laws to the U.S. Code.

For example, the Constitution grants to the federal government the power to tax and spend in order to provide for the general welfare of the nation. Since a strong educational system serves the interests of the nation's well-being, Congress has used this power to pass laws that financially support a variety of causes, including ones covering the provision of subsidized meals to poor students and the increase in the number of computers and other technological resources in rural schools.

Another constitutional power that Congress has used to justify passage of at least one school-related law is the power granted by the commerce clause to regulate commerce between the states. Congress passed the Gun-Free School Zones Act in 1990, which made it a federal offense to carry a gun onto school property. When a high school student charged under the act challenged its validity, the case ultimately reached the Supreme Court. The gist of the government's argument in support of the law was that guns in school threaten a healthy learning environment, which in turn leads to poorly educated citizens, which in turn leads to a less productive work force, which in turn is bad for the nation's economy. The Court rejected this argument and held the law to be an unconstitutional exercise of federal power in *United States v. Lopez*. [115 S. Ct. 1624 (1995)] This case promises to have an impact far beyond the field of education law, since Congress has frequently used similar reasoning in the past 50 years to pass other laws impacting areas traditionally considered to be state matters.

Congress often uses money to give teeth to the laws it passes concerning education. In some cases, Congress will offer additional money to states that agree to abide by a particular act. Goals 2000 is an example of one such law. Goals 2000 provides grants of federal money to states that pledge to implement reforms in their educational systems in order to help the entire nation reach eight goals, including a 90 percent graduation rate and complete literacy among U.S. adults.

Another way in which Congress uses money to encourage compliance with new laws is by threatening to cut off all federal educational funds that a school already receives if the school violates the tenets of the new law. For example, under Title IX of the 1972 Education Act Amendments "no person shall, on the basis of sex, be excluded from participation in, be denied the benefits of, be treated differently from another person or otherwise be discriminated against in any interscholastic, intercollegiate, club or intramural athletics offered by a recipient [of federal funds]." If a school violates this requirement, its federal support for all programs may be terminated, even if the discrimination occurred in a program that itself received no federal money.

STATE CONSTITUTIONS AND STATUTES

Unlike the federal government, which must draw its power to influence education from its other powers, states have an absolute right to pass laws governing how their citizens are to be educated. This right is reflected in the constitutions of each individual state, most of which spell out a duty on the part of the state government to provide education. Constitutions vary from state to state as to how much detail is offered regarding education and how much is left for the state's statutes to flesh out.

Besides offering specifics on education, many state constitutions also provide protections that are similar to those found in the U.S. Constitution. While a state may not offer less protection than is guaranteed by the Constitution, it may offer the same—or even more—protection in areas such as freedom of speech and religion, which impact the field of education law, since these are some of the freedoms at issue in the area of student and teacher rights.

State statutes spell out the details covering a host of education topics, such as how public schools are to be financed, what topics (like creationism and evolution) shall or shall not be addressed, and how long the school year and day are to be. It is important to remember that the statutes of any particular state apply only to students and schools within that state and not to those of other states.

Each state, either through its constitution or its statutes, provides for a state department of education, which acts as a clearinghouse of education-related information; a state school officer, usually known as the superintendent or commissioner; and a state board of education. The state boards usually have the power to issue policies and regulations to help in the implementation of state legislation.

LOCAL REGULATION

In every state except Hawaii, an additional level of governance over education exists at the local level. These states have local school boards that administer the day-to-day operation of the schools. In most states, board members are elected by the local citizens of the school district.

The amount of control delegated to the school boards by the state legislatures varies from one state to another. Some states have very structured educational codes, which do not leave the local boards much room to maneuver. Others delegate a great deal of authority to the local level. In either case, a local board works within the framework of laws passed by the state legislature and state board of education to issue rules covering how certain issues, such as student attendance and discipline, are to be handled within the schools of its district. Some local boards delegate a certain amount of authority down to the school level and allow schools to make some decisions for themselves.

CASE LAW

State and federal codes are not the only source of education law. Principles governing education issues also come from the decisions of courts in the many school-related cases heard each year. Under the doctrine of *stare decisis,* a court generally—but not always—follows the decisions already made in similar cases. As a result, these decisions become precedent and are enforced in later cases. It is important to note, however, that a court may go against precedent that it decides is no longer valid. Perhaps the most striking example of this in the field of education law is the decision by the Supreme Court in the 1954 case *Brown v. Board of Education of Topeka* [347 U.S. 483 (1954)] that "separate but equal" schools for blacks and whites were not constitutional. This decision went directly against precedent that had stood for many years.

The U.S. judicial system is actually composed of a federal system as well as the systems of each individual state. Each system, in turn, is made up of different levels of courts. At the first level, there are the trial courts. In the federal system, these courts are called district courts; in the state systems, these courts have a variety of names, such as district courts and circuit courts.

The trial court is where most of the action one associates with Perry Mason and other television lawyers happens. In a typical case, a plaintiff files a lawsuit against a defendant, and the two parties (and sometimes more, since there can be multiple plaintiffs and defendants) go to a trial court, where the plaintiff attempts to prove to a judge or jury that he or she is in the right. (This type of case is a civil case. Trial courts also hear criminal cases, in which the government brings a defendant into court and attempts to prove that he or she committed a crime. Except for the occasional prosecution of a student in which an issue arises over the admissibility of evidence found during a search at school, criminal cases are not much of a presence in education law.) Each side is allowed to present witnesses and evidence to support his or her argument as well as to dispute the witnesses and evidence presented by the other side. It is important to note that in education-related cases, courts are not inclined to substitute their judgment for that of educators on issues that are properly decided by educators. Therefore, a student who believes that his or her project should have won first prize in the school district's science fair is unlikely to find satisfaction in a courtroom.

In many disputes between individuals and schools, the individual must exhaust any administrative avenues for solving the problem before he or she can resort to the judicial system. For example, some states require that the dispute first be heard before the state superintendent or commissioner. Many disputes are settled at the administrative level, which cuts down on the court system's burden.

Once a plaintiff has decided to pursue a claim through the courts, he or she cannot simply decide whether to go through the state system or the federal system. Only cases that meet certain qualifications may be brought in a federal district court. An education case may go to federal court if it meets certain jurisdictional requirements, such as parties who are citizens of different states. Other cases make it to federal court if they deal with a federal question, such as a violation of a federal statute or the U.S. Constitution.

Once the trial court has rendered its decision in a case, the losing party may choose to appeal the decision to a higher, appellate court. If the case began in a state system, it stays in that system and goes on to the mid-level appellate courts. If the case began in federal district court, it goes on to the appropriate circuit court of appeal.

These appellate courts will not reconsider issues of fact; instead they are concerned only with the question of whether the law was properly applied at the lower level. At the appellate level, the parties submit briefs in which they outline their cases and why they believe that the lower court did or did not correctly apply the law to the facts of the case. At the hearing, which is called an oral argument, each side sends an attorney (or attorneys) who appears for a set period of time before a panel of judges that then makes a decision.

Once the mid-level appellate court has given its opinion, the dissatisfied party may attempt to take his or her case to the highest appellate court. In the federal system, the highest court is the U.S. Supreme Court. Many state systems also call their highest courts supreme courts (except for New York, where supreme courts are actually trial courts).

If a party to a case that has gone through a state judicial system all the way to the state's highest court is not happy with that court's ruling, he or she can attempt (along with those in the federal system who have not found satisfaction at the circuit-court level) to be heard by the U.S. Supreme Court. The Supreme Court, however, is a very selective body. Of the many petitions it receives each year, it hears only a handful and refuses to consider the rest. A refusal by the Court to take a case is not a comment on its merits—it is simply a decision made necessary by the limits of time. When the Supreme Court agrees to hear a case, the parties file briefs, as they did at the lower appellate level. Oral arguments, however, are strictly limited to 30 minutes for each side regardless of the importance of the case.

While Georgia courts may disagree with Florida courts on a particular issue and the First Circuit may settle a dispute contrary to the way in which the Tenth Circuit would handle it, once an issue has been decided by the Supreme Court, that holding becomes the law of the land. As a result, when a school-related case is accepted for review by the Supreme Court, the decision sets off waves of excitement within the U.S. education community. The Court's holding means that yet another aspect of education law has been settled for the entire nation.

HISTORICAL DEVELOPMENT OF EDUCATION LAW

Today, when people think about the reasons behind education—either for themselves or for their children—they generally see education as a means of improving life for the individual. We implore teenagers to stay in school in the hopes that with more education, they will be able to secure better jobs and find greater personal fulfillment. When viewing education from a historical perspective, however, one quickly sees that the complex U.S. educational system grew out of a desire to improve and protect the nation rather than each individual citizen. The field of education law as set out in the previously discussed sources initially developed as a means of ensuring this protection of society through education of the individual.

Beginning in 1642, the colony of Massachusetts required that all children be taught a trade and how to read. Initially, children were taught in their homes, in their churches, and through apprenticeship programs. Later, some children began attending dame schools, which were offered in private homes, and eventually towns began building local schools. Massachusetts passed a law in 1647 requiring towns with 50 or more households to hire a teacher of reading and writing; towns with 100 or more households were also required to provide Latin grammar schools, which prepared students for education at the university level. Much of this early schooling was religiously motivated, the premise being that citizens who could read the Bible were less likely to fall into the grasp of Satan. In fact, the 1647 Massachusetts law became popularly known as the "Old Deluder Satan Law."

Following the American Revolution, the nation faced the issue of how to make the former colonists into a new nation of citizens having one national identity. A common view at the time was that education should play a meaningful role in establishing this national identity and transmitting it to the new citizens.

Despite the nature of education as a state—rather than federal—issue, Congress left its first clear marks on public education with the passage of the Land Ordinance Act of 1785 and the Northwest Ordinance Act of 1787. These acts dealt with the territories between the Ohio and Mississippi rivers.

The 1785 act required that the land be divided into townships measuring six miles on each side. The townships were to be further divided into 36 sections of one square mile each, and the 16th section of each township was to be used for the support of public schools. Rather than mandating that a school be built on the 16th lot, Congress instead gave the money raised by the sale or lease of this land to the township to use for educational purposes. Unfortunately, a great deal of the money from the land grants was lost due to speculation and mismanagement. As a response to this local mismanagement, the federal government began giving control over the land-grant money to the states instead of the townships, beginning with Michigan in 1835 and including all states admitted after 1858.

The 1787 act contained language that is often quoted to show the federal government's view of education at that time: "Religion, morality, and knowledge being necessary to good government and the happiness of mankind, schools and the means of education shall forever be encouraged." Together, these two congressional acts demonstrate federal commitment to building the nation through education of its citizens. This commitment was echoed by the states: half of the first 14 states made specific mention of education in their constitutions. Later, Congress required that Montana, North Dakota, South Dakota, and Washington establish systems of free, nonsectarian (or nonreligious) public schools as a prerequisite for statehood.

In the early nineteenth century, a movement developed in favor of establishing free schools that were open to all. These common schools were the forerunners of today's elementary schools. The idea behind them was that the children of newly arrived immigrants should be "Americanized."

During this same time, the line between private and public education became clearer. Many states began to prohibit—at least in theory—the spending of public funds in sectarian schools and the teaching of religious topics in the public schools due to the constitutional separation of church and state. In practice, however, what was viewed as nonsectarian by the Protestant majority was in fact generic Protestantism.

The reading of the King James Bible and the singing of Protestant hymns in the public schools were common practices, which offended the many Catholic immigrants who arrived in the 1830s and 1840s. The Catholics responded by establishing private church schools. Many Protestants already held prejudices against the Catholics due to the jobs lost to the new immigrants and to suspicions that the Catholics' loyalty to the pope would outweigh their loyalty to their new homeland. As a result, these new Catholic schools were viewed with mistrust by many, who worried that they would instill "antidemocratic values" in their students. Protesters sometimes went so far as to damage—even burn—the Catholic schools.

Besides this type of harassment, Catholic parents then shared a concern with today's parents of private school students. Since the Catholic parents were supporting the public education system through their tax dollars and were paying tuition to their church schools as well, they were in effect paying twice to educate their children. New York briefly subsidized Catholic schools in the 1870s but then stopped, citing the separation of church and state.

During the second half of the nineteenth century, attendance was high in the nation's private and public education institutions, although states that had compulsory attendance laws seldom enforced them. Starting at the turn of the century and continuing into the 1930s, however, enforcement of these laws became a priority. This was partially in response to the vast number of immigrants who arrived from 1876 to 1926. During those 50 years, the nation's population grew by 60 percent, which meant there were vast numbers of foreigners to be Americanized and assimilated. Again, the schools were perceived as the best means of reaching this end. Some states took this idea to extremes.

In 1919, the state of Nebraska passed a law prohibiting the teaching of school subjects in any language other than English and forbidding the teaching of other languages to students before the eighth grade. Over half the states had such laws, inspired in part by anti-immigration sentiment and in part by patriotic fervor following World War I. At that time, it was common for even some public schools to teach in the first language of the local population, which frequently was not English. The Supreme Court overturned such English-only laws in *Meyer v. Nebraska* [262 U.S. 390 (1923)] as an impermissible burden on the rights of parents to educate their children as they see fit within certain boundaries.

Similar anti-immigrant feelings inspired the Ku Klux Klan in 1922 to lead a movement in Oregon to require children between the ages of 8 and 16 not just to attend school, but to attend a *public* school. This crusade was prompted by the fear that education of students in diverse private schools—which were presumed to teach dangerous, antidemocratic ideals—would lead to the destruction of U.S. society and government through the destruction of America's public schools. The measure passed, but was promptly challenged in court by operators of Catholic schools and a private military academy. The controversy ultimately reached the Supreme Court, which held in *Pierce v. Society of Sisters* [268 U.S. 510 (1925)] that the law unconstitutionally infringed on the rights of parents to direct their children's education and on the rights of private schools to conduct business.

Nationalism was not the only value solidified in the educational system by means of the legal system. At various times throughout history other special-interest groups have been given state blessing for promotion of their agendas in U.S. schools. Toward the end of the nineteenth century, for example, the Women's Christian Temperance Union, which condemned the consumption of alcohol, conducted a vigorous campaign that eventually lead many states to pass laws promoting the temperance movement through the schools. By 1895, all states had made scientific temperance a mandatory part of the curriculum; some states went so far as to require that 25 percent of physiology textbooks be devoted to the issue of temperance.

While even nonsectarian schools had often included practices such as Bible reading in their daily activities during the 1800s, only the state of Massachusetts required it. During the 1900s, however, many states that had relied on voluntary action to transmit religious values to their students began instilling religion in their schools by passage of new laws. Such laws often mandated Bible reading, prayers, and the posting of the Ten Commandments and prohibited the teaching of Darwin's theory of evolution, which contradicts the biblical account of creation.

During the nineteenth century, very few disputes surrounding education made it into the court system. Part of this was due to the expense of going to court. Many dissenters simply left the public school system for private schools; those who stayed often settled their disputes through local and state administrative channels. There were two other important reasons for a lack of education cases before the early 1900s: (1) Many unpopular laws were simply ignored rather than enforced; and (2) the public schools were a source of such intense nationalistic pride and support that those who disagreed with the schools' administration had little chance of finding satisfaction in the local courts.

Near the beginning of the twentieth century, however, states began actually enforcing their education laws and began passing others that, like those at issue in *Pierce* and *Meyer*, offended a number of people. Cases such as these represented a major milestone in education law, since they were some of the earliest examples of judicial recognition that the states' right to control education was not absolute. In the years that followed, the number of cases in which individuals alleged denial of their constitutional rights by the state schools and won in court increased dramatically.

Gradually, the U.S. Supreme Court, whose opinions carry the force of law in every state, began holding in favor of those oppressed by state education. It decreed the practice of providing separate but equal schools for whites and blacks to be unconstitutional and ordered the states to integrate their public schools. It held that ordering the children of Jehovah's Witnesses to take part in a flag salute violated their rights to freedom of religion. It maintained that students could exercise their right to freedom of speech on public school campuses, subject to certain limitations. It found that a state could not deny the children of illegal immigrants access to a free, public education. This is not to say that anyone who challenged a school district in court automatically won, but the strides made in favor of individual rights were enormous.

During this period of time, Congress also got into the business of protecting the rights of individuals within the public schools. It mandated that disabled children, who were almost completely ignored by the schools until the 1970s, be afforded the same educational opportunities available to other children as well as the services they required in order to benefit from these opportunities. It directed that religious and political clubs be given the same access to school facilities as other clubs. It declared that schools that discriminated against students on the basis of sex could lose their federal financial support. This interplay between the rights of students and their parents and the rights of the states in controlling public education has continued as one of the biggest legal issues facing education today.

ISSUES FOR TODAY AND TOMORROW

Many of the controversies in the field of education law today deal with rights: the rights of students, the rights of their parents, the rights of teachers, and the rights of the state. A court that faces a case involving competing rights must perform a precarious balancing act.

These cases sometimes arise when a state attempts to deal with a new social crisis through education and people disagree with the chosen solution. For example, not so very long ago violent gangs were virtually unheard of in most schools. Today, however, they are a very real and very dangerous presence in many schools. In an attempt to address this danger, a number of school districts have implemented policies prohibiting the wearing of gang-related clothing and accessories, such as baseball caps. Some districts have even grappled with the idea of requiring school uniforms for public school students. One could argue that the government has a legitimate interest in ensuring the safety of its schools. On the other hand, students may argue that such measures abridge their rights to freedom of expression.

Another new social crisis that has required attention by schools is the spread of acquired immune deficiency syndrome (AIDS). Early reaction to students infected with the human immunodeficiency virus (HIV), which causes AIDS, was often one of sheer panic. Infected students were sometimes banned from school. Under section 504 of the Rehabilitation Act, however, people infected with HIV qualify as disabled and may not be excluded from public education based on their disabilities. As a result, school districts have been forced to develop policies for dealing with infected students and staff that protect the rights of those who carry the virus as well as the safety of those around them.

In recent years, religion in the public schools has been a source of contention. Following the movement during the first half of the twentieth century to reinstate religion in the classroom, the trend since the 1960s has been on the side of strict separation of church and state. Some would argue that this separation has gone too far and that, in an effort to be as nonjudgmental as possible when it comes to differing value systems, schools are producing students who are taught no values. One interesting argument that has been offered by Christian fundamentalists on the side of religious involvement is that the "nonreligion" currently in place is actually secular humanism, which, they argue, is indeed a religion, and that its very presence in the curriculum is a violation of church and state separation.

Perhaps the biggest issue currently under review in the field of education law is the alleged crisis within education itself. Public schools are generally perceived as being mediocre at best. In 1983, a commission created by the secretary of education released a study of U.S. schools entitled *A Nation at Risk.* The report stated, "If an unfriendly foreign power had attempted to impose on America the mediocre educational performance that exists today, we might well have viewed it as an act of war." Some of the indications the study offered to show that something has gone awry in U.S. education included low test scores compared with other industrialized nations, a startling number of functionally illiterate adults and teenagers, and 20 years' worth of declining scores on the Scholastic Aptitude Test.

When President Ronald Reagan received the report, he urged the states to assume responsibility for improving their educational systems. Many states responded during the 1980s by raising graduation requirements, requiring teacher-competency testing, and increasing the time students actually spent in school each year. When George Bush became president in 1988, he proposed a number of reforms, including Goals 2000, which was eventually passed by Congress and signed by President Bill Clinton in 1994.

The Goals 2000 program is designed to encourage states to initiate their own reform programs in order to meet certain federal goals, such as raising U.S. high school graduation rates and making schools safer. States that sign up to participate in the plan are given federal funds to help in the implementation of their reforms.

Whether participating or not in Goals 2000, states have been very concerned with education reform in recent years. Some states are experimenting with new answers to the question of who should control the schools. Some states allow charter schools, which receive money from the state but are not required to adhere to the many administrative requirements that control regular public schools. Some school districts have turned over control of their schools to private, for-profit companies that claim they can produce positive results by running the schools like businesses. Critics of these reform movements argue that turning over education funds in these ways provides too many opportunities for misuse of public money, while supporters contend that the state and local governments have not shown that they are up to the job of effectively managing the money themselves.

One reform initiative that has proved popular among educators is the idea of site- or school-based management. In schools operating under such a system, the power has been delegated to the administrators and teachers at each school to determine the policies covering its day-to-day operations. The theory here is that control should be vested at the lowest level possible, since the people who work at this level know their own weaknesses and are therefore in the best position to adopt policies addressing these weaknesses. Whatever the details, these reforms show the general tendency to localize control to the greatest possible extent.

At the same time that interest in local autonomy is growing, many educators are becoming increasingly aware of the need for some sort of standardization within school curriculums. The United States has a mobile society in which a move from one state to another is not unusual. Moving can have a negative impact on a child's education, however, when he or she goes from a math class that is just beginning to learn division into one that is just finishing division. Children of military personnel are especially vulnerable to the risk of winding up in their senior year of high school in a state with graduation standards that are significantly higher than those of the state from which they moved. Debate about this issue centers on whether standardization is something that should be achieved through voluntary consensus, if at all, or whether it should come about through use of the legal system and, if so, who should be in charge of legislating what will be taught.

Many of the issues receiving attention today will continue to affect the area of education law for years to come. Few would argue that the increased recognition of the rights of individuals has been a positive change. Most would agree that students should not be treated differently based on their racial differences, that states should attempt to educate disabled students in an effective manner, and that students should be free to express themselves without incurring the wrath of the state in the form of public school administrators. Some educators, however, are concerned that this broadening of individual rights has lead to a generation dominated by unruly students who feel that they are the ones in control of the schools. These educators are waiting for a backlash. Many teachers argue that the rights of the many to a safe, effective education are violated when the rights of the individual are overzealously guarded.

Teachers sometimes feel frustrated by a lack of support on the part of litigation-shy administrators when it comes to dealing with students and their parents. Administrators, in turn, are often confused about exactly how far a student's rights extend. When a student or parent yells "Lawsuit!" the urge to yield is understandable. This is why all the players in the field of education—students, parents, teachers, and administrators—must be aware of their rights and the rights of others.

Suppose, for example, that an English teacher assigns students the task of writing an essay based on a personal experience, and one student chooses to use the assignment as a forum for extolling the virtues of getting high. When the teacher refuses to accept the paper and tells the student that the topic is inappropriate, the student's mother goes to the principal claiming that her child's right to express himself has been unconstitutionally squelched. The principal agrees with the mother and directs the teacher to accept the paper and to grade it on its technical merits.

Such a scenario may sound incredible, but situations like this happen every day in schools across the country. Americans today live in a litigious society, where being sued is never beyond the realm of possibility. While nobody wants to get dragged into court, even if he or she will eventually win, it is important for teachers and administrators to understand the boundaries of students' rights so they will not feel intimidated by students who use their rights as battering rams. In a situation such as the one depicted above, it is important for the teacher and principal to know that courts are loathe to substitute judicial judgment for that of educators in such matters. It is also important for them to realize that when the Supreme Court recognized that even students have a right to free speech, it also held that such a right does not extend to expression that materially disrupts class work or violates the rights of others.

Education assumed its important role in U.S. society as a means of nation building. Over the years, it has also become common to address social ills through the educational system. When children came to school hungry, Congress developed a program to provide them with subsidized meals. When teenagers began getting pregnant in record numbers, schools responded by offering sex education and even birth control. When concern grew that students suffered from low self-esteem, schools and school districts used the power delegated to them by the state governments and implemented new policies designed to validate the students' sense of worth, such as giving "I"s for "Incomplete"—or "In progress" in particularly sensitive schools—instead of the traditional "F" for "Failure." Given this tradition of using the schools to solve problems, it is safe to assume that education law—as derived from statutes, case law, and local regulations—will continue to evolve to address new social problems as they arise.

A

Academic Freedom Freedom of teachers to teach and students to learn without recrimination. This right is more limited in public schools than in colleges, universities, and private schools because of greater regulation of the public school curriculum by state and local school boards.

As a general rule, a teacher may not use his or her position to advocate personal or political viewpoints and may not make immoral statements or commit immoral acts in class. Occasionally, a teacher's outside activities may affect his or her professional fitness. The Supreme Court case *Keyishian v. Board of Regents* [385 U.S. 589 (1967)] centered on state university professors whose jobs were at stake over their refusal to sign statements attesting that they had never been members of the Communist Party. The Court held that although the state of New York did have a legitimate interest in "protecting its education system from subversion," the law requiring these statements was too vague in defining exactly what conduct was forbidden. This vagueness could potentially have a chilling effect on permissible activities as teachers attempted to "steer far wider of the unlawful zone." The Court set out a famous and often quoted idea that "the classroom is peculiarly the marketplace of ideas" and that First Amendment freedoms such as speech and association should be carefully guarded there.

A more recent example of a teacher's outside conduct having bearing on his or her professional suitability occurred in 1994 in Virginia. Controversy erupted in a high school when an extremely effective guidance counselor was sentenced to serve three months in prison for tax fraud. The scandal divided the school community over whether or not the counselor should be retained by the school following his release from jail. Ultimately, the state Board of Education revoked his teaching license, and the counselor was transferred to an administrative position.

Usually, however, academic freedom issues center on conduct within the classroom. One landmark Supreme Court case, ***Meyer v. Nebraska,*** held unconstitutional a 1919 state law forbidding the teaching of modern foreign languages to school children who had not completed the eighth grade.

The teacher in that case had been convicted of giving German-language training to a ten-year-old child. Although it seems strange in a contemporary context to punish someone for teaching German, that was indeed a touchy area in post-World War I America.

Today, many academic freedom issues revolve around the topics of religion (particularly the theories of **creationism and evolution**) and sex. For example, in 1993, a university biology teacher generated a great deal of controversy by teaching that life on earth had been created by an "intelligent designer." The university reassigned the professor to teach classes other than the one in which the issue of creation occurred. The teacher, however, received support from many of his colleagues as well as from the American Association of University Professors, an association concerned with upholding academic freedom. The professor was eventually reinstated to his regular classes.

A California high school biology teacher was not as successful in his 1994 crusade against the school district's requirement that he teach evolution. The teacher claimed that this requirement showed hostility to religion and violated his academic freedom. His case was eventually thrown out because, the federal appellate court said, his religion was not affected by requiring him to teach evolution.

Sex is another sensitive topic in academic freedom. While many states have set out regulations for sex education classes as part of the curriculum, controversies sometimes arise when teachers talk about sex in other classes. For example, a court held in favor of a teacher whose eighth-grade students badgered her into defining homosexuality. [*Brown v. Coffeeville Consol. School Dist.*, 365 F. Supp. 990 (N.D. Miss. 1973)] The court's support of the teacher rested in part on her use of objective language in discussing the subject. On the other hand, a teacher who told stories to his 12th-grade boys' speech class as if he were recalling with relish his own wild days was not ordered rehired. [*State v. Board of School Dirs.*, 111 N.W.2d 198 (Wis. 1961)] Teachers have also fallen into trouble for assignments that contain vulgarity, as in the case of a teacher who was fired for assigning a Kurt Vonnegut book that contained a great deal of sexual slang. Because the court found the book to be comparable to other works of literature that were deemed acceptable for the students and because the school was not disrupted, the court ordered the teacher to be reinstated. [*Parducci v. Rutland*, 316 F. Supp. 352 (M.D. Ala. 1970)] In general, words may be offensive and still protected by academic freedom if they are educationally necessary, such as for understanding a story. Where they are unnecessarily offensive, however, they are not protected.

Sometimes it can be difficult to determine the educational necessity of the teacher's chosen language. For example, a state university professor found himself in deep trouble when seven female students complained about two comments he made in a technical writing class. First, he compared focus in writing to sex: "You seek a target. You zero in on your subject. You move from side to side. You close in on the subject. You bracket the subject and center on it. Focus connects experience and language. You and the subject become one." Later, he gave the following as an example of a simile, which is a figure of speech involving comparison, usually by use of the words "like" or "as": "Belly dancing is like Jell-O on a plate with a vibrator under the plate." The university declared that the professor's language had violated the school's sexual-harassment policy and suspended him from teaching. He sued, and in 1994 a federal district court ordered him reinstated while his claim for damages and back pay went to trial. The court stated that the professor had educational reasons for using the language and that the university had violated his right to free speech. [*Silva v. Univ. of N.H.*, 888 F. Supp. 293 (D.N.H. 1994)]

Academic freedom controversies in primary and secondary schools generally pit the right of teachers to use their discretion in deciding how to teach a subject against the right of parents to exercise some degree of control over what their children see and hear. A California woman, for example, balked when she heard that her seventh-grade son's science teacher planned to dissect a pregnant cat in front of the class, as he did each year. The school board backed the teacher's decision, because the class was always conducted with sensitivity and contributed to the students' understanding of mammalian studies.

Teachers do not always win such conflicts, however. When parents complained about satanic overtones in a fantasy spelling game, a California school district banned the game from its classrooms. A teachers' union sued, claiming the action violated the academic freedom rights of the teachers. The trial judge upheld the ban, however, because it was "reasonably related to legitimate educational concerns."

ACADEMIC SANCTIONS Administrative punishments, such as the reduction of a grade or suspension from extracurricular activities, given instead of other types of discipline, such as **corporal punishment,** suspension, or expulsion [see **suspension and expulsion**], to students who break certain rules. Most courts agree that academic sanctions are a proper response to academic misconduct. Few would argue, for example, that a student who is caught cheating on a test or plagiarizing a term paper is a victim of inappropriate discipline when the student's grade for the test, paper, or class is lowered as a result. Controversy tends to arise, however, when the sanction and the misconduct are unrelated. A New York student who was accused of attacking her school principal, for example, successfully sued after she was punished by being prohibited from taking part in the school's graduation ceremony. The court held that there was no relationship between the student's actions and the school's response.

In recent years, many school districts have adopted **attendance policies** that punish absences from class with grade reductions. A number of courts have upheld such policies, since absenteeism is related to academic performance. In 1984, a Connecticut court found in favor of a school district that was sued by a student whose grades were reduced in three classes due to a number of unexcused absences. [*Campbell v. New Milford Bd. of Educ.*, 475 A.2d 289 (Conn. 1984)] That same year, however, a Pennsylvania court found in favor of a student who had two points deducted for each absence in her classes. [*Katzman v. Cumberland Valley School Dist.*, 479 A.2d 671 (Pa. Commw. Ct. 1988)] The difference was that in the Connecticut case, the absences were a result of the student's decision not to attend school. In the Pennsylvania case, however, the absences were due to a five-day suspension that was administered for violation of the school district's policy against alcohol use by students. Therefore, the court found, the sanction was not related to the actual underlying misbehavior.

Four years later, a Michigan student sued the Board of Education when her grades were all reduced because she failed to attend required study-hall sessions to make up time lost in class due to five excused absences. [*Slocum v. Holton Bd. of Educ.*, 429 N.W.2d 607 (1988)] The student offered arguments against the policy that are commonly given in such challenges: that the policy was an *ultra vires* act (one that is beyond the powers granted to the school district by the state) and that it violated her **due process** rights. The court, however, rejected these arguments.

In considering the *ultra vires* claim, the court found that even though no state statute specifically gave local school boards the power to establish such attendance policies, such power could be inferred from statutes giving school boards extensive powers in deciding how to achieve the goals of the compulsory attendance law. In examining the student's assertion that the board's action took away both a protected property interest and a protected liberty interest, therefore violating her constitutional right to due process, the court held that the reduction of the student's grade did not deprive her of either type of interest. According to the court, a higher grade was not a property interest, since the grade could not be considered earned until after attendance was factored in (as opposed to cases in which a grade is earned by the student and then reduced by the school). Nor did the student's academic reputation constitute a liberty interest, because reputation alone, without injury to employment or some other tangible interest, is not protected under either the state or federal constitutions.

ACCOUNTABILITY Making individual schools directly responsible for their successes and failures by giving them a certain amount of freedom from governmental interference. The concept of accountability developed in the 1980s and gathered steam in the 1990s in response to alarming reports about the overall performance level of U.S. students. The 1983 report *A Nation at Risk* stated, "If an unfriendly foreign power had attempted to impose on America the mediocre educational performance that exists today, we might well have viewed it as an act of war." Five years later, former U.S. Secretary of Education William J. Bennett echoed this view and offered a possible explanation for the shortcomings of the U.S. educational system, saying, "There are greater, more certain, and more immediate penalties in this country for serving up a single rotten hamburger in a restaurant than for repeatedly furnishing a thousand children with a rotten education."

It is slightly misleading, however, to speak of the "U.S. educational system," because education is a function of the local and state, rather than federal, governments. Some state legislatures have recognized that their current systems have shortcomings and have begun to enact laws to pass decision-making powers down to the individual schools in an effort to effect positive change. For example, South Carolina and New Jersey adopted legislation in the 1980s designed to improve student achievement by developing tougher performance standards while at the same time freeing the schools to a greater extent to develop their own methods for achieving this goal. In 1991, the state of Florida passed a similar accountability program entitled "Blueprint 2000."

Some argue that state efforts to pass along the responsibility to the schools for their performances cannot work if the necessary funds (and the freedom to spend them as the schools see fit) are not passed along as well. This has led to a rethinking of certain school finance issues. For example, site-based management, a financing scheme in which districts give money to schools instead of spending it for them, is gaining in popularity.

Even though education is technically a state and local power, the federal government has also entered the fight for school accountability. For example, in 1994 Congress passed **Goals 2000,** a reform package initially introduced by President George Bush. The legislation sets out eight goals for U.S. schools to strive to meet and provides money to states that adopt plans for meeting those goals.

The federal government has also funded a project to ease the path toward accountability by setting out national standards in core subjects that all U.S. students should know. The National Standards for United States History, however, came under fire almost immediately after their unveiling in 1994. Many critics of the project felt that the standards were biased against inclusion of the white male heroes and organizations traditionally included in U.S. history courses in favor of "politically correct" examples, such as Harriett Tubman and the National Organization for Women. The Senate passed a nonbinding resolution in response to the ensuing public outcry that federal money should go to support only programs that "have a decent respect for the contributions of western civilization and United States history, ideas and institutions, to the increase of freedom and prosperity around the world."

ADVERTISING In an effort to make up for budgetary constraints, school districts occasionally raise money by allowing private enterprises to advertise within the schools. This is not necessarily a new concept. For quite a few years, schools have taken part in programs in which students and their families collect items such as grocery store receipts or soup labels, the schools receive supplies such as playground or computer equipment, and the companies receive the advertising benefit. The advertising nature of such programs has gone largely unnoticed.

Recently, however, advertising within the school forum has grown more blatant and harder to ignore. In 1994, a Colorado school district began to allow companies to buy advertising space in school gyms and hallways, on school buses, and even on team jackets. The district hopes eventually to earn $300,000 a year from the campaign, and the initial reaction from parents and students has been favorable.

While the advertising program in Colorado has been generally viewed as a harmless way of raising much-needed money, at least one other program has created storms of controversy nationwide. In the late 1980s and early 1990s, a communications company introduced Channel One, an advertising scheme in which the company would provide equipment such as televisions, VCRs, and even satellite dishes to schools that would, in return, promise to air a daily news program, including two minutes of commercials.

While schools raced to sign up for the program, critics began to speak out against it in the media, as well as in the judicial and legislative systems. Some critics, for example, worry that the commercials aired on Channel One undermine the schools' educational interests by promoting commercialism among the students with the not-so-subtle message that buying a particular expensive stereo or drinking a certain soft drink will enhance one's social status. This argument goes along with the issue of whether requiring students to watch television commercials violates their right to a free public education as guaranteed by state constitutions and laws.

A related legal issue is whether mandatory exposure to the commercials violates the students' First Amendment free speech rights by violating their right to be free from unwanted speech. Compulsory education laws require school-aged children in each state to attend school. The Supreme Court held in 1948 that public schools could not bring clergy members into the classrooms to conduct religious instruction, because separation of church and state would not allow the use of the compulsory education laws of the state to form a captive audience for the promotion of religion. While the Channel One controversy does not implicate issues of religion, a number of critics have attempted to make similar arguments against its presence in the classrooms.

At least one court has recognized a right to be free from unwanted speech, although the facts of the case did not involve a school environment. In 1989, a Nevada court held in favor of parents whose son killed himself after listening to music by the band Judas Priest that contained subliminal messages advocating suicide. [*Vance v. Judas Priest,* 16 Media L. Rptr. 2241 (Nev. Dist. Ct. 1989)] The court based its decision on the idea that "if an individual has the right to receive information and ideas expressed by others with whom he may philosophically, socially, religiously, or politically agree or disagree, he must also have the reciprocal right to refuse to receive such information and ideas." Because a student is not free to leave school or to turn the channel to escape the commercials (most

Channel One contracts stipulate that a certain percentage of the student body must watch the programming each day), such an argument might be successful against programs like Channel One.

Another legal issue that arises in such disputes is what level of government has authority over whether or not the program will be allowed as part of the curriculum. For example, in 1991 the North Carolina State Board of Education sued to stop schools from contracting with Channel One, as prohibited by a board regulation. [*North Carolina v. Whittle Communications*, 402 S.E.2d 556 (N.C. 1991)] The schools argued that this constituted improper interference with local authority. The court held in favor of Channel One, saying that the program was supplemental in nature and that a 1969 law gave local school boards the power to select "supplementary instructional materials." While this case was pending, the North Carolina General Assembly passed another law expressly giving local school boards "sole authority to select and procure supplementary instructional materials, whether or not the materials contain commercial advertising."

AFFIRMATIVE ACTION Programs intended to rectify past discrimination through the hiring and promotion of blacks, women, and other minorities. The ***Brown v. Board of Education of Topeka*** Supreme Court decisions of the mid-1950s, which mandated **desegregation** of the nation's public schools, did not address the issue of faculty desegregation. Courts soon began demanding an end to racial segregation among teachers, but resistance to putting black teachers into formerly white schools was strong. The Court held in 1965 that black students could challenge segregative faculty assignments [*Rogers v. Paul*, 382 U.S. 198 (1965)], and in 1968 it upheld the order of a lower court that required a school board to reassign teachers so the racial makeup of the faculty of each school reflected the racial composition of the faculty in the whole system. [*Green v. County Sch. Bd.*, 391 U.S. 430 (1968)]

Based on this indication from the Supreme Court that faculty segregation must cease, lower courts began to grapple with the issue of how to accomplish this task. Some courts adopted quotas for hiring, which required a certain number of jobs to be set aside for minority applicants. Other courts approved such measures as race-based layoffs of white employees to maintain racial proportions. Such measures inevitably led to claims of reverse discrimination by majority applicants and employees who were denied jobs in order to remedy past discriminatory employment practices, but the Supreme Court has held that remedying specific acts of past discrimination is a "compelling government interest" that justifies race-based affirmative action programs and policies. [*Wygant v. Jackson Bd. of Educ.*, 476 U.S. 267 (1986)]

The issue of when affirmative action is permissible becomes murkier when it is applied in a setting in which there have been no allegations of prior discriminatory employment practices. For example, a New Jersey school board adopted an affirmative action program in the mid-1970s in response to a directive from the state Board of Education requiring each school board to develop such a plan. No charges of racial discrimination had ever been leveled at the local board and, in fact, the percentage of minorities it employed was higher than the percentage of minorities in the population at large that was qualified for teaching positions. Nevertheless, the plan called for the hiring of the most qualified job candidates when one was clearly better qualified but the hiring of a minority candidate when qualifications appeared to be equal.

In 1989, the board decided to eliminate one member of its high school business staff and had to choose between two similarly qualified teachers, Sharon Taxman and Debra Williams. Both had been hired on the same day 14 years earlier and both had received tenure at the same time. Normally, the board would have solved such a problem by drawing lots and laying off the unlucky teacher. In this case, however, the board decided to lay off Taxman and retain Williams for the simple reason that Taxman was white and Williams was black. The purpose of the decision was not to remedy past instances of discrimination but rather to promote racial diversity.

Taxman and the Justice Department filed suit in federal court for lost wages, alleging that the school board's actions violated her civil rights. The court held in favor of Taxman and awarded her a $144,000 judgment based on the board's reasoning in choosing to lay her off solely on the basis of her race. [*United States v. Board of Educ.*, 832 F. Supp. 836 (D.N.J. 1993)] The board appealed the decision, and in an interesting twist, the Justice Department, which had supported Taxman under President George Bush, switched sides in favor of the board as part of President Bill Clinton's commitment to expansion of affirmative action programs.

Controversies over affirmative action have not been limited to employment situations; they also appear in the issue of whether or not public universities should use race as a factor in deciding which students to accept. In the 1960s, the Medical School of the University of California at Davis instituted a special admissions program for minority students who did not qualify for admission through the regular program. Under the special program, the university set aside 16 of 100 slots for minority students; therefore, a minority applicant could potentially be admitted to fill one of the 84 regular slots or one of the 16 reserved slots, while white applicants had to compete for the 84 regular slots. A white applicant who had been rejected sued, alleging violation of his civil rights. In *Regents of the University of California v. Bakke* [438 U.S. 265 (1978)], the Supreme Court held against the use of quota systems like the one at Davis. On the other hand, the Court said that admission programs could certainly consider race as a factor but not as the *only* factor. For nearly 20 years, the University of California abided by this decision and considered race as one of a number of factors in its admission policy. Then, in 1995, the Board of Regents voted to end consideration of race as a factor in both hiring and admissions. The decision provoked a firestorm of debate, and the university decided to postpone implementing the change in its admission policy until 1998.

One year after the controversial decision by the University of California, the attorney general of Georgia instructed its state universities and colleges to stop giving preferential treatment to minorities as part of its admission policies.

AFROCENTRIC CURRICULUM A course of study using the cultures and traditions of Africans and African Americans as its reference point. There is a growing movement in support of replacing the Eurocentric **curriculum,** with its emphasis on the white, male perspective, upon which U.S. schools have historically focused their attention, with an Afrocentric curriculum—especially in inner-city schools that have predominately black populations. At first glance, this appears to be a strictly pedagogical (or teaching-related) issue. It is actually a legal issue, however, since the curriculum of public schools is mandated, to some extent, by state legislatures, state boards of education, and local school boards.

In 1992, the Eurocentric focus came under attack in the court system when a group of plaintiffs sued under various civil rights statutes, claiming that the racial and cultural bias of the New York City public school curriculum psychologically injured black children and diminished their ability to receive an education. The court eventually dismissed the case, because the plaintiffs failed to show discriminatory intent on the part of the defendants.

From a sociological perspective, proponents of replacing Eurocentrism with Afrocentrism argue that it will enhance the self-image of black students and give them a deeper understanding of their cultural heritage. Some schools that have implemented such programs point to improved test scores and attendance rates as proof of their success. Critics of the approach, on the other hand, argue that such programs will serve only to further divide students along racial lines and that they will actually do a disservice to the black students they hope to help by making them less competitive on standardized tests, which are very important in U.S. school systems.

From a legal standpoint, some critics worry that setting up a specific curriculum for African-American children creates the same sort of "separate but equal" conditions established in 1896 in *Plessy v. Ferguson* [163 U.S. 537 (1896)] and discarded nearly 60 years later in ***Brown v. Board of Education of Topeka.*** Also, many critics charge that by exchanging Eurocentrism for Afrocentrism, schools are merely swapping one prejudiced approach for another and that a more balanced, multicultural approach is required to fix any imbalances caused by reliance on the Eurocentric position over the years. Many supporters counter such arguments with the proposition that even though Afrocentrism might be a form of separatism, a curriculum in which the achievements of blacks are exalted will remove the "badge of inferiority" that the *Brown* court found to be the result of racially separate schools. Also, supporters say, forbidding a teacher from using an Afrocentric approach in his or her classes infringes on the principle of **academic freedom,** which protects a teacher's right to teach and a student's right to learn and be exposed to a number of viewpoints. If the prohibition of Afrocentric teachings is motivated by political reasons or a desire to deny students access to ideas that are unpopular, such prohibition also infringes on the free speech rights protected in ***Board of Education, Island Trees Union Free School District v. Pico.***

AGE DISCRIMINATION

Federal law prohibits discriminating against employees between the ages of 40 and 70 on the basis of age. Even so, many courts have found in favor of mandatory retirement ages. The Supreme Court has upheld mandatory retirement ages for police officers and Foreign Service employees, since the statutes had rational reasons: ensuring a fit police force and creating a "relatively small, homogeneous and particularly able corps of foreign service officers." [*Massachusetts Bd. of Retirement v. Murgia*, 427 U.S. 307 (1976)]

Teachers have challenged mandatory retirement laws with mixed success. In 1977, for example, the Seventh Circuit Court of Appeals ruled in favor of a teacher who objected to being forced to retire at a certain age, because there was no evidence that the teacher was unfit to teach. The court reasoned that, theoretically, an older person could be a better teacher than a younger person. [*Gault v. Garrison*, 569 F.2d 993 (7th Cir. 1977)] Three years later, however, the Second Circuit reached the opposite conclusion and upheld a mandatory retirement age for teachers, explaining that the statute could serve other rational purposes, such as opening up the field for young teachers and minorities and keeping the profession from growing stale. [*Palmer v. Ticcione*, 576 F.2d 459 (2d Cir. 1978)] In 1986, a Florida court followed the Second Circuit's reasoning and upheld a state statute allowing school boards to refuse to continue to employ teachers over the age of 70 strictly on the basis of age. [*Duval County Sch. Bd. v. State Dep't of Admin.*, 500 So. 2d 458 (Fla. Dist. Ct. App. 1986)]

Teachers are not the only people to have claimed age discrimination by schools. In 1993, a Texas court considered the case of two 19-year-old high school seniors who sued the University Interscholastic League (ULI), an organization that regulates high school athletes in Texas, for refusing to grant waivers to the rule forbidding students 19 and older from participating in varsity sports. The ULI argued that the rule served a legitimate purpose by ensuring that competing students were roughly equal in size and by discouraging "red shirting," a practice in which students repeat grades in order to be bigger when they compete in high school. In this case, however, each student had repeated two grades due to recognized learning disabilities. Since one student was average in size and the other below average, they argued that the purpose of safety was not at issue in their case and that, instead, the rule discriminated against them on the basis of their disabilities in violation of the **Rehabilitation Act.** The court agreed with the students and held that waiving the over-19 rule was a reasonable accommodation as required by the Rehabilitation Act for programs that receive federal assistance. [*University Interscholastic League v. Buchanan*, 848 S.W.2d 298 (Tex. Ct. App. 1993)]

A dental student did not fare as well in another 1993 age-discrimination case brought before an Illinois court. The student, who was 40 years old when he began dental school, had been dismissed from the program for repeatedly failing to live up to the required academic and clinical standards. The student claimed that he had been discriminated against on the basis of his age, since younger students had received similar grades for inferior work and since the faculty offered greater remedial assistance to struggling younger students. The student presented no real evidence to back up these claims, however. He also asserted that three Australian professors were against him for having changed from an engineering career to pursue a career in dentistry. This allegation was based on a conversation with one of the professors in which the professor had stated that he passed up a chance to go into medicine, since he had already finished dental school. From this, the student inferred that the professor and his colleagues shared a prejudice against older people who change professions. The court disagreed, however, stating that it could not "reasonably infer from the autobiographical data relayed to plaintiff by a single Australian professor that plaintiff was the victim of some subtle scheme involving a ring of Australian professors to oust him from dental school." [*Frederick v. Northwestern Univ.*, 617 N.E.2d 382 (Ill. App. Ct. 1993)]

AIDS EDUCATION Many schools are becoming actively involved in educating students about acquired immune deficiency syndrome (AIDS), in part to teach tolerance for persons infected with the deadly disease, but also to instruct students on how they can protect themselves against contracting the human immunodeficiency virus (HIV), which causes AIDS. Schools base their right and duty to cover this sensitive topic on the right of the state to oversee, to some extent, the health of its students. This is the same right that justifies other health-related classes such as physical education and **sex education.** High school students are particularly at risk of exposure through sexual contact. The Centers for Disease Control released a survey in 1992 in which 19 percent of the students surveyed (and 29 percent of the seniors in that group) had had four or more sexual partners, but less than half of the students who had had sex in the preceding three months had used condoms. Educating students on the risks of AIDS requires dealing frankly with topics such as drug use and the use of **condoms** during sexual intercourse.

Some schools have even gone so far as to distribute free condoms to students who request them. Such programs have at times been challenged in court by irate parents for one of two reasons. First, many worry that distribution of condoms gives students a sense of approval for premarital sex in contradiction to their religious beliefs. Second, many are concerned that emphasis on condom usage can lull students into a false sense of security, since condoms can break or leak, allowing HIV transmission. Some state legislators have sided with parents who object to their children being exposed to emphasis on condoms. Louisiana and Arkansas have passed laws requiring teachers to point out that sexual abstinence is the only sure means to avoid contracting AIDS through sex. The governor of New Jersey, on the other hand, vetoed a law requiring public school teachers to emphasize abstinence when dealing with the topic in class.

Those who support providing information on "safe sex" worry that such measures infringe on the **academic freedom** of teachers to teach and students to learn. In 1994, a California school district bowed to pressure from conservative parents and suspended the production of an award-winning play about a teenager with AIDS. The parents were concerned that the play was not strong enough in its emphasis of abstinence as the most effective means of avoiding sexual transmission of HIV, as required by state law.

AIDS, STUDENTS WITH A number of schools across the country have faced controversy when a student with acquired immune deficiency syndrome (AIDS) wishes to attend classes. AIDS is a deadly condition caused by the human immunodeficiency virus (HIV). The virus is transferred through the exchange of contaminated bodily fluids, such as those involved in sexual contact, blood transfusions, and the sharing of needles by intravenous drug users. The Public Health Service and the Centers for Disease Control have declared that the virus is not contagious through routine daily contact with an infected person or even by sharing toilets and water fountains. Despite this advice, the attitude of the public has at times verged on hysteria in its fear of infected persons.

Two early examples of the impact of this hysteria on schools and their communities are the cases of Ryan White of Kokomo, Indiana, and the Ray brothers of Arcadia, Florida. The boys contracted the virus from contaminated blood products they received to combat hemophilia, a genetic disorder in which the blood does not clot and the victim can literally bleed to death from what would otherwise be a relatively minor injury. When the communities learned that the infected boys wished to attend the area public schools, panic ensued, and the boys were barred from attending. Both families won their court battles to have their children enrolled in the public schools. [*Ray v. School Dist. of DeSoto County*, 666 F. Supp. 1524 (M.D. Fla. 1987)] Public outrage continued, however, and a number of parents, including the mayor of Arcadia in the case of the Ray brothers, withdrew their children from school. Both families eventually moved to new communities to escape the pressure. (The Rays relocated after their home was destroyed in a suspicious fire.)

Specific policies on dealing with students infected with HIV can help schools and their students and parents through potentially difficult times. More and more schools are adopting such policies as the number of children, especially teenagers, infected with the virus increases steadily. The courts, however, will not uphold just any policy.

For example, a policy of total exclusion will not be tolerated by the courts for two reasons. First, a school's policy must be founded on scientific evidence rather than on the fears and pressures of parents. There are no known cases in which HIV has been caught from an incontinent child or one who bites, so even though parents might feel squeamish at the thought of their children being exposed to infected bodily fluids in such ways, that would not justify reassigning the infected child to a more restrictive educational environment, such as homebound instruction. Second, a student infected with HIV qualifies as disabled under section 504 of the **Rehabilitation Act,** which makes excluding such students from public education based on their disabilities illegal.

Some policies provide for the temporary exclusion of students with AIDS for their own protection during outbreaks of disease within the school community. Such measures are probably permissible when there is, for example, an epidemic of chicken pox or some other highly contagious disease. After all, in normal, day-to-day contact among people the various germs carried by the rest of the students pose a far greater risk to the student with AIDS than the fragile HIV poses to the rest of the student body. Even so, a policy may not exclude infected students "for their own protection" from such normal risks.

An effective AIDS policy should give guidance on protecting the privacy of the infected child. This is because communities have, at times, treated infected children and their families as virtual pariahs. Courts and legislatures have generally recognized an increased need for confidentiality with regard to HIV status.

See also **AIDS, teachers with** and **AIDS education.**

AIDS, TEACHERS WITH

AIDS, TEACHERS WITH While cases of teachers infected with the human immunodeficiency virus (HIV), which causes acquired immune deficiency syndrome (AIDS), have not caused the same level of nationwide panic as have cases of students with AIDS [see **AIDS, students with**], individual instances have created uncomfortable situations for a number of schools and their communities. Legal issues involving HIV-infected teachers tend to arise when a teacher who carries the virus wishes to return to his or her duties and meets with resistance from the administration or the parents of the students. Despite the fact that the virus can be transmitted only through direct contact with contaminated bodily fluids, such as blood and sexual fluids, many parents are leery of having their children exposed to an infected person on a daily basis. In an effort to keep the peace, a school might reassign a teacher with the virus to a nonclassroom position or even dismiss the person from employment. Various cases and federal statutes indicate that such discrimination will not be tolerated.

Two important federal statutes, the Vocational Rehabilitation Act of 1973 [see **Rehabilitation Act**] and the **Americans with Disabilities Act (ADA),** address the issue of employing people with disabilities. Congress passed the Rehabilitation Act to promote the hiring of the disabled and to prohibit employers who receive funds under the act from discriminating against disabled workers who are otherwise able to perform their duties. Following a case brought by an employee with tuberculosis against a Florida school board [*Arline v. School Bd. of Nassau County,* 480 U.S. 273 (1987)], the act was amended to state that while a person with a contagious disease such as AIDS does qualify as disabled, the act does not apply to individuals who pose a health or safety threat to others or who are unable to perform their duties due to their illness. The effect of the Americans with Disabilities Act, which became effective in July 1992, is not as clear, since there has not been as much opportunity for judicial analysis of it as there has been of the Rehabilitation Act.

Both statutes require "reasonable accomodation" of the employee's disability. In the case of a teacher with AIDS, that includes accomodations necessary to allow the teacher to continue in his or her job without posing a health threat to others. Where the teacher is a high school social studies teacher with little, if any, physical contact with the students, little accomodation may be necessary. In the lower grades, however, and particularly in special education, where the teacher may be involved in activities such as changing diapers, the level of accomodation required would probably be greater. A school might arrange to have an uninfected person take over such duties. Courts have generally held, however, that a school is not required to make accomodations that impose an unreasonable financial hardship, such as a poorly funded school being made to hire additional staff.

See also **AIDS education.**

ALCOHOL TESTING As awareness grows of the number of students who occasionally or regularly use alcohol, schools continue to look for new ways to enforce policies against under-age drinking. While not as widespread as **drug testing** of students, some schools have begun using Breathalyzer tests to detect alcohol use.

In 1990, the Supreme Court upheld a program conducted by state police to catch intoxicated drivers. Under the program, the police established roadblocks to stop cars and administered breath tests to drivers on whom they detected the scent of alcohol. The 1990 decision shows what level of police intrusion is permissible with private citizens in searching for alcohol impairment. Given that the landmark case involving searches of students, ***New Jersey v. T.L.O.,*** holds school officials to a lower standard of cause necessary in conducting a search of a student, it seems reasonable to believe that Breathalyzer tests of students might be permissible in certain circumstances.

A high school in South Dakota implemented a policy of giving breath tests to students wishing to attend school dances. If a student tested positive, school officials called his or her parents; if the parents were unavailable, the police were contacted. The policy was not challenged in court, but critics claimed that such blanket testing lacked the required individualized suspicion. The policy was eventually modified to require more chaperones at school functions and testing only where a chaperone had a reasonable suspicion that a student had been drinking. In a similar case that did make it into court, a Colorado court upheld the suspension of two high school students for violation of the school's alcohol policy. A chaperone at a school dance required the two obviously intoxicated students to blow in his face, so he could determine for certain if they had been drinking. Even if this action constituted a "search" of the students, it was not unreasonable under the circumstances. [*Martinez v. School Dist. No. 60,* 852 P.2d 1275 (Colo. Ct. App. 1992)]

At the college and university level, Breathalyzer machines have occasionally been available at fraternity parties. The purpose for providing the machines was originally to warn students that they had had too much alcohol to be able to drive safely. Unfortunately, some students take the presence of the machines as a challenge to drink even more in an effort to "max out" their scores. School liability could foreseeably result from a situation such as this, where the presence of Breathalyzer machines arguably "causes" a student to drink even more alcohol than he or she would have normally and where the student's impairment leads to a traffic accident or other injury.

ALTERNATIVE SCHOOLS Public schools that use innovative programs to reach a particular type of student. Some alternative schools, such as **magnet schools,** cater to children with particular interests and talents, while others provide one last chance at a public education to students who, for whatever reason, fail to do well in traditional schools. This latter type of alternative school aims to curb dropout rates among students who are commonly viewed as "troublemakers."

Los Angeles established such a program of alternative schools called Alternative Education and Work Centers (AEWC) in 1987 to combat the district's 40 percent dropout rate. The centers focus on providing their students with the educational skills necessary either to return to a traditional high school or to pass the General Education Diploma (GED) examination. They also teach students vocational skills that could lead to employment in a variety of fields, from clerical work to automobile repair.

While the Los Angeles centers initially focused on students with academic problems in traditional schools, they have recently begun to focus on another segment of students: gang members. Such students are often viewed as troublemakers by regular schools. Less obvious, however, are the risks encountered by gang members who are assigned to schools located on another gang's territory. By implementing strict policies, including a dress code that forbids baseball caps, earrings, and other types of **gang clothing,** the centers provide a neutral environment where these students can concentrate on scholastics rather than warfare.

Some criticize programs such as the AEWC as ushering in a new era of segregation in which "good kids" go through one school system and "bad kids" go through another. Supporters, however, question why "good kids" should be forced to tolerate "bad kids" in order to get a public education.

Many alternative schools have had success in dealing with troubled students who probably would have failed to graduate from a regular program. Given that these alternative programs can be so beneficial, the question then arises as to whether school systems should be required to establish them. One North Carolina trial court attempted to impose such a requirement to provide an alternative educational program for a student who had been suspended for assaulting another student and teacher. A few days after the attacks at school, the student was charged with a host of crimes, including carrying a concealed weapon and breaking and entering. The judge in the resulting delinquency hearing decided that while the student did not need to be placed in a juvenile detention facility, he should not be "left free to roam at will." Accordingly, the judge ordered the school system, which had no alternative programs in place, to design a program for this student. The appellate court, however, reversed the ruling, saying that while the lower court could order participation in an existing program, it had no power to order the development of new programs. [*In re Jackson*, 352 S.E.2d 449 (N.C. Ct. App. 1987)]

AMERICAN CENTER FOR LAW AND JUSTICE (ACLJ)

Conservative nonprofit organization founded in 1990 by Pat Robertson in Virginia Beach, Virginia. Its motto is "To defend the rights of believers."

The ACLJ focuses on First Amendment rights—particularly those concerning speech, religion, and assembly, and particularly as they affect Christians. The ACLJ offers free legal advice in a number of cases involving these issues. For example, it assisted a California high school teacher in his fruitless attempt to free himself from being required to teach evolution [see **creationism and evolution**]. The organization was more successful when it teamed up in cases involving the **Equal Access Act** with a student prayer group (in *Board of Education of Westside Community Schools v. Mergens,* [496 U.S. 226 (1990)]) and a local church (in *Lamb's Chapel v. Center Moriches Union Free School District,* [113 S. Ct. 2141 (1993)]), both of which had been refused use of school facilities that other organizations were allowed to use. Both cases ultimately made it to the U.S. Supreme Court, which held in favor of the religious organizations.

Besides its courtroom pursuits, the ACLJ is also concerned with educating citizens and government officials about their rights. In an effort to reach Christian students, it publishes a brochure entitled "Students' Rights and the Public Schools," which is available by writing to The

American Center for Law and Justice, P.O. Box 64429, Virginia Beach, Virginia 23467. The ACLJ is also developing a site on the World Wide Web (http://www.aclj.org).

AMERICAN CIVIL LIBERTIES UNION (ACLU)

Organization founded in 1920 to defend civil liberties in the United States. The ACLU now has 275,000 members nationwide and a staff of over 60 attorneys who work with more than 2,000 volunteers in handling thousands of cases each year. The ACLU's national headquarters are in New York City, but it also maintains a legislative office in Washington, D.C., and affiliate offices in most major cities.

The ACLU frequently gets involved in school-related issues, such as freedom of speech, freedom of religion, and racial discrimination. In 1925, it defended a Tennessee teacher who had been convicted of violating the state's antievolution statute in the case of ***Scopes v. State.*** Thirty years later, the ACLU championed the cause of school desegregation in ***Brown v. Board of Education of Topeka.*** In 1981, the ACLU successfully challenged an Arkansas law that required the teaching of creationism [see **creationism and evolution**] in the public schools, and in 1994, it negotiated a settlement with a Pennsylvania school district to stop teaching creationism in science classes.

Not all of the ACLU's lobbying is carried on in courts. The organization occasionally contacts schools and school officials directly to offer its position on certain controversial subjects. For example, when the **American Center for Law and Justice (ACLJ)** sent letters in 1993 to school superintendents heralding a recent Fifth Circuit case as allowing voluntary prayer at graduation ceremonies, the ACLU fought back with its own letter, sent to 15,000 superintendents, in which it claimed that the circuit court's decision misconstrued the holding by the Supreme Court in ***Lee v. Weisman.*** In 1994, the ACLU sent a letter to the president of Carnegie Mellon University to voice its disapproval of the university's decision to censor material available to students from certain Internet sites containing sexually explicit material [see **Internet censorship**].

The ACLU publishes a 181-page handbook called *The Rights of Students* and has produced a video entitled *America's Constitutional Heritage: Religion and Our Public Schools,* both of which may be ordered by writing to: The American Civil Liberties Union, Department L, P.O. Box 794, Medford, New York, 11763.

The ACLU also maintains an Internet site called the American Civil Liberties Union Free Reading Room, which contains many of the organization's publications, newsletters, and news releases. The Reading Room can be accessed by Gopher (aclu.org.6601) or by FTP (aclu.org). The ACLU also has a home page on the World Wide Web (http://www.aclu.org).

AMERICAN FEDERATION OF TEACHERS, AFL-CIO (AFT) A union for teachers founded in 1916 with a membership today of over 800,000. As a union, the AFT is concerned with protecting teachers from unfair treatment and championing their causes in matters of salary and working conditions.

The AFT also has a long history of lobbying for the improvement of U.S. schools. The union has traditionally favored aggressive, innovative school-reform measures. Recently, however, it unveiled its "Lessons for Life: Responsibility, Respect, Results" campaign, which emphasizes safe, orderly schools as its priority. Some have criticized the "back-to-basics flavor" of this campaign, which advocates methods such as placing disruptive students in **alternative schools.**

The AFT produces a number of publications for its members, such as *American Teacher,* which comes out monthly, and *American Educator,* which is distributed quarterly. The AFT may be reached at: 555 New Jersey Avenue NW, Washington, DC 20001-2079.

AMERICANS WITH DISABILITIES ACT (ADA) Federal legislation passed in 1990, 20 years after passage of the **Rehabilitation Act,** that makes most of the provisions of the Rehabilitation Act applicable to the private sector. The ADA incorporates the earlier law's prohibition against discriminating against disabled persons who are otherwise qualified to perform the task at hand. The act sets out a list of conditions that are not protected, including current use of illegal drugs (former users and those in rehabilitation are covered); use of alcohol on the job; failure to meet performance standards; failure to pass drug testing; transvestism; other sexual conditions (such as homosexuality, bisexuality, transsexualism, pedophilia, exhibitionism, and voyeurism); and other behavior disorders (such as compulsive gambling, kleptomania, and pyromania).

The ADA does not set quotas for the number of disabled persons to be employed, nor does it require favoring a disabled person over one who is not disabled. It does, however, require an employer to make reasonable accommodations to permit an otherwise qualified individual to perform his or her job—unless such an accommodation would be an undue hardship on the business.

The ADA prohibits asking job applicants questions designed to determine whether they are disabled, but it does allow inquiry into an applicant's ability to perform job-related functions by describing the function and asking if the person can do it. The act allows an employer to require medical examinations of all new employees, but if a disability is discovered during the exam, the reasonable-accommodation requirement arises.

The potential effects of the ADA have yet to be determined because of its relative newness. However, it has already had an important impact by adding to the remedies that were recoverable under the Rehabilitation Act and by making the spirit of the act applicable to private employees. The passage of the ADA has had the immediate effect of allowing persons with discrimination cases against many private schools (those that meet the requirements, such as by employing 15 or more employees) to bring their cases to court.

ANTITRUST LAWS Federal antitrust laws are statutes established under the commerce clause of the Constitution, which gives Congress the power to regulate commerce among the states. Such statutes are designed to protect competition in the economic marketplace by forbidding practices such as price-fixing and monopolization, which inhibit competition. Over the past 20 years, antitrust laws have developed an increasingly greater impact on institutions of higher education, which have come under scrutiny for a number of reasons.

For example, colleges and universities often act as sellers of products such as books and computers to their faculty members and students. In fact, they usually offer these products at prices well below those of nearby merchants, which may raise antitrust issues. In 1982, a book dealer accused a university bookstore of predatory pricing when the bookstore consistently undercut his prices until he was forced to sell books at below cost in order to compete. [*Sunshine Books, Ltd. v. Temple Univ.*, 697 F.2d 90 (3d Cir. 1980)]

Another pricing issue that has recently made its way into the judicial system is that of price fixing tuition and financial aid packages. In the 1980s, the Justice Department investigated the Overlap Group, an organization of Ivy League and other schools. Each year the member schools would independently figure out financial aid packages for the applicants that they had chosen to accept for admission. Later, they would compare notes on the amount each institution had figured for family contribution of students who had been accepted by more than one of the schools. If the differences were greater than $500, the universities would negotiate until they reached a compromise figure that would be used by all member schools offering a package to that student.

Many of the schools entered into an agreement with the Justice Department to cease this practice. The Massachusetts Institute of Technology, on the other hand, elected to fight out the issue in court. In 1992, a federal district court held that the practice was clearly anticompetitive and "interfered with the natural functioning of the marketplace." Since a student who was accepted would be offered an identical package from each potential school, the student lost the ability to shop around for the best bargain. [*United States v. Brown Univ.*, 805 F. Supp. 288 (E.D. Pa. 1992)]

Yet another facet of higher education that sometimes runs into antitrust challenges is college athletics. For example, the National Collegiate Athletic Association (NCAA), which controls intercollegiate athletics to a great extent, was sued for creating an unreasonable restraint of trade by limiting the number of games each team could broadcast on the two television networks with which the NCAA had contracts. Although the NCAA argued that the plan was intended to limit the effect that televising games would have on attendance at live games, the Supreme Court declared in 1984 that the plan violated federal antitrust laws. [*NCAA v. Board of Regents*, 468 U.S. 85 (1984)]

Six years later, the NCAA had greater success in withstanding antitrust challenges to its "no agent" and "no draft" rules. These rules revoke the college eligibility of athletes who either hire an agent or enter the NFL draft, regardless of whether or not the athlete is able to establish a professional career. In two separate cases, federal trial courts held against college football players who argued that the rules were anticompetitive. Instead, the courts agreed with the NCAA that the rules had the procompetitive purpose of preserving amateurism and deterring college athletes from forsaking their education for the allure of a professional career before graduation. [*Banks v. NCAA*, 746 F. Supp. 850 (N.D. Ind. 1990) and *Gaines v. NCAA*, 746 F. Supp. 738 (M.D. Tenn. 1990)]

"AT-RISK" STUDENTS Students who have been identified as being at a higher risk of school failure or dropout and placed into special programs, such as HeadStart. As federal and local governments have begun to recognize the importance of such programs and, therefore, to lend financial support for their efforts, an issue has arisen as to who, exactly, should be deemed "at risk."

Congress answered this question at the federal level in 1988 through legislation that included the following definition:

> The term "at risk" means students who, because of learning deficiencies, lack of school readiness, limited English proficiency, poverty, educational or economic disadvantage, or physical or emotional handicapping conditions face greater risk of low educational achievement and have greater potential of becoming school dropouts.

State definitions, naturally, vary from state to state. Some states that have legislation aimed at helping such students do not include any definition at all, preferring instead to leave it up to state or local boards of education to determine who is at risk. Definitions at the state level depend on any of a number of factors, including a student's race or family income, or such obstacles as being the child of teenage parents, having a non–English-speaking background, or having a history of alcohol or drug abuse in the family. California and Massachusetts, on the other hand, focus on schools with the lowest test scores rather than on the problems of individual students.

Once the issue of who is at risk has been settled, the potential issue arises of whether the definition will withstand a constitutional challenge based on either the equal protection clause [see **equal protection**] or the due process clause [see **due process**] of the Fourteenth Amendment. In an equal protection challenge, a court applies one of three levels of scrutiny in examining the statute. Which level should be applied is determined by whether the statute affects a fundamental right and how the people affected by the statute are classified. Since the Supreme Court has found that the Constitution does not include a fundamental right to education, the level of scrutiny to be applied in such challenges hinges on how at-risk students are classified. For example, if students are deemed to be at risk based on their race (a "suspect class" in legal jargon), the statute will pass muster only if a compelling governmental interest is at stake and there is no less discriminatory alternative. If students are classified based on factors other than race, such as income, the statute need only be rationally related to a legitimate governmental purpose.

Where students are classified based on factors other than race or national origin, the statute might still be challenged under a procedural due process argument. Like placement in a special-education class for disabled students, the placement of at-risk students in special programs benefits them. Even so, such special placement can carry with it a stigma of being labeled as somehow inferior to students in regular programs. Some might argue that children who are placed in special programs should be entitled to procedural safeguards such as those afforded disabled students under the **Individuals with Disabilities Education Act (IDEA).**

ATHLETICS, ELIGIBILITY AND High school students who wish to take part in their schools' athletics programs usually must comply with rules and regulations established not only by the schools themselves, but also by voluntary organizations in each state that govern athletic competition. More students are challenging these regulations as the stakes, and the potential payoff, increase for a college sports scholarship and maybe even a professional career.

In the 1980s, a number of states began implementing policies known as "no pass-no play" rules that require students to meet certain academic standards before being allowed to compete in extracurricular activities, including athletics. In 1984, a West Virginia court heard a case in which a high school basketball player challenged the county board of education's modification of the state rule requiring students to maintain a 2.0 grade point average in order to take part in extracurricular activities. The student had met the state requirement for overall grade point average but had failed his English class, which left him ineligible to play under the county requirement that students pass each individual subject. The court upheld the state requirement as having the rational purpose of encouraging scholarship and the county requirement as being a legitimate exercise of the board's power to regulate extracurricular activities. The same court, however, limited application of the rule to only nonacademic extracurricular activities; "academic" activities would be exempt. [*Bailey v. Truby,* 321 S.E.2d 302 (W. Va. 1984)]

Besides meeting academic requirements, potential athletes must also meet age requirements. Such rules generally forbid students older than 18 from playing. The purpose of these rules is to discourage the practice of "red shirting" in which students repeat grades with the goal of being a bigger and better athlete during the varsity years and also to promote safety by ensuring that all athletes are roughly the same size. In some cases, however, students have alleged that application of these rules constitutes **age discrimination.** For example, students who have "aged out" of eligibility due to grades repeated as a result of diagnosed learning disabilities have met with some success in challenging age requirements. In such cases, the students generally argue that application of the requirements without any consideration of special circumstances discriminates against them on the basis of their disabilities.

Another area of athletic eligibility that is receiving a great deal of attention lately is application of school-transfer rules, which require that a student who transfers from one school to another loses his or her eligibility for a certain period of time (usually one year) before being allowed to compete on behalf of the new school. The rules serve a legitimate purpose by discouraging athletic recruiting at the high school level—any incentive to switch schools for athletic reasons is weakened by the loss of a year's eligibility. The problem, however, is that across-the-board application of such rules also affects students who transfer schools for reasons totally unrelated to athletics.

The number of "innocent" students affected by school-transfer rules has grown in recent years as divorce rates have risen and families have been forced to move for economic reasons. Such students have at times sought relief in the judicial system. For example, a student who had moved from Florida to Indiana to live with his older brother challenged Indiana's rule. The student's move had been motivated by extensive drug use among his peers on his school's basketball team and a home environment that consisted of 13 people living in a two-bedroom home. The court held in favor of the student and declared that application of the transfer rule to every student who changed schools created an irrebuttable presumption that each of those students had been recruited, which rendered the rule overbroad as applied. [*Sturrup v. Mahan,* 305 N.E.2d 877 (Ind. 1974)]

ATHLETICS, LIABILITY FOR INJURIES AND In order for a student athlete to recover a judgment against a coach or school district for negligence, certain conditions must be met. First, the defendant must have breached a duty owed to the student. Second, the breach must have been the proximate cause of the athlete's injury. This breach can occur either by action, such as when a coach moves a hurt player and aggravates the player's injuries or when a coach bullies a reluctant player into taking extraordinary risks, or by inaction, such as when a coach fails to warn players of the dangers of certain sports or to supervise practices or when a school district fails to provide necessary safety equipment.

Coaches and school districts accused of negligence have several possible defenses. One such defense is the doctrine of assumption of risk. For example, a baseball player who slides headfirst onto base in spite of being warned against such behavior might be deemed by a court to have assumed the risk of his or her injuries, which would preclude recovery from the defendant. Another possible bar to recovery is the doctrine of contributory negligence, which completely relieves the defendant of liability if the plaintiff was partially liable for his or her own injuries. Finally, many states today apply the doctrine of comparative negligence, which apportions recovery along with fault. For example, if a plaintiff and defendant were both liable for the plaintiff's injuries, the plaintiff would be able to recover from the defendant only the amount that could be attributed to the defendant's, rather than the plaintiff's, liability.

ATHLETICS, SEX DISCRIMINATION AND

A good deal of recent attention has been focused on the issue of **sex discrimination** and athletic programs. Some cases are brought under Title IX of the Education Amendments of 1972, which provides that "no person shall, on the basis of sex, be excluded from participation in, be denied the benefits of, be treated differently from another person or otherwise be discriminated against in any interscholastic, intercollegiate, club or intramural athletics offered by a recipient [of federal funds]." Other cases are grounded in the equal protection clause of the Fourteenth Amendment of the U.S. Constitution [see **equal protection**], which requires that a government action treating males and females differently must be substantially (rather than merely rationally) related to a legitimate government purpose.

In 1989, the Ninth Circuit Court of Appeals heard a case in which a male high school student challenged a rule of the Arizona Interscholastic Association (AIA) that restricted interscholastic volleyball competition to single-sex teams. Since the student's high school maintained only a girl's volleyball team, he was precluded from participating in interscholastic volleyball. The appellate court affirmed the decision of the lower court to enter judgment in favor of the AIA without trial. It explained that in the past women had been discriminated against in interscholastic athletics and that maintaining a women-only volleyball team was a legitimate means of redressing the past discrimination. To allow men to compete for places on such a team would have the effect of displacing women and thus would further diminish athletic opportunities for women. Accordingly, the exclusion of men from such teams was substantially related to the governmental goal of providing equal opportunities for women. [*Clark v. Arizona Interscholastic Ass'n*, 886 F.2d 1191 (9th Cir. 1989)]

Also in 1989, the Supreme Court of Appeals of West Virginia considered an equal protection case brought by a female high school student who alleged gender discrimination after she was forbidden to play on her school's boys' baseball team. Instead, the school said, she could play on the girls' softball team. The trial court granted judgment in favor of the defendants, but the appellate court reversed. The appellate court acknowledged that equal protection does not prohibit the maintenance under certain circumstances of separate teams for boys and girls as long as the teams are substantially equivalent. It held, however, that the trial court erred in finding that the games of baseball and softball are substantially equivalent, when evidence was offered that the two sports are actually quite different. [*Israel v. West Virginia Secondary Schools Activities Comm'n*, 388 S.E.2d 480 (W. Va. 1989)]

Four years later, the Third Circuit heard a case brought under Title IX of the Education Act Amendments. In that case, parents sued on behalf of their son, who had been excluded from his high school's girls' field hockey team based on his gender. Under the regulations that implement Title IX, a school that sponsors single-sex teams must allow a member of the excluded sex to try out for the team if athletic opportunities of the excluded sex have previously been limited, unless the sport involved is a contact sport. The district court entered summary judgment for the student and his parents, holding that "field hockey is not a 'contact sport' and that males 'have previously been denied athletic opportunities.'" The appellate court, however, held that the lower court had erred in summarily concluding that field hockey is not a contact sport simply because it is not included in the list of examples of contact sports provided by the regulations. Furthermore, the court held, even though girls had been allowed for nearly 20 years to try out for almost twice as many teams as boys could, this did not mean that boys were denied athletic opportunities. The school's director of athletics testified, "In the 27 years I have been in this business, I believe I have seen two girls that had tried out for a given sport and at best were carried on the team. It did not displace any boys." Such evidence created a factual issue of whether athletic opportunities for boys had previously been limited. Accordingly, the appellate court reversed the decision of the lower court and sent the case back for further proceedings. [*Williams v. School Dist. of Bethlehem*, 998 F.2d 168 (3d Cir. 1993)]

ATTENDANCE POLICIES Many schools formulate attendance policies as a means of enforcing state compulsory education laws, which require the formal education of children between certain ages, usually 6 or 7 and 16. Controversy sometimes arises over how to treat 18-year-old students, who are neither minors nor required to attend school under the compulsory education laws. Such students may argue that having to provide parental excuses when they are absent or tardy violates their rights, since technically they have reached the age of majority. Reaching the age of majority, however, does not confer upon young people all the rights of adulthood. They still, for example, must wait until they are 21 before they can legally purchase alcohol. It is generally accepted that school boards may adopt and apply uniform rules in the interest of the orderly functioning of the schools. Accordingly, an 18-year-old student who chooses to continue his or her education past the age mandated by law must obey the rules set out by the school.

Sometimes, however, application of rules requiring students to provide parental excuses could violate rights that the student holds independently from his or her parents. For example, in states where abortion is available to minors without parental notice or consent, legal issues could arise if application of the school's attendance policy somehow led to notification of a student's parents against her wishes.

Sometimes students claim that their rights have been violated when schools link their attendance policies with **academic sanctions,** such as grade reduction. Courts generally uphold such policies, since class attendance and grades are closely related. In at least one case, however, a court sided with a student whose absences had occurred due to school action by suspension than by personal choice.

B

Bethel School District No. 403 v. Fraser

Supreme Court case construing ***Tinker v. Des Moines Independent School District*** as allowing a school to punish a student for giving a speech full of sexual insinuations at an official school assembly. [478 U.S. 675 (1986)]

Matthew Fraser, a high school student, delivered the following speech to his fellow students:

> I know a man who is firm—he's firm in his pants, he's firm in his shirt, his character is firm—but most of all, his belief in you, the students of Bethel, is firm.
>
> Jeff Kuhlman is a man who takes his point and pounds it in. If necessary, he'll take an issue and nail it to the wall. He doesn't attack things in spurts—he drives hard, pushing and pushing until finally—he succeeds.
>
> Jeff is a man who will go to the very end—even the climax, for each and every one of you.
>
> So vote for Jeff for A.S.B. vice-president—he'll never come between you and the best our high school can be.

The school determined that the sexual innuendo in the speech violated a school rule against "conduct which materially and substantially interferes with the educational process . . . , including the use of obscene, profane language or gestures" and suspended Fraser for three days and dismissed him as a possible graduation speaker.

When the school district, after reviewing the case, refused to overturn his punishment, Fraser sued, claiming that the school district had violated his First Amendment right to free speech [see **freedom of speech**]. He succeeded at the trial level, where the court agreed that the sanctions violated his rights and that the school's rule against profanity was "void for vagueness." A law is void for vagueness when it is not sufficiently explicit as to what behavior it prohibits, which could lead people to refrain from permissible actions in an effort to comply with the law or rule. The court awarded him money damages and issued an injunction to prohibit the school from interfering with Fraser's speech at the graduation ceremony, which he had been elected by his classmates to give as a write-in candidate.

The school district appealed, but the appellate court affirmed the judgment, finding that Fraser's speech did not differ from the silent antiwar protest upheld by the Supreme Court in *Tinker.* The district appealed again, and the Supreme Court agreed to review the case.

The Court held that the lower courts had misunderstood the holding in *Tinker.* While it is true that students' rights to free speech and expression follow them into their schools, only speech that neither disrupts the educational process nor violates the rights of others will be protected. The evidence in the *Fraser* case showed that the speech created chaos within the student body. Some students responded by shouting; others used sexually explicit gestures to demonstrate the activities to which Fraser alluded; still others seemed bewildered and embarrassed. One teacher stated that she had to cancel part of her planned lesson to discuss the speech with her class. Because of the disruptive effect of Fraser's speech and the embarrassment it caused some teachers and students, and because the school was not attempting to squelch a particular political viewpoint, as had been the case in *Tinker,* the Court held that the school district did not act improperly in punishing Fraser as it did.

BIBLE READING AND DISTRIBUTION The Supreme Court struck down state and city laws requiring beginning the public school day with a prayer and the recitation of Bible verses in the 1963 case ***School District of Abington Township v. Schempp,*** which combined two state cases. Parents (Unitarians in one case, atheists in the other) objected to this practice, because it exposed their children to doctrines that went against their religious beliefs. Even though participation was voluntary and children who objected could leave the room during the ritual, the Court held that by injecting such activities into the school schedule, the states had violated the establishment clause of the First Amendment of the U.S. Constitution [see **establishment and free exercise clauses**], which forbids government promotion of religion.

Nearly 30 years later, a federal court examined the policy of allowing members of Gideon International into the public classrooms of Indiana to distribute free Bibles to fifth graders. Although the teachers usually were present when the Bibles were handed out, they did not participate, and the

Bibles were not used for teaching purposes afterward. The trial court upheld the distribution, saying it was no different than a baseball coach passing out materials about Little League. The appellate court, however, reversed this decision based on the establishment clause, because it found that students could not help but believe that the school endorsed the activity. The court rejected the Gideons' argument that refusing to allow them to hand out Bibles to school children violated their First Amendment rights to free speech and pointed out that they remained free to distribute Bibles anyplace that did not carry the seal of the state, based on a concept set out in a Supreme Court case dealing with **released-time programs** that held that religious organizations cannot use the compulsory education laws to gather a captive audience. [*Berger v. Rensselaer Cent. Sch. Corp.*, 766 F. Supp. 696 (N.D. Ind. 1991)]

Even though the *Schempp* Court banned using the Bible for religious purposes in public schools, it specifically declared the Bible "worthy of study for its literary and historic qualities." In spite of this endorsement, the presence of a Bible in a public classroom often generates anxiety for school officials who fear crossing the line that separates church and state. In 1989, a federal district court upheld the decision of a school principal who ordered a fifth-grade teacher to conceal his Bible in his desk during school hours and to remove two books, *The Bible in Pictures* and *The Story of Jesus,* from his classroom library of over 200 books. The court overruled the principal on one issue, ordering the Bible restored to the classroom library because of its literary value.

Although using the Bible as a religious text in the public schools is prohibited, that certainly does not mean that it does not still happen. In 1994, the **American Civil Liberties Union (ACLU)** teamed up with People for the American Way to sue a Mississippi school district on behalf of a woman and her five children who were harassed for objecting to daily Bible readings and prayers as part of the official school curriculum.

BOARD OF EDUCATION, ISLAND TREES UNION FREE SCHOOL DISTRICT v. PICO

Supreme Court case dealing with the removal of **library books** from school libraries. [457 U.S. 853 (1982)]

Members of a local school board became aware that certain books listed as "objectionable" by a conservative parents' organization were in the high school and junior high school libraries. As a result they ordered the books, which they termed "anti-American, anti-Christian, anti-Semitic, and just plain filthy," removed despite the advice of the superintendent and a book review committee. Students sued to stop the book removal, claiming it violated their First Amendment rights.

The trial court granted summary judgment in favor of the school board, meaning that the students had presented no factual issues worthy of debate and that the board was entitled to win as a matter of law without a trial. An appellate court reversed the summary judgment and sent the case back to the trial court, and the school board appealed to the U.S. Supreme Court.

The issue before the Court was whether the rights guaranteed by the First Amendment limit the discretion of a school board to remove books from school libraries. The Court began by stating that as a general rule, "local school boards have broad discretion in the management of school affairs" but pointed out that they must use this discretion within the restrictions of certain constitutional rights. One right that limits the use of such power is the right to free speech, which is meaningless without the corresponding right to receive ideas. The Court held that the board's motivation for removing the books would determine whether this action violated the free speech rights of the students. If the board members intended to deny the students access to ideas with which they disagreed, then the board did in fact infringe on the students' rights.

Seven years later, a California court heard a similar case, in which a school board tried to remove books from the school library. The court held that while the board did have the power to create school libraries, it did not have the power to remove books once they were in the libraries. According to this case, once books are in a library, they obtain "shelf tenure" and may not be removed. [*Wexner v. Anderson Union High Sch.*, 258 Cal. Rptr. 26 (Cal. Ct. App. 1989)]

Board of Education of Kiryas Joel School District v. Grumet Supreme Court case considering the validity of a state statute designed to allow a religious group to run its own public schools. [114 S. Ct. 2481 (1994)]

In 1977, a group of strictly conservative Jews known as the Satmars formed their own village, the Village of Kiryas Joel, within the town of

Monroe, New York. Village lines were carefully drawn so as to include only land owned and inhabited by Satmars, and the Satmars avoided mixing with the modern world whenever possible.

Most Satmar children attend religious private schools that do not provide any special-education programs for disabled children. Accordingly, disabled Satmar children were sent at first to the public schools of the Monroe-Woodbury school district. Most Satmar parents, however, claimed that it traumatized their children to be sent to schools outside the village and withdrew them from school.

In order to provide free, public educations for these children, the state of New York declared the Village of Kiryas Joel to be its own separate school district. This gave the village the power to run its own public schools. The village elected to run only a special program for disabled students, leaving regular students in their private schools. The New York State School Boards Association sued, claiming that the statute under which the Kiryas Joel school district was created was unconstitutional. The case ultimately reached the U.S. Supreme Court, which upheld the lower courts' decision that despite its nonreligious purpose of educating the disabled children, the statute did, in fact, violate the establishment clause [see **establishment and free exercise clauses**] of both the state and federal constitutions.

The Court explained that states must walk a fine line in respecting both the establishment clause and the free exercise clause and should strive for neutrality on religious issues. As a result, no state may assign its governmental powers to a group chosen because of its religious affiliation. When it does, as in the case of the Satmars, problems could develop if other religious and nonreligious groups are not given the same accommodation. If the Kiryas Joel school district had been established "simply as one of many communities eligible for equal treatment under a general law," the Court said that would have been permissible. Since, however, the statute was directed at only the Satmars, the result was state-supported establishment of their religion.

The Court recognized that striking down the statute and, thus, the Kiryas Joel school district, left Satmar parents of disabled children back where they started. However, the Court pointed out, if the parents disagreed with the educations designed for their children by the Monroe-Woodbury school district, they should seek relief through the review process established under the **Individuals with Disabilities Education Act (IDEA).**

BONDS Securities representing a borrower-lender relationship between the issuer and the buyer of the bonds. In the case of school funding, the borrower is often a local school district. The buyers of the bonds earn money through payment of interest on the money lent. School districts usually make payments on the bonds with money raised from **property taxes.** In recent years, issues have arisen in some states that have forced them to consider changing how they deal with school funding through the issue of bonds.

For example, in 1990, the Florida Supreme Court heard a case brought by three school boards to validate certain agreements with nonprofit organizations under which the organizations would receive title to land on which they would build new schools or improve existing ones. The organizations would then lease the land back to the school boards for money raised in part through the issuance of bonds that would be payable from property taxes. The state argued that the Florida Constitution requires voter approval through a referendum prior to a school district issuing such bonds. The court, however, disagreed and held that a referendum would not be required. [*State v. School Bd. of Sarasota County,* 561 So. 2d 549 (Fla. 1990)] Critics of this decision argue that such judicial interference with the state constitution was improper. They believe that if the people of Florida wanted to do away with the referendum requirement, the constitution should have been amended.

The state of California has also recently dealt with confusion over school bonds. In 1992, a state trial court heard a case that had the potential for changing the way many California municipalities and school districts raise money. In that case, a school district issued $9.8 million worth of certificate of participation bonds and secured the debt with school property. Such bonds are often issued in California to raise money for capital projects, such as building schools and jails. In this case, however, the money raised was used for operating expenses. When the school district ultimately went bankrupt, the state stepped in to save it. In straightening out the district's financial problems, the state argued that it should not have to repay the money to the bondholders, because the arrangement violated the state constitution. The lower court dismissed this argument, but the state appealed. Since the arrangement at issue here mirrored other certificate of participation bond schemes in California, a decision allowing default on the payment of the bonds could have consequences that reach far beyond the area of education.

One year after the county court decided this case in favor of the investors, California voters considered a proposal that would allow local school boards to pass school bond measures with a majority vote instead of the two-thirds vote previously required. Developers in the state favored the ** to the constitution, because it went hand-in-hand with a law limiting the amount of school construction fees that could be levied on developers of other projects. For example, the fee cap would mean that a developer of a $3 billion resort project would pay $2.5 million in school construction fees; without the cap, such fees would rise to $220 million. Voters rejected the measure, however, largely out of fear that it would result in higher property taxes to pay for the increased number of bond issues that would pass under the lower majority requirement.

Brown v. Board of Education of Topeka

Landmark Supreme Court decisions calling for an end to racial segregation [see **desegregation**] in the public schools. [347 U.S. 483 (1954) and 349 U.S. 294 (1955)] *Brown* was actually a consolidation of four cases in which black children had been denied admission to white schools under state statutes that either allowed or required segregation of the races. The case from which the opinion takes its name was from Kansas, and the other three were from South Carolina, Virginia, and Delaware.

Although most people think of *Brown* as a single decision, there were actually two separate Supreme Court opinions. First, in 1954, the Court considered the issue of segregation in the public schools. In the 1896 transportation case *Plessy v. Ferguson* [163 U.S. 537 (1896)], the Court upheld the doctrine of "separate but equal," which allowed division of the races to separate facilities as long as the facilities were of substantially equal quality. The lower courts had denied the request of the *Brown* plaintiffs on the basis of this doctrine, except in the case from Delaware, where the lower court upheld the doctrine but found that the white schools were superior to the black schools.

In evaluating the applicability of the separate but equal doctrine in education, the Court considered the role of public education in modern American life. Education, the Court determined, "is perhaps the most important function of state and local governments." The significance of education is shown by the enactment of **compulsory attendance** laws as well as by the amount of public money spent on education. Where a state chooses to provide such an opportunity, it must make it available to all on an equal basis. Accordingly, the Court held that even where "tangible factors" may be equal, the very fact that children were separated on account of race "generates a feeling of inferiority as to their status in the community that may affect their hearts and minds in a way unlikely ever to be undone. . . . Separate educational facilities are inherently unequal." Such segregation denies the children the equal protection of the laws guaranteed by the Fourteenth Amendment [see **equal protection**].

Having announced the end of the separate but equal doctrine, the Court turned its attention to the problem of accomplishing desegregation on a nationwide scale. It announced its opinion on this matter the following year. After soliciting the views of the U.S. attorney general and the attorneys general of all segregated states, the Court determined that the lower courts would be best suited to oversee desegregation because of their "proximity to local conditions." So, after determining that U.S. public schools must desegregate "with all deliberate speed," the Court remanded the cases to the lower courts to allow them to work out the details of how that goal could best be accomplished at each local level.

Over 30 years later, the federal district court in Kansas reopened *Brown* when a group of intervening plaintiffs alleged that their local school district still suffered from the effects of *de jure* segregation, or segregation mandated by law. The court placed the burden on the plaintiffs to prove that racial imbalances were caused by intentional discrimination. Accordingly, the court held in favor of the school district, saying that any racial imbalances that remained were the result of forces like population movements, which were beyond the control of the district, and declared the district to be unitary, or fully desegregated.

The case went on to the circuit court of appeals, which reversed the district court's opinion on the grounds that the lower court had misplaced the burden of proof. [*Brown v. Board of Educ. of Topeka*, 892 F.2d 851 (10th Cir. 1990)] The appellate court held that plaintiffs in such a case are entitled to a presumption that disparities are related to past intentional conduct; a school district that has been deemed a product of *de jure* segregation bears the burden of proving otherwise. In this case, the school district failed to meet its burden. In 1992, however, the dispute eventually reached the U.S. Supreme Court, which vacated the judgment of the appellate court and sent it back for reconsideration in light of other recent desegregation cases heard by the Court.

BUCKLEY AMENDMENT Federal law officially entitled the Family Educational Rights and Privacy Act but more popularly known as the Buckley Amendment after its sponsor, New York Senator James Buckley. Passed in 1974, its two main goals are: (1) to allow parents of students (and students themselves once they have reached the age of 18 or are enrolled in a postsecondary program) access to their children's educational records; and (2) to prevent schools from releasing those same records to outsiders without written consent of the parents (or the students, in the case of those who meet the age or education requirements). Like many federal laws regarding education, the Buckley Amendment accomplishes its aims by threatening to withhold federal financial support from any school that does not follow the requirements of the act.

The Buckley Amendment was inspired, at least in part, by cases such as one that occurred in Pennsylvania in 1973. [*Merriken v. Cressman*, 364 F. Supp. 913 (E.D. Pa. 1973)] In that case, a junior high school implemented a special program to identify students who might be potential drug abusers. The court found that since the school did not obtain parental consent before enrolling children in the program, it violated the privacy rights of the parents and their children. Buckley argued that his bill should be passed to protect against such a "violation of confidentiality and abuse of personal data" by "governmental and other busybodies."

The act is quite explicit in defining certain "directory information" that may be released by the school unless a parent or student requests it be withheld. This directory information includes:

> The student's name, address, telephone listing, date and place of birth, major field of study, participation in officially recognized activities and sports, weight and height of members of athletic teams, dates of attendance, degrees and awards received, and the most recent previous educational agency or institution attended by the student.

On the other hand, the act is rather vague in defining records that must be protected:

> Those records, files, documents, and other material which contain information directly related to a student and are maintained by an

> educational agency or institution or by a person acting for such agency or institution.

As a result, the issue that arises most often in conjunction with the Buckley Amendment is the question of what, exactly, constitutes "educational records."

For example, the Georgia Supreme Court heard a case in 1993 in which a student newspaper at the University of Georgia sued the Board of Regents for access to records from the disciplinary hearings of fraternities on charges of alcohol and hazing offenses. The court held in favor of the newspaper on the grounds that the Georgia Open Records Act gave it a right of access to the records and that the Georgia Open Meetings Act [see **open-meeting laws**] gave it a similar right with regard to the hearings themselves. Critical to the court's holding was its decision that the records in question were not educational records protected by the Buckley Amendment as the university argued, since the records did not relate to academic issues such as "academic performance, financial aid, or scholastic probation." [*Red & Black Pub. Co. v. Board of Regents,* 427 S.E.2d 257 (Ga. 1993)]

Critics of the court's holding assert that it places a school administrator who is faced with a request for records in a predicament. On the one hand, he or she may comply with the request and risk running afoul of the Buckley Amendment, therefore losing valuable federal assistance. On the other hand, if the administrator refuses to comply, the institution could wind up as the defendant in a potentially costly civil suit.

Another issue that has cropped up in regard to the question of what records are covered by the Buckley Amendment is whether or not records relating to campus crime are protected educational records. In 1991, Congress passed a law regarding **campus security** that requires all schools receiving federal funds to publish their crime statistics and security policies. Even so, school administrators sometimes argue that Buckley forbids the release of such records.

In one case heard in 1991, the editor of a student newspaper at Southwest Missouri State University sued for access to the crime reports maintained by the university's campus security. [*Bauer v. Kincaid,* 759 F. Supp. 575 (W.D. Mo. 1991)] The school argued that the records were protected by Buckley, but a federal court disagreed, finding that "the fact that the statute specifically exempts records maintained for law enforcement purposes demonstrates that Congress did not intend to treat criminal investigation and incident reports as educational records." Furthermore, the court found, the actions of the university violated the First Amendment rights of the students to receive information. In another case heard later that same year, a federal judge enjoined the U.S. **Department of Education** from using the Buckley Amendment to keep colleges and universities from releasing campus crime records to the public. [*Student Press Law Ctr. v. Alexander,* 778 F. Supp. 1227 (D.D.C. 1991)]

The possible repercussions of violations of the amendment are another interesting issue. The consequences to the offending institution are obvious: it could potentially lose its federal financial backing. The act does not, however, provide a private cause of action for the people who are injured by violations of the act. They must seek alternate avenues of redress.

For example, in 1995, a federal court in South Dakota heard a case in which the parents of an autistic child sued the school district for releasing certain records regarding their child's education. [*Maynard v. Greater Hoyt Sch. Dist.,* 876 F. Supp. 1104 (D.S.D. 1995)] In that case, the child had been sent to a special school in Connecticut at the cost of the school district. To cover the cost of this special education, the district had to raise its property taxes. The child and his parents were identified through subsequent news coverage and public hearings on the issue of reducing the local tax burden. As a result, family members were harassed in what they felt were efforts to force them to move. Since there was no private cause of action available to the family under the Buckley Amendment, the court allowed them to maintain a suit under federal civil rights legislation.

An additional issue that sometimes arises is who should be denied access to educational records under Buckley. Some institutions have taken the directives of the Buckley Amendment to what some would argue are absurd lengths, even to the point of denying faculty members access to their own students' records. Critics of such policies point out that the amendment allows access to records by "other school officials, including teachers within the educational institution . . . who have been determined by such . . . institution to have legitimate educational interests." One professor in particular has pointed out that "while a university may accept a policy of denying faculty access to student records, it should be clear that the Buckley Amendment does not compel that result."

BUSING Transporting children away from neighborhood schools and into "racially identifiable" schools in an effort to achieve racial balance within a school district. The Supreme Court upheld busing in *Swann v. Charlotte-Mecklenburg Board of Education* [402 U.S. 1 (1971)] as a legitimate remedy for school systems in which *de jure* segregation, or segregation mandated by law, once existed.

In *Swann,* the Court held that busing does not conflict with the Civil Rights Act of 1964, which was enacted in part as a congressional response to the lack of progress made in school desegregation. The act states, however, that desegregation "shall not mean the assignment of students to public schools in order to overcome racial imbalance," and that "nothing herein shall empower any official or court of the United States to issue any order seeking to achieve a racial balance in any school by requiring the transportation of pupils or students from one school to another or one school district to another in order to achieve such racial balance." This, the Court explained, was the result of congressional concern that the act might be applied to schools that are racially imbalanced as a result of *de facto* segregation, or segregation by neutral circumstances such as population shifts, rather than due to state discrimination. Busing opponents, however, argue that these same restrictions were added to the act in an effort to appease southern representatives.

Critics also point to "white flight" as a way in which busing has hurt some of the school districts it was intended to help. This refers to the fact that many parents who are economically able to afford private schools withdraw their children from the public school system rather than put up with busing, which leaves the public schools with less of a white presence than before busing. For example, court-ordered busing began in Norfolk, Virginia, and Oklahoma City in 1972, at which time Norfolk schools were 57 percent white and Oklahoma City schools were 77 percent white. Some ten years later, the number of students attending Norfolk and Oklahoma City public schools had fallen dramatically. Of the students remaining in the public schools, the percentage of white students had fallen to 42 percent in Norfolk and 50 percent in Oklahoma City. Critics argue that the loss of these white students and their parents hurts the public schools and the students who remain behind in them. Membership in the Parent Teacher Association in Norfolk, for example, fell from between 15,000 and 20,000 in 1971 to 3,500 in 1981. Supporters of busing, on the other hand, argue that consideration of such statistics is evidence of a school district's continuing racism and the need for further remedies.

Perhaps the most pressing issue concerning court-ordered busing as a remedy for segregation today is when it will end. The most recent answer from the Supreme Court came in 1992, when it declared that a lower court could gradually relinquish control over a school district's desegregation process as it becomes apparent that the district has become "unitary," or desegregated, in different aspects of its operations, such as student assignments. [*Freeman v. Pitts,* 112 S. Ct. 1430 (1992)] The year before, the Court had held that a desegregation order should be lifted "after the local authorities have operated in compliance with it for a reasonable period of time," although the Court did not specify the length of a "reasonable period of time." [*Board of Educ. v. Dowell,* 498 U.S. 237 (1991)] Supporters of busing, however, worry that racially identifiable schools might reappear once such orders are dissolved.

C

CAMPUS SECURITY College students have traditionally considered their campuses to be safe havens from criminal activity—a view that now seems naïve in the face of recent publicity and litigation concerning crime at colleges and universities. The past several years have seen a trend toward lawsuits by student victims of crime to hold the colleges liable for negligence.

As in all cases alleging negligence, the plaintiff must prove that the defendant owed a duty, that the duty was breached, and that the breach of that duty was the proximate cause of the plaintiff's injuries. Courts sometimes find that a "special relationship" exists between a school and its students, which in turn gives rise to several duties. First, the college has a duty not to cover up crime or to misrepresent the safety of its campus. Second, the college has a duty to warn of foreseeable dangers of criminal incidents. The key word here is "foreseeable." One court, for example, held in favor of a student who was attacked in a stairwell on the campus of a community college. Since the college knew of other crimes committed in the same location it was foreseeable that more crimes might occur there, but college authorities never warned the students. [*Peterson v. San Francisco Community College Dist.*, 685 P.2d 1193 (Cal. 1984)]

Finally, the college has a duty to provide a certain level of security in order to prevent crimes from happening in the first place. The issue in cases based on this duty is how much security is enough. For example, in 1993. one court held that a university credit union customer who was raped on the university grounds had not proved causation, since her expert witness testified that the university's security measures were inadequate but was unable to say what measures would have been adequate. The court explained that causation of injuries from inadequate security is more easily proved in cases where the injury could have been prevented by "a lock or a fence or a chain across a driveway or some other physical device." [*Nola M. v. University of Southern Cal.*, 20 Cal. Rptr. 2d 97 (Cal. Ct. App. 1993)]

That same year, another court applied similar reasoning in finding against a dormitory resident who was attacked while in his room. In that case, the perpetrator had entered the building by scaling nearly three stories of exterior metal grating to find an unlocked fire door and then broke down the plaintiff's door in spite of a locked deadbolt. By placing two locked doors between the plaintiff and his attacker, the court held, the university had fulfilled its duty to provide security. [*Vangeli v. Schneider,* 598 N.Y.S.2d 837 (N.Y. App. Div. 1993)]

In an effort to be more forthcoming about the incidence of campus crime, Pennsylvania became the first state in 1991 to enact a crime-reporting law, following the murder of a student at Lehigh University. Soon after, 13 states had passed such laws. The requirements of these laws, however, varied greatly state to state, and most states still had no such statutes, which made it difficult for potential students to compare schools based on crime rates.

In an effort to solve this problem, Congress passed the Crime Awareness and Campus Security Act of 1991 to provide uniform reporting requirements. This act applies to all schools that receive federal funds, whether directly or through the financial aid awarded to their students. Under the terms of the act, each school must make annual reports detailing both crime statistics and security policies and distribute these reports to potential and current students and employees who request copies. Schools that do not comply with the terms of the act face suspension or termination of their federal money or fines up to $25,000 for each violation. The act does not, however, create a private cause of action upon which students could base a lawsuit.

CENSORSHIP Suppression of speech, sometimes occurring through the pressure of special-interest groups and sometimes originating within the schools themselves. In examining cases in which censorship is alleged, courts apply different levels of scrutiny depending on the nature of the arena in which the complained-of action occurred. For example, if a state agency attempts to stifle free expression in a public or limited public forum, such as a public park, the court will apply strict scrutiny, which is a very high standard of review. If the action occurs in a nonpublic forum, the court will apply only reasonable scrutiny.

A public school is generally considered to be a nonpublic forum, because even though it is a public facility, not just anyone is entitled to walk in from the street and begin speaking his or her mind. Even speech by those entitled to be there can be limited in certain conditions. For example, while the Supreme Court case ***Tinker v. Des Moines Independent School District*** held that students do not leave their First Amendment rights at the schoolhouse gate, school officials may suppress student expression that disrupts the orderly functioning of the school or violates the rights of others. Nearly 20 years after *Tinker,* the Supreme Court upheld the actions of a school principal who removed several pages of what he deemed objectionable material from the school newspaper. That case, ***Hazelwood School District v. Kuhlmeier,*** followed the reasoning in the 1983 Supreme Court case *Perry Education Association v. Perry Local Educators' Association* [460 U.S. 37 (1983)], which stated that school facilities are nonpublic, assuming school officials have not opened them up for use by the general public.

In 1991, the Ninth Circuit Court of Appeals considered a case in which school officials refused to sell advertising space in the high school newspaper to Planned Parenthood in an effort to steer clear of controversy. [*Planned Parenthood v. Clark County Sch. Dist.,* 941 F.2d 817 (9th Cir. 1991)] Planned Parenthood sued the school district for violating its free speech rights.

Even though the school gave the student editors broad latitude in decisions relating to the management of the newspaper, the school's written policy with regard to advertising standards stated that "the school reserves the right to deny advertising space to any entity that does not serve the best interests of the school, the school district, and the community." Even so, the school had sold advertising space to just about every organization, except Planned Parenthood, that sought it, including bars, churches, and political candidates. Although Planned Parenthood initially won, the decision was later overturned in the wake of *Hazelwood* on the basis that a school newspaper is not a public forum. Critics of this decision, however, contend that the school had opened up the paper for use by the general public by selling advertising space to all other organizations in spite of its written policy.

CHARTER SCHOOLS Schools that receive money from the state but operate independently of the bureaucracy inherent in the state educational system. Minnesota passed the first charter school law in 1991 and over a dozen other states have followed suit.

Supporters of the charter school movement claim that independence at the school level allows the schools to be more innovative in their approaches. Some schools, for example, emphasize the arts; others stress community service. Almost all require parental involvement as a condition of admission. In these respects, charter schools resemble private schools. Because they are public schools, however, children whose parents could not afford to pay tuition are not excluded.

Even so, not everyone supports charter schools. Many school districts oppose the movement, because state money follows the students. Fewer students in district schools means less funding for the schools. Other school districts, however, are cautiously supportive, seeing charter schools as a slightly less radical alternative to school **vouchers,** which would send public money to private and religious schools.

Teachers' unions tend to oppose charter schools as well. Their reasons range from concern over the quality of education provided by charter schools to distress over lack of collective bargaining agreements for teachers in charter schools. In an effort to pacify the unions, many states with charter laws have set limits on the number of charters that can be awarded. For example, the state of California has limited its number of charter schools to 100 and Massachusetts permits only 25.

Charter schools were the subject of two legal attacks in the fall of 1994, but each case had a vastly different outcome. In Colorado, Hispanic parents challenged the law based on the closing of two neighborhood schools and the funding of a charter school for the arts. The parents claimed that the law unconstitutionally discriminated against them and that the money that went to fund the charter school should have been used to keep the other two schools open. The court disagreed, saying the law applied equally to all racial groups and was a genuine effort toward school reform.

A Michigan law did not fare so well. At the center of the Michigan controversy was the Noah Webster Academy, a network of **home schools** that was slated to receive approximately $11 million in state aid. Various organizations backed the challenge, including the Michigan Education Association and the Michigan chapter of the **American Civil Liberties Union (ACLU).** Concerns over Noah Webster's eligibility for charter money ranged from the fact that many of the home schoolers enrolled in the academy chose overtly religious courses of study, in violation of the separation of state and religion, to the school's violations of the requirements to operate from a single location and to use only certified teachers. The state Department of Education eventually ruled that due to the latter violations Noah Webster Academy was ineligible for charter aid. Shortly after that, however, a state court ruled that the law allowing for charter schools violated a state ban on spending public money on private schools and was, therefore, unconstitutional [see **private schools, government money and**]. [*Council of Organizations v. Governor of Mich.*, 548 N.W.2d 909 (Mich. Ct. App. 1996)]

CHILD-BENEFIT THEORY Principle established by the U.S. Supreme Court in 1930 to support its holding that a statute requiring the state of Louisiana to purchase textbooks and lend them to all children, regardless of whether the children attended public schools or private schools, did not violate the establishment clause of the U.S. Constitution [see **establishment and free exercise clauses**], even though many of the private schools had religious affiliations. [*Cochran v. Louisiana State Bd. of Educ.*, 281 U.S. 370 (1930)] Seventeen years later, the Court applied the child-benefit theory to a case in which parents of private school students were reimbursed by the state for the cost of their children's bus fare to and from school; the Court upheld the statute authorizing the reimbursements. The Court directed that in order for a law to be valid under this theory, it must meet two requirements: (1) the legislature must have intended to help the state's school children, not its private schools, and (2) the children must, in fact, be the ones who receive the benefit of the law, not the private schools. [*Everson v. Board of Educ.*, 330 U.S. 1 (1947)]

In the 1970s, the Supreme Court heard several more cases dealing with textbook lending programs. Each time, it applied the child-benefit theory and upheld the practice. State courts, however, have generally rejected using public funds to finance textbooks for private school students. Such holdings do not conflict with the Supreme Court opinions, because while a state constitution cannot take away from the rights guaranteed in the federal Constitution, it can extend rights even further. So, even if a state statute, such as one establishing a textbook lending program, does not violate the U.S. Constitution, it may still run afoul of a state constitution that takes separation of church and state even further.

CIVIL SUITS Sometimes students who are injured at school or on their way to or from school bring civil suits in an attempt to recover money damages to compensate them for their injuries. Many of these cases rely on a theory of negligence. In order for a party to be liable for negligence, several factors must be met: (1) there must be a duty on the part of the defendant toward the victim either to act or to refrain from acting in a particular way, (2) this duty must be breached through failure to exercise a reasonable standard of care, and (3) there must be an injury caused by this breach.

Suppose, for example, that a student athlete suffers a concussion while sliding headfirst onto base. The physical education instructor has not taught the students that this sort of maneuver is dangerous. The student could make a case that the teacher was negligent. The teacher did have a duty to protect the well-being of the students. Under a reasonable standard of care, one way in which a physical education instructor fulfills this duty is by instructing students in how to participate safely in sports. And, finally, the student suffered an actual injury as a result of this breach of duty by the teacher.

If sued for negligence, a teacher, administrator, or school district may assert any of a number of possible defenses in an attempt to avoid liability. At common law, for example, school districts were immune from suit, since they were agents of the government. Teachers, however, were not entitled to this defense. Some states have done away with, or at least limited, this immunity either legislatively (by passing laws) or judicially (by decree of a court).

Because of the difficulty in many states of successfully suing a school district for injuries sustained by a student, more and more constitutional tort actions are brought instead—especially where the school has failed to protect the student against **violence** or **sexual harassment.** The Constitution restricts the government from depriving a person of his or her constitutional rights, but it does not set out a means for punishing one who, as an agent of the state, engages in such behavior anyway. Under 42 U.S.C. § 1983, however, one can sometimes recover money damages in such situations.

Section 1983 also covers situations in which the government could have prevented a constitutional deprivation but failed to do so. For example, courts have held that prison inmates and involuntarily committed mental patients have a "special relationship" with the state that gives rise to a duty on the part of the state to look out for their safety. This is because the inmates and the patients are at the complete mercy of the state and are incapable of acting on their own behalf.

On the other hand, the Supreme Court held that no special relationship existed between a county department of social services and a young child whom the department had good reason to believe was abused by his father. The department continued to hand the child back to the father despite blatant evidence of abuse. When the father finally beat the child so severely that he destroyed parts of his son's brain, the child and his mother sued under section 1983, claiming that the department violated the boy's right to liberty by failing to rescue him from his father. The Court disagreed, since the injuries were inflicted by the father rather than by an agent of the state. [*DeShaney v. Winnebago County Dep't of Social Servs.*, 489 U.S. 189 (1989)] Had the same abuse occurred in the context of a foster-care situation, the result might have been different.

This leads to the question of whether public schools and their students have a "special relationship" that would support recovery under section 1983. The answer varies among lower courts. For example, the Fifth Circuit held that because of state **compulsory attendance** laws requiring children to attend school, the schools do have such a relationship with their students. Accordingly, the teachers and administrators of a high school had an affirmative duty to intervene when nearly everyone knew that a coach was sexually molesting one of his students. [*Doe v. Taylor Indep. Sch. Dist.*, 15 F.3d 443 (5th Cir. 1994)]

On the other hand, in the case of a special-education student who fought during school with several other students who later chased him away from the school and to a site where he either died accidentally or was killed, a Pennsylvania federal district court granted summary judgment in favor of the school district in the mother's section 1983 claim. The court reasoned that the compulsory education laws did not restrict a parent's capability to protect his or her child (or the capability of the child to protect him- or herself). Furthermore, in this case especially, since the child was disabled and therefore covered by federal legislation requiring parental approval of his educational plan, it was the mother who ultimately decided where her son should go to school. [*Hunter v. Carbondale Area Sch. Dist.*, 829 F. Supp. 714 (M.D. Pa. 1993)]

COMMUNITY SERVICE Since the late 1980s, many schools have begun requiring their students to perform community service as part of the educational **curriculum.** In 1993, the Third Circuit Court of Appeals became the first federal appellate court to consider the constitutional implications of such demands.

Two high school students and their parents filed a lawsuit against the school district and superintendent, challenging a requirement that students perform 60 hours of community service in order to graduate. The district had adopted the program to "help students acquire life skills and learn about the significance of rendering services to their communities . . . [and] gain a sense of worth and pride as they understand and appreciate the functions of community organizations." As part of the program, the high school maintained a list of some 70 organizations for which students could work to obtain their community service credit. The list included such organizations as the Girl Scout Council, a local museum, Meals on Wheels, and Planned Parenthood, but students and their parents were encouraged to suggest other organizations to be added to the list. Students could also exercise the option of designing an "experiential situation" in which they created their own community service program.

The plaintiffs alleged that this program violated their First Amendment rights to **freedom of speech** and their Thirteenth Amendment rights to freedom from involuntary servitude. The trial court, however, disagreed and granted judgment in favor of the defendants without trial.

On appeal, the circuit court first considered the plaintiffs' free speech claims. [*Steirer v. Bethlehem Area Sch. Dist.*, 987 F.2d 989 (3d Cir. 1993)] The students argued that requiring them to take part in the program compelled them to declare a belief in the value of altruism and explained that "when a student goes out and works for others in his community, it is natural for an observer to assume that the student supports the idea that helping others and serving the community are desirable." The court agreed that actions can constitute protected speech when they amount to expressive conduct—when the actor intends to express a message and those who view the action are likely to understand the message. Courts have held that symbolic actions such as black armbands, flag salutes, and recitation of the **Pledge of Allegiance** are protected as speech, while the length of a student's hair [see **hair codes**] is nonexpressive conduct and, therefore, not constitutionally protected. The court found that the performance of community service under such a program fell into the second category of conduct and was not protected. Rather than believing that the students were expressing support for altruism, the court concluded that observers were just as likely to view them "merely as students completing their high school graduation requirements."

The court agreed that if the community service program required the students to work for a particular organization whose views conflicted with their own, it would possibly raise First Amendment concerns. This, however, was not the plaintiffs' argument. They were free to choose a charity from an extensive list of approved organizations, add other charities to the list, or even create their own programs.

Next, the court considered the plaintiffs' claim that the community service requirement violated the Thirteenth Amendment, which states, "Neither slavery nor involuntary servitude, except as punishment for crime whereof the party shall have been duly convicted, shall exist within the United States." The amendment was intended to abolish slavery and other similar types of compulsory labor. The plaintiffs argued that the amendment applied to the program, saying, (1) "the program is servitude because the students provide unpaid service to the community for the benefit of others" and (2) "participation in the program is involuntary because the threat of not receiving a diploma is prima facie coercion."

The court, however, disagreed, pointing out that "not every situation in which an individual faces a choice between labor or legal sanctions constitutes involuntary servitude." Military service and jury duty, for example, have been found by courts to be civic duties for which the government may impose legal sanctions to ensure compliance. Courts have also upheld requirements that attorneys provide a certain number of hours of *pro bono*, or free, work as a condition of maintaining a law license and have allowed the collection of money damages from physicians who accepted National Health Service Corps scholarships and then refused to perform the required services after graduation. Based on this history, the court concluded that it could not analogize the community service requirement, which was designed primarily to benefit the students' education, to slavery simply because the students would not receive money for their work.

A New York high school student and his parents also challenged a similar requirement on the grounds that it violated his Thirteenth Amendment right to freedom from involuntary servitude. [*Immediato v. Rye Neck Sch. Dist.*, 873 F. Supp. 846 (S.D.N.Y. 1995)] The plaintiffs based their case on a violation of the student's right to privacy under the Fourteenth Amendment by requiring him to choose between revealing the types of organizations he truly believed to be worthy of helping and choosing only those of which his teachers and classmates would approve. The parents also alleged a violation of their right to control their child's education and upbringing. The court was unpersuaded by these assertions. It referred to the *Steirer* decision in overruling the slavery argument. In the two points that were not addressed by *Steirer*, the court concluded that a student's choices, such as which class to take, which book to write a report on, or which organization to assist, do not implicate any constitutionally protected interest and that parents do not have a constitutionally protected right to remove their children from classes and programs they disapprove of on purely secular (nonreligious) grounds. The court of appeals agreed and upheld the lower court's opinion.

COMPULSORY ATTENDANCE State compulsory attendance laws are rooted in the concept of *parens patriae,* a common law doctrine meaning that the government acts as a sort of super-parent over all of its citizens, both adults and minors. Although parents have a general right to control the upbringing of their children, the state can restrict that right to some degree in order to protect the children and further its own interests. Since the state has a legitimate interest in having an educated population, it can require children to have some form of education, even against the wishes of their parents.

Compulsory attendance laws often work in conjunction with other types of laws, such as child labor laws, to prevent the exploitation of children and to ensure their attendance at school. The city of Chicago passed an ordinance that prohibited children under the age of 17 from playing video games during school hours. Again, the aim of that law was to do away with a possible hinderance to school attendance. A federal court upheld the statute in 1991 when it was attacked as a violation of freedom of expression. [*Rothner v. City of Chicago,* 725 F. Supp. 945 (N.D. Ill. 1989)]

Children have both a right and a duty to attend school. Children who fail to attend school regularly or at all are said to be truant [see **truancy**]. While a child might be excused from attending school due to illness or disability, truant children and their parents can face criminal punishment.

Compulsory attendance laws work to benefit not only children but also the state, which has a legitimate interest in setting certain requirements that children must meet in order to attend school. For example, most states demand that children submit to routine **vaccinations** to prevent the spread of disease through the schools. Also, a state may require that children live in a certain area in order to attend a certain public school, but it may not deny the children of **illegal aliens** residing in the state admission to the schools. States still try sometimes to do just that: California passed Proposition 137 in 1994, which was aimed specifically at excluding illegal aliens from public benefits, including education and health care.

The government does not, however, have unlimited power over education matters. For example, in ***Pierce v. Society of Sisters,*** the U.S. Supreme Court held that a state law requiring children to attend only public schools was unconstitutional. Parents who elect not to send their children to public schools can comply with compulsory attendance laws by enrolling them in private schools or **home schools.**

The Court also held, in ***Wisconsin v. Yoder,*** that although the state does have an interest in educating its children, Amish children could be excused from attending after the eighth grade because attending high school violates their religion. Since the *Yoder* decision, a number of parents have attempted to get around compulsory attendance laws by pleading infringement on their religious beliefs. Proof that school attendance runs contrary to religious beliefs, however, must be very strong for a child to be excused. For example, one court held that the children of parents who believed that desegregated schools were sinful were not excused from complying with the compulsory education laws.

CONDOMS In an effort to prevent the spread of AIDS [see **AIDS education**] and to reverse the increasing frequency of pregnancy among high school students, some schools have begun distributing free condoms to students who request them. In 1992, an organization of parents of Philadelphia high school students challenged a program that presumed parental consent for condom distribution unless the student's parents returned a letter "opting out" of the program. [*Parents United for Better Schools v. School Dist. of Philadelphia Bd. of Educ.*, 646 A.2d 689 (Pa. Commw. Ct. 1994)] The court initially dismissed the claim, but an appellate court ordered the case to be sent back for trial. In its opinion, the appellate court pointed out that parental consent and parental veto are two very different procedures, with parental consent providing more protection for parental rights. Also, the court pointed out, affirmative parental consent is required under Pennsylvania law before minors may engage in a number of activities, such as applying for a driver's or marriage license, waiving *Miranda* rights, or donating blood. It would not, therefore, be unreasonable for such affirmative consent to be required before a child could obtain birth control devices through his or her public school.

Also in 1992, New York City parents challenged a slightly different program in the city's public schools. [*Alfonso v. Fernandez*, 606 N.Y.S.2d 259 (N.Y. App. Div. 1993)] Not only did this AIDS-education program not require affirmative parental consent, it also did not allow parents to opt out of the program on behalf of their children, who could obtain condoms for free in health resource rooms set up at the schools. Although counseling was available to the students, they were not required to participate in it to receive the condoms. The trial court held that since handing out condoms did not constitute a health service, such as the dispensing of prescription drugs, the schools were not in violation of state statutes requiring parental consent. The court also held that the program interfered with neither the parents' **due process** rights to bring up their children in accordance with their own views nor their rights to free exercise of their religious beliefs.

The appellate court agreed that the program did not violate any First Amendment religious rights, since it merely offended their beliefs rather than denied them the ability to practice their religion. However, the appellate court disagreed with the decision reached by the lower court on the other two arguments.

First, the court concluded that distribution of condoms is, in fact, a health service. Although the statutes requiring parental consent before health services are offered to minors do provide certain exceptions, such as the distribution of birth control to minors through clinics or as part of public assistance programs, distribution of condoms through the public schools is not a recognized exception to the general rule.

Next, the court found that the parents did have a constitutionally protected due process right to direct their children's upbringing. The court pointed out, however, that even without the program at the schools students have ready access to condoms, which "are now displayed next to vitamins and cold remedies" at drug stores and that "a condom may be purchased for about the same price as a slice of pizza." Students can also obtain condoms through publicly funded programs outside of school. While the prevention of AIDS among high school students is a worthy goal, the school district failed to show that this goal could be met only by interfering with the parents' due process rights.

In 1996, the Supreme Court turned down the opportunity to review a case in which parents challenged a high school's policy of providing condoms to students who requested them. [*Curtis v. School Comm. of Falmouth*, 652 N.E.2d 580 (Mass. 1995) , cert. den., 116 S. Ct. 753 (1996)] The Massachusetts state court that heard the case agreed with the parents, who were supported by the **American Center for Law and Justice (ACLJ),** that parents do have a constitutionally protected right to direct the upbringing of their children. In this case, however, the parents had not shown how the school's condom policy burdened that right. The refusal by the Court to hear the case is not legal support in favor of such policies. The Court could, at any time, agree to hear a case involving similar issues and find in favor of the parents.

Controversy occasionally arises concerning students and condoms even when the school is not the distributor. In fact, officials at one California high school confiscated nearly 400 condoms in the spring of 1995 that a group of students had planned to hand out in "safe-sex kits" for prom goers. The kits included a note stating that the condoms were provided by students, not by the school, but the officials decided that the kits violated a district policy of promoting abstinence.

Conduct off School Grounds, Students and

Teachers and school administrators have the right to control the actions of students under the doctrine of *in loco parentis,* which means that the school stands in the place of the parent. That doctrine was historically interpreted as giving school personnel nearly unlimited authority in disciplinary matters, both at school and away from school if the actions committed away from school had a bearing on the good order of the school. A classic example of this is the "old Jack Seaver" case from the mid-1800s, in which a court upheld as proper the beating of a boy who disrespectfully referred to the headmaster in the presence of other students but away from school as "old Jack Seaver." [*Lander v. Seaver,* 32 Vt. 114, 76 Am. Dec. 156 (1859)]

Today, however, the increasing respect for the rights of students makes such a result unlikely. In 1986, for example, a federal court in Maine held that a high school could not suspend a student for "giving the finger" to a teacher in a restaurant parking lot after school hours. [*Klein v. Smith,* 635 F. Supp. 1440 (D. Me. 1986)] The school had based the suspension on a rule against "vulgar or extremely inappropriate language or conduct directed to a staff member" and argued that allowing such an action to go unpunished would undermine discipline and respect at school. The court disagreed, however, pointing out that any possible connection between the offense and discipline at school was very weak, since neither the student nor the teacher had been engaged in any school activity.

In 1995, an interesting situation arose concerning the authority of a school to discipline a student for off-campus activities conducted on the Internet [see **Internet censorship**]. A high school student with an exceptional academic record constructed, on his own time and using his own resources, a World Wide Web home page lampooning his school. The Web page listed "sex" as one of the favorite subjects of the student body and included hypertext links to other Web areas that included graphic sexual content. The student's home page was accepted for listing on Yahoo, a popular directory of Web pages.

Even though the title of the home page declared it to be "unofficial" and the text contained a number of disclaimers disassociating the page from the school, school officials were not amused. When an assistant principal and guidance counselor confronted the student, he responded by removing the home page from the Internet. Even so, the assistant principal retaliated by revoking the school's endorsement of the student for a National Merit scholarship and sending letters to all the colleges to which he had applied, withdrawing any recommendations.

The student, backed by the **American Civil Liberties Union (ACLU),** threatened to sue for violations of his constitutional rights to free speech [see **freedom of speech**] and **due process.** The school district finally settled, agreeing to compensate the student for the $2,000 scholarship that the assistant principal's actions had cost him. As part of the settlement, the district also issued a public statement apologizing to the student and affirming the district's respect for the constitutional rights of its students.

CONDUCT OFF SCHOOL GROUNDS, TEACHERS AND

Until relatively recently, entering the field of education involved teachers sacrificing a great deal of personal privacy in order to be positive role models for their students. In 1954, for example, one education law scholar wrote, "When he enters the teaching profession, a person legally surrenders a measure of his freedom of action. It should be remembered that a teacher may legally be free to be immoral, so long as he violates no law, but he is not legally free to be a teacher and engage in immoral conduct."

Until the 1960s, a teacher could be discharged on the basis of mere rumor or speculation without any real proof. In 1969, however, a court recognized a teacher's right to a private life so long as his or her activities did not make the teacher professionally unfit. In *Morrison v. Board of Education* [461 P.2d 375 (Cal. 1969)], the Supreme Court of California overturned a decision to revoke the certificate of a teacher for a homosexual encounter with another teacher three years earlier, since the board was unable to show that Morrison's behavior made him unfit to teach.

Many courts since *Morrison* have followed its "nexus" requirement, meaning that a school board may not fire a teacher for his or her private activities unless the board can show a substantial relationship between the off-campus activities and the teacher's professional effectiveness. For example, in 1993, a Tennessee court upheld the termination of a band director who engaged in homosexual acts at his home with some of his students and who then used his authority at school to punish the students who refused to accommodate him. [*Morris v. Clarksville-Montgomery County Consolidated Bd. of Educ.*, 867 S.W.2d 324 (Tenn. Ct. App. 1993)]

CONFEDERATE FLAGS Protests over the presence of Confederate battle flags at public schools began to reach the courts in the early 1970s as part of school desegregation cases. In some cases, the flags were sponsored by school officials. In 1970, for example, a federal trial court heard a case in which a Louisiana high school principal refused to remove a Confederate flag from his office, where it was displayed along with the American and state flags. [*Smith v. St. Tammany Parish Sch. Bd.*, 316 F. Supp. 1174 (E.D. La. 1970)] The court held that the rebel flag had to be removed since it expressed an official desire to maintain segregated schools and hindered efforts to eliminate racial discrimination in the school.

In ordering the removal of such flags, the court specifically stated that "this shall not prevent individual students from wearing or displaying buttons, signs, or symbols." Many subsequent protests, however, have been sparked by precisely such individual action.

For example, a federal court considered a case in which a high school student challenged the constitutionality of his suspension for wearing a jacket that had a Confederate flag patch on the sleeve. [*Melton v. Young*, 465 F.2d 1332 (6th Cir. 1972)] In 1969, the year before the jacket incident, the school had abandoned the Confederate flag and the song "Dixie" as its official school flag and pep song after students held protests that had far-reaching effects, such as disruption of classes and imposition of a city-wide curfew for several nights. The protests led the school board to adopt a code banning the flag from school premises and prohibiting "provocative symbols on clothing."

When the student wore his jacket to school, the principal asked him either to remove the flag patch or not wear the jacket while at school, but the student refused and was allowed to return to class. A number of students and teachers complained, and the student was once again asked to remove the jacket. When he continued to refuse, the principal declared that the flag was "provocative" and therefore forbidden by the policy and suspended the student. The student sued, claiming that the regulation and his suspension violated his constitutional right to free speech.

The court held that the statute against provocative symbols was unconstitutionally vague and therefore void. (In order to be valid, a reasonable person must be able to tell from reading a statute exactly what conduct is prohibited. Otherwise, there is a risk that people might refrain from engaging in allowable conduct in an effort not to cross over the invisible line.) Even though the statute was ruled unconstitutional, however, the court upheld the student's suspension as valid. The court cited the Supreme Court case ***Tinker v. Des Moines Independent School District*** as precedent for not giving constitutional protection to students' speech where that speech disrupts class work or invades the rights of others. In view of the disruption resulting from flag protests the year before, the principal was reasonable to anticipate that the patch on the jacket could lead to similar violence.

More than 30 years after these cases, controversy continues to flare up occasionally in educational institutions over the Confederate flag. For example, in 1991, 100 students were suspended from a South Carolina high school in the chaos that ensued after students began demanding the right to wear the flag on their clothes. Three years later a similar conflict arose at a Texas high school when a student was forced to change out of a T-shirt displaying the Confederate flag and the slogan: "It's a white thing, you wouldn't understand." Fears of violence lead quite a few parents to keep their children home from school temporarily, but the incident eventually passed after students agreed to a 30-day ban on race-related clothing.

Confederate flag controversies are not limited to public secondary schools; they have reached the realm of higher education as well. In 1983, the University of Mississippi was persuaded to abandon the flag as its official emblem. The display of a Confederate flag was also listed among the actions that could lead to punishment under **hate-speech codes** promulgated by the University of Michigan in 1987 and later declared unconstitutional by a federal court. Even the Virginia Military Institute, where black cadets caused a furor in 1971 for refusing to turn eyes right to the Confederate flag during a ceremony in honor of cadets who died in the Civil War, no longer uses the flag symbol on its official class rings.

COPYRIGHT A right giving the holder the exclusive power to reproduce copies of literary, musical, or artistic materials and to sell those copies for a certain number of years. Such rights are protected by federal statutes that attempt to balance society's need for access to such materials with the creator's need for recognition and compensation.

An understanding of basic copyright issues has an important place in the field of education, because of the amount of copy-making that occurs in the educational environment. For example, sometimes schools might order one copy of a piece of music or a videotape and then reproduce as many of their own copies as they need. Such actions, while seldom malicious, can violate the copyright laws.

In 1991, a federal district court heard a case that provides an excellent analysis of modern copyright law as it applies to education. In *Basic Books, Inc. v. Kinko's Graphics Corp.* [758 F. Supp. 1522 (S.D.N.Y. 1991)], a group of publishers sued a photocopying business for copyright infringement stemming from the business's practice of photocopying copyrighted materials at the request of college professors for inclusion in anthologies that the business then sold to the students. These anthologies often included entire chapters from other sources, and none of the excerpts contained the required copyright notice. The court found in favor of the publishers and ordered Kinko's to pay $510,000 in damages, which it eventually agreed to pay along with attorneys' fees of over $1.3 million.

One of the principle defenses asserted by Kinko's was that of the fair-use doctrine. This doctrine attempts to forge a compromise between copyright holders and educational institutions by giving one other than the holder the privilege to use the material in a reasonable manner without consent. In determining whether the action in controversy constituted a "fair use" or copyright infringement, courts weigh four factors. First, the court must consider the "purpose and character of the use," such as whether it serves educational or commercial purposes. In *Kinko's,* the court held that even though one purpose was to provide educational materials for university students, Kinko's actions showed profit-making intentions.

Second, the court must consider the nature of the copyrighted work. Factual, informative works are given less protection than creative, fictional works, because copyright laws work to protect expression of ideas rather than particular facts. Since most of the works copied by Kinko's were factual, the court found in favor of Kinko's on this particular element.

The next factor to be weighed is the amount of material copied and the significance of this amount in relation to the whole work. Kinko's lost on this issue, because it had copied entire chapters from other texts. The court declared that the action of copying 110 pages from another work and selling it to 132 students was "grossly out of line with accepted fair-use principles."

Finally, courts must consider the market effect the unauthorized copying has on the original. In *Kinko's*, the court found that the reproduction had a significantly detrimental market effect on the copyrighted works, because without the anthologies provided by Kinko's, the students would have been forced to buy the original books from the publishers.

The *Kinko's* court also applied the Guidelines for Classroom Copying in Not-for-Profit Educational Institutions, which are found in the legislative history of the Copyright Act. The guidelines set out a three-part test for determining when teachers may make multiple copies of copyrighted works: (1) the copying must meet brevity and spontaneity tests, (2) the copying must meet a cumulative effect test, and (3) each copy must include a copyright notice.

The brevity standard set out in the guidelines specifies certain numerical limits on the number of words and the percentage of an entire work that may be reproduced, while the spontaneity element requires that there must be insufficient time to go through the proper channels for requesting permission. Kinko's failed to meet both of these standards, given the amount of materials photocopied and the fact that the copying was done at the beginning of the semester, even for works that would not be used until much later in the semester. The cumulative effect test, which Kinko's failed to meet, requires that "there shall not be more than nine instances of . . . multiple copying for one course during one class term." Finally, Kinko's failed to meet the third requirement by not including copyright notices in its anthologies.

The effect of the *Kinko's* decision has been substantial. Companies such as Kinko's no longer offer anthology services, and the permission process is burdened by professors who have renewed interest in operating "by the book." Many other professors changed the content of their courses rather than go through the permissions process or take a risk with unauthorized photocopying.

Even after *Kinko's*, misunderstandings about copyright issues in education abound. Many teachers and school officials, for example, believe that they can get around the copyright laws by having students do any questionable photocopying. The laws, however, apply to students just as much as they apply to anybody else, and a teacher who attempts to use a student in such a way could find him- or herself held liable anyway.

Another common misunderstanding is the notion that copyright laws do not apply to out-of-print materials. Some courts, including the court in *Kinko's*, have indicated that they would be more likely to find a fair use in cases where the reproduced material was out of print, since that would serve society's need for material that might otherwise be unavailable. On the other hand, one who holds the copyright to out-of-print material has no means of making money from the material without charging a fee for permission to copy.

Another area that raises copyright questions in the field of education is who to designate as the proper copyright holder when a teacher creates a work, such as a textbook. If the teacher does not have a contract that covers copyright issues, it may be difficult to prove who holds the copyright, whether the teacher, the school district, or the university that employs the teacher, unless the teacher is able to show that he or she created the work completely independently.

A basic understanding of copyright law is especially important now, since the stakes associated with infringement have recently increased. Spurred on by lobbying from the Software Publisher's Association, Congress passed a law in 1992 that lowered the level of copyright infringement that would qualify as a federal felony. While the old statute imposed felony penalties for reproducing extremely high numbers of sound recordings, motion pictures, or audiovisual works, the new statute makes it a felony to willfully and wrongfully reproduce within 180 days "at least 10 copies . . . of 1 or more copyrighted works, with a retail value of more than $2500" and broadens the application of the old law to also cover books, computer software, and magazines. Potential penalties include imprisonment of up to five years and fines of up to $250,000. The amount of the fines may be doubled when an organization rather than an individual is convicted under the statute.

CORPORAL PUNISHMENT Infliction of physical pain to punish a student for disobedience. Pain inflicted by a school official against a student in self-defense or in the defense of other persons or of property is not corporal punishment.

Most people think of beatings when they hear the words "corporal punishment," but it can also include a student being stuck with pins, shaken, locked in a closet, denied bathroom privileges, or made to endure excessive physical training. In at least one aversion therapy program used on unruly students, it has on occasion included mild electrical shock administered to the sole of a student's foot through a small, remote-controlled device that fits inside a sneaker.

Teachers and other school officials have a historically recognized right to use force against students when reasonably necessary to maintain order in the schools. Such a right is said to have arisen out of the common law. No federal statute exists that outlaws the use of corporal punishment against students. In addition, in ***Ingraham v. Wright,*** the U.S. Supreme Court refused to extend constitutional protection to students who received corporal punishment. This does not, however, mean that all corporal punishment is perfectly legal in all U.S. schools.

In the first place, a number of states have outlawed corporal punishment on their own, starting with New Jersey in 1867. By 1994, 27 states had enacted laws prohibiting corporal punishment of students. Many places in states that continue to permit corporal punishment have banned it at the county, city, or school board level. For example, the cities of Miami, Florida; Boulder, Colorado; and Pittsburgh, Pennsylvania, forbid the practice even though the state statutes of Florida, Colorado, and Pennsylvania allow it.

Many jurisdictions that allow corporal punishment have enacted **due process** safeguards, such as requiring witnesses or hearings. Many of these states and localities have set specific limits on exactly what force may be used. For example, it may be illegal to strike the student's head or to require the student to remove articles of clothing. Or, there may be a state or local requirement that the school notify the student's parents before administering corporal punishment (although in the absence of such a rule, schools do not have to give parental notification or get parental consent). A school official who uses corporal punishment in violation of state or local rules may face a variety of consequences. He or she may be subject to administrative discipline (such as suspension or firing), criminal penalties (imposed by the state as monetary fines or even imprisonment), or civil penalties (damages in the form of money paid to the injured party).

Even in a state that allows corporal punishment but gives absolutely no guidance about how or when it should be used, a school official could still be found liable in the judicial system for assault and battery. The injured student may file a civil suit in court or the state may pursue a criminal conviction. In order for either of these actions to be successful, the injured student must show to the court (1) that the force used was unreasonable and unnecessary under the circumstances and (2) that he or she suffered an actual injury.

A court might also find in favor of a student who received corporal punishment if the punishment involved racial issues. For example, a court might find a school official liable for damages if the student can prove that his or her paddling was motivated by racial prejudice. Likewise, if a student could prove that children of one race receive paddlings or other physical punishments while children of another race who commit the same offense are not physically punished, the school officials might be found guilty of discrimination.

The incidence of corporal punishment varies widely across the nation. The National Coalition to Abolish Corporal Punishment in Schools asserts that a child in the South is 4,000 times more likely to experience corporal punishment than a child in the Northeast. Many opponents of corporal punishment would like to see federal legislation to guarantee all students equal freedom from such punishment. So far, however, all attempts by Congress to legislate corporal punishment have been unsuccessful. In 1992, the Hon. Major R. Owens introduced a bill that would prohibit corporal punishment in schools that receive federal funds. The bill went to the Committee on Education and Labor, where it languished and died. Support for the bill continues, however, and it was subsequently reintroduced.

CREATIONISM AND EVOLUTION

Theories that attempt to explain the beginning of the world. Creationism, sometimes called "creation science," accepts the biblical account that God created the world and all its people, while evolution is Charles Darwin's theory that mankind descended gradually from members of the ape family. Controversy sometimes arises over which theory should be taught in the public school curriculum.

Early in the twentieth century, some states enacted antievolution legislation to prohibit public schools from teaching the evolution theory, since many people believed it ran against biblical teachings. In the 1927 case ***Scopes v. State,*** popularly known as the "Scopes monkey trial," the Tennessee Supreme Court upheld the constitutionality of the Butler Act, a state law forbidding the teaching of evolution in Tennessee public schools and universities. Forty years later, however, Tennessee repealed its antievolution act, and only Arkansas and Mississippi still had such laws.

Then, in 1968, the U.S. Supreme Court struck down the Arkansas antievolution statute, saying such a law violated the establishment clause of the Constitution [see **establishment and free exercise clauses**], which forbids the government to enact laws to further any particular religion. [*Epperson v. State,* 393 U.S. 97 (1968)] Rejecting the teaching of evolution only because it conflicts with Christian teachings, the Court declared, amounted to endorsement by the state of Christian doctrine. Two years later, the Mississippi Supreme Court struck down Mississippi's antievolution statute on the grounds that it violated the free exercise clause of the Constitution.

The revocation of the antievolution laws offended many supporters of creationism who claimed that their theory is as "scientific" as Darwinism and that Darwin's theory is in itself a religion: secular humanism. In an effort to get creationism back into the curriculum, Arkansas enacted a law that required teaching creation-science along with evolution. A federal court struck down this statute as a violation of the separation of church and state in 1982. In the 1987 case *Edwards v. Aguillard* [482 U.S. 578 (1987)], the U.S. Supreme Court agreed that a state could not mandate the teaching of creationism because of the religious intentions of the legislature.

In 1994, a California high school biology teacher sued his school district for requiring him to teach evolution as fact rather than theory, which he claimed showed support for atheism and hostility to religion. A federal court dismissed his case as frivolous (meaning without basis), but an appellate court reopened the case. The appellate court, however, later reversed itself and declared that he could not sue after all, because requiring the teaching of evolution does not affect religion. [*Peloza v. Capistrano Unified Sch. Dist.,* 37 F.3d 517 (9th Cir. 1994)]

The controversy over which theory to teach has also reached into the sphere of higher education. In 1993, the administration of the Biology Department at San Francisco State University reproached a teacher who had been teaching that an "intelligent designer" created life on earth. Although the professor avoided mentioning God in his lectures, the administration decided that he was indoctrinating students with religion and reassigned him to teach other courses. The teacher received support from many of his fellow faculty members as well as from an organization devoted to maintaining academic freedom. He was eventually reinstated in his regular class.

CURRICULUM Courses offered by a school. In public schools, the course of study is generally set out by the state legislature, which mandates that students obtain a certain number of credits in required classes, such as English. Local school boards often have power to set out their own requirements, as long as the local rules do not violate state standards.

Even the federal government has gotten into the business of curriculum planning with the passage by Congress of the **Goals 2000** legislation, which is aimed at establishing voluntary goals for teaching standards. Many objected in 1994 when the national standards for teaching world history in grades 5 through 12 were released. The standards attempt to replace the emphasis on Western contributions commonly taught as world history with a more multicultural view that recognizes the achievements of African Americans, Native Americans, and women. Some, however, decry this as revisionist history, which edits out the accomplishments of many white males, such as Paul Revere and Thomas Edison.

Problems often occur on a state or local level when either the legislature or a school board goes beyond setting out broad requirements and attempts to dictate the substance of what is to be taught. For example, Florida legislators introduced a bill in 1994 that would require Florida students to learn about the extermination of Jews and other minorities in World War II as a case study of the effects of hatred. Conservative groups opposed the measure, fearing it might lead to establishing acceptance of homosexuality as part of the curriculum based on a Florida Department of Education bulletin that listed homosexuals as a group to be valued for its diversity.

The small Florida town of Tavares, on the other hand, offended many liberals when its school board ordered that students be taught "our republican form of government, capitalism, a free enterprise system, patriotism, strong family values, freedom of religion and other basic values that are superior to other foreign or historic cultures." A number of students, parents, and teachers filed suit, claiming that the policy violates First Amendment rights to free speech [see **freedom of speech**] and teachers' rights to **academic freedom.**

Parents sometimes disagree with state mandates dealing with the teaching of other sensitive subjects such as **creationism and evolution, sex education,** and **AIDS education.** Some attempt to remedy this problem by demanding that a certain class be dropped entirely from the curriculum. Such efforts usually are not successful. For example, in 1992, a Colorado father sued to force his son's high school to drop its requirement of an eight-week mythology segment in tenth-grade world literature because he believed studying pagan gods conflicted with his religion. A judge dismissed his case, calling it "frivolous and without any foundation." Although the school refused to drop the course requirement or set up a course on Christianity and the Bible, as requested by the father, it did allow parents who objected to having their children exposed to the subject matter to withdraw their children from the class.

Schools are not always amenable, however, to allowing students to opt out of required classes. In 1979, students who were members of the United Pentecostal Church sued to prevent the state from requiring them to attend coeducational gym classes in which class members wore "immodest apparel." Because the students' objections were based on deeply held religious convictions against such attire in mixed company—not simply on shyness or some other reason—the court held that the state's requirement burdened the free exercise of their religion. [*Moody v. Cronin*, 484 F. Supp. 270 (C.D. Ill. 1979)]

Where a court finds that state action burdens the exercise of religion, it must next determine whether the government's interest in that action justifies the burden or whether there are less restrictive alternatives. In this case, the court acknowledged the state's right to educate its young people but ruled that the state's right did not justify hindering the children's religious rights. The court pointed out that the state had less restrictive options: it could provide sex-segregated or individual physical education classes, since it was the attire and not the subject matter to which the students objected. If the state did not like that idea, it could simply exempt the students from the offending classes. It could not, however, punish the students in any way for not taking part in the classes.

Students and parents who object to course requirements cannot invariably count on the courts to back them up, however. In the early 1980s, a group of born-again Christians in Tennessee objected to their children using readers that contained what they perceived as offensive material. Among their complaints were stories and poems dealing with evolution, magic, and gender-role reversal, such as a story where a boy had fun cooking. At first, the school arranged for an alternative program for the children whose parents opposed the reading series. The school board, however, voted to eliminate the alternative programs. When the children refused to read from the books, some were suspended, while others opted for private schools or home schools.

Some parents took their case to court. They sought to have their children excused from classes that used readers containing the offending material, or, alternately, to have the school board pay for the cost of sending their children to private schools. The case, *Mozert v. Hawkins County Board of Education* [827 F.2d 1058 (6th Cir. 1987)], became popularly known as *Scopes II*, in reference to the famous antievolution case ***Scopes v. State***, which took place 150 miles away.

The trial court held in favor of the parents, because it found that the mere exposure to ideas contrary to their beliefs constituted a burden on the free exercise of their religion. The school board was ordered to allow the students to opt out of the classes and to pay over $50,000 in damages to cover the costs of the trial and tuition that had been paid to private schools. The appellate court, however, reversed the decision and threw out the damages award.

The appellate court compared the *Mozert* case with other cases in which the U.S. Supreme Court found religion to be unduly burdened. In one case, a government employee was required to work on the Sabbath. In another, a Jehovah's Witness was denied unemployment benefits when he quit a job rather than work on military tanks. Unlike the plaintiffs in those cases, these students were never forced to affirm or deny their religious beliefs and were never made to actually do something contrary to those beliefs. Since the court found that mere exposure to contrary teachings did not constitute a burden of the students' religious rights, it was not required to analyze the state's compelling interest in requiring the children to use the reading series adopted by the state. The parents appealed to the U.S. Supreme Court, but the Court refused to hear the case.

D

Department of Education The original U.S. Department of Education was founded in 1867, but it was abolished approximately one year later. The modern department was established in 1980 and is lead by the secretary of education, who is also a member of the president's Cabinet.

The Department of Education claims six major responsibilities as its mission. First, it is responsible for addressing and providing national leadership on critical educational issues. For example, *A Nation at Risk*, the 1983 report to the secretary of education, was responsible for inspiring a number of states to increase their graduation requirements.

The second part of the department's mission is to act as a national clearinghouse for innovative ideas that pertain to education. For example, it maintains the Educational Resources Information Center, the world's largest education database. Better known as ERIC, this database provides education information to more than 500,000 people annually and can be reached by telephone at 1-800-LET-ERIC or by e-mail at askeric@ericir.syr.edu. The department also supports innovations such as the development of **charter schools** by providing money to states that wish to establish such schools.

Another innovation supported by the Department of Education is the Star Schools Program. This program began in 1988 with the goal of providing computer technology to poor and isolated schools to give their students access to special courses they would otherwise lack. This program came under fire in 1995 in the Republican push to balance the national budget, with House Republicans opting to eliminate it and Senate Republicans advocating no increase in its funding.

The third part of the department's mission is to help students bear the financial cost of higher education. Nearly three-quarters of **financial aid** for U.S. college students comes from such federal government programs as the Federal Pell Grant program and the Federal Work-Study Program and through low-interest loans guaranteed against default by the federal government. Concern has risen recently over the high rate of default on such loans and the subsequent financial burden placed on the government.

Fourth, the department strives to assist local communities in meeting the needs of their students. To achieve this goal, the Department of Education gives almost $13 billion annually to states and local school districts. Much of this money is distributed under special federal legislation such as **Goals 2000** and the **Individuals with Disabilities Education Act (IDEA).**

Fifth, the department tries to make the educational experience translate into positive career opportunities for students. To accomplish this, it provides money for vocational training programs and backs the efforts of communities who wish to implement school-to-work systems to prepare students for their first jobs.

Finally, the department, through its Office for Civil Rights (OCR), is concerned with ensuring that schools that receive federal money do not discriminate on the basis of "race, color, national origin, gender, disability, or age." The threat of losing financial backing is a powerful motivator—of the 5,000 or so complaints received each year by the OCR, over 95 percent are settled out of court.

The Department of Education maintains a home page on the World Wide Web (http://www.ed.gov/index.html). From this site, one has access to a directory of department offices and staff, information and publications about a variety of department programs, and links to other education-related sites.

DESEGREGATION The process of moving from segregated, or racially separate, schools to integrated ones. U.S. courts have historically dealt with two types of segregation, *de facto* and *de jure.* In *de facto* segregation, schools are identifiable by race due to factors beyond government control, such as housing patterns. *De jure* segregation, on the other hand, existed where the law mandated that children of a particular race go to a particular school.

One of the earliest important cases concerning *de jure* segregation was not, in fact, an education case. In 1896, *Plessy v. Ferguson* [163 U.S. 537 (1896)] dealt with separate railroad facilities for blacks and whites. In that case, the U.S. Supreme Court decreed that separate facilities were constitutional if they were "equal." Sixty years later, however, the Court rejected the separate but equal doctrine as applied in the nation's public schools. In the ***Brown v. Board of Education of Topeka*** opinions, the Court held that "separate educational facilities are inherently unequal" and ordered public schools to desegregate "with all deliberate speed." The Court then returned the cases to the district courts with the intention that the district courts retain jurisdiction until desegregation was complete.

Many states, however, failed to work toward accomplishing desegregation. As a result, the Court declared in 1968 in *Green v. County School Board* [391 U.S. 430 (1968)] that, "The burden on a school board today is to come forward with a plan that promises realistically to work, and promises realistically to work *now.*" The *Green* court used the term "unitary" to describe a successfully desegregated school system.

In response to *Green,* a number of federal district courts ordered school districts within their jurisdictions to come up with immediate desegregation plans. Many schools implemented programs such as **busing** and changing the manner in which students and teachers were assigned to particular schools. As a result of such programs, the racial composition of many schools finally began to change toward a unitary status.

Recently, the Supreme Court has dealt with the issues of exactly what "unitary" means and at what point a district court can declare desegregation to have been accomplished and so relinquish jurisdiction. In 1991, the Court rendered an opinion in *Board of Education v. Dowell* [498 U.S. 237 (1991)] that dealt with the Oklahoma City public schools. The district court had terminated jurisdiction in 1977 based on a finding that the school board had substantially complied with the requirements of desegregation through a program implemented in 1972. In 1985, the school board sought to reassign young black students to different schools to alleviate burdens placed upon them by changes in housing patterns. This reassignment plan would resegregate approximately half of the elementary schools, which lead to an attempt to reopen the case. When the case reached the Supreme Court, the Court declared that rather than quibbling over the meaning of "unitary," the following standard should be applied in determining whether to lift or modify a desegregation order:

> The District Court should address itself to whether the Board had complied in good faith with the desegregation decree since it was entered, and whether the vestiges of past discrimination had been eliminated to the extent practicable.

In 1992, the Court dealt again with the issue of when a desegregation order may be lifted. In *Freeman v. Pitts* [112 S. Ct. 1430 (1992)], a district court found that the DeKalb County School System of Georgia had become unitary with regard to "student assignments, transportation, physical facilities, and extracurricular activities," but not with regard to "teacher and principal assignments, resource allocation, and quality of education." Accordingly, the district court sought to relinquish jurisdiction over the areas in which unitary status had been achieved. The Supreme Court held that the lower court could relinquish jurisdiction over those matters, since there was no necessity for maintaining judicial control.

Recently, critics have argued that certain programs originally established under court order to further the cause of desegregation are actually hurting minority children. For example, in 1995, controversy arose concerning busing and **magnet schools** in Prince Georges County, Maryland, which lies just outside Washington, D.C. When ordered to desegregate its schools in the early 1970s, the county implemented a plan under which students would be bused away from neighborhood schools to ensure racial diversity within the schools. As the racial composition of the county's students changed, however, from 78 percent white and 22 percent black in 1972 to over 70 percent black and 20 percent white 20 years later, busing was no longer as effective in achieving racial diversity, since most schools remained predominately black.

In response to this problem, the county created magnet programs at neighborhood schools in 1985. The idea behind such programs is that by offering special themes, such as "talented and gifted" classes, the schools would attract white students from outside the neighborhoods, which would help achieve racial balance. In order to ensure that the programs themselves would not become segregated, policies were set in place forbidding any magnet program from having a black enrollment of more than 80 percent.

When the 1995 school year began, over 4,000 black students were on waiting lists to get into these special magnet programs. Many programs had openings but could accept only white students due to the race restrictions. At one elementary school, for example, there were 50 openings in a special talented and gifted program, but all 67 children on the waiting list were black. The school board agreed that it would become more aggressive in its pursuit of white students for these programs but that if such efforts did not work, it would petition the court that oversees its desegregation plans to relax the race-based admissions restrictions.

Even in counties where no desegregation court orders exist, efforts to ensure racial balance sometimes have an adverse effect on minority students. Montgomery County, Maryland, for example, implemented efforts to maintain racial diversity voluntarily after being criticized by a Harvard

University study on desegregation. One such effort was a rule against allowing Asian students to transfer out of a particular elementary school because of the small number of Asian students enrolled there compared with the countywide proportion of Asian students. In 1995, the school board sought to enforce the rule by forbidding two kindergarten students who each had one Asian parent and one white parent from transferring out of the school into a special French immersion program at another elementary school in the same county.

Supporters of the students and their parents argued that the girls would be an asset to the racial balance at the other school, which had an Asian population almost as small as Takoma Park's. Faced with intense media pressure, the board eventually reversed its decision and allowed the students to transfer.

DIPLOMAS A diploma is a certificate of achievement granted upon completion of a particular educational program. As such, many view the diploma as the "grand prize" or "finish line," so withholding it can be the ultimate academic sanction [see **academic sanctions**]. In 1988, for example, a court overturned a decision to withhold a high school diploma from a student who had fulfilled all the graduation requirements but who had been found guilty of drug violations. [*Shuman v. Cumberland Valley Sch. Dist. Bd. of Dir.*, 536 A.2d 490 (Pa. Commw. Ct. 1988)]

Some states, concerned that some students who receive diplomas do not actually deserve them, have passed laws requiring students to pass competency exams in order to graduate. In 1979, when the state of Florida began requiring students to pass a functional literacy test before being allowed to graduate, a federal lawsuit ensued in which the plaintiff claimed that the test was racially discriminatory, since many more minority students than white students failed it. A federal appellate court eventually upheld the decision that the state could require students to pass the test before they could receive their diplomas, since the subject matter covered on the test was included in the **curriculum** and since students who failed the test over the course of five tries between their sophomore and senior years were given remedial assistance. [*Debra P. v. Turlington*, 730 F.2d 1405 (11th Cir. 1984)] By 1996, at least 16 states required students to pass competency tests in order to receive their diplomas.

In the area of higher education, legal issues concerning the withholding of diplomas sometimes arise under breach of contract theory. The college promises to award a degree to its students who, in return, promise to live up to certain standards, such as by maintaining a minimum grade point average and by paying all necessary fees. Courts have sometimes found that this sort of a contract exists between a college and a student where the college sets out its expectations in the form of a catalogue. This does not mean, however, that a college or university is always prohibited from withholding a diploma from a student who has fulfilled his or her promises but has also committed some other serious misdeed.

Courts generally prefer not to become involved in academic controversies unless the action by the academic institution is plainly arbitrary. Furthermore, a number of courts have held that there are certain situations in which the withholding of a diploma is a legitimate and appropriate way to protect the interests of a college or university. For example, a college has an interest in protecting its academic reputation. Awarding degrees to students who will likely prove incompetent in their chosen field devalues the college's diplomas, which might eventually lead to fewer students choosing to enroll in its programs. In 1986, the Ohio Supreme Court expressed this sentiment in a case involving the revocation of university degrees that "[t]o hold that a university may never withdraw a degree effectively requires the university to continue making a false certification to the public at large [which] would undermine public confidence in the integrity of degrees." [*Waliga v. Board of Trustees of Kent State Univ.*, 488 N.E.2d 850 (Ohio 1986)]

Less controversial than the protection of academic reputation is the protection of a university's financial interests. Most colleges and universities make receipt of a diploma contingent upon the payment of all outstanding fees and tuition before graduation, and courts tend to look favorably upon this arrangement. For example, in 1985, the Texas Court of Appeals upheld a university's decision to withhold a law degree from a student who had failed to pay his university-issued parking tickets. [*Haug v. Franklin*, 690 S.W.2d 646 (Tex. Ct. App. 1985)]

Finally, courts have sometimes found that a university has a legitimate interest in protecting its moral atmosphere and reputation. For example, in 1893, a New York court allowed a law school to withhold a diploma from a student who had completed all the requirements for graduation but who was quite vocal in protesting the school's choice of graduation speaker. [*People ex rel. O'Sullivan v. New York Law Sch.*, 22 N.Y.S. 663 (1893)]

Such a decision would be unlikely to stand today in the face of First Amendment protection of speech for students, but schools still sometimes deny students their diplomas for private actions unrelated to academic performance. For example, while an Illinois court held in 1986 that a private Christian college could not arbitrarily withhold a diploma from a student based on charges that the student might be homosexual [*Johnson v. Lincoln Christian College,* 501 N.E.2d 1380 (Ill. Ct. App. 1986)], just seven years earlier a Kentucky court allowed a seminary to deny a divinity degree to an admitted homosexual based on language in the school's catalogue that implied that homosexuals would be excluded from the ministry. [*Lexington Theological Seminary v. Vance,* 596 S.W.2d 11 (Ky. Ct. App. 1979)]

DISCIPLINE Schools keep order among students in a variety of ways. Some schools allow **corporal punishment,** in which a child is physically punished for certain acts, while others only allow suspension [see **suspension and expulsion**], where the child is removed from the classroom or the school for a period of days. The most serious offenses, such as bringing guns to school, can result in expulsion, where the student is kicked out of school.

One problem that schools often face in disciplinary matters is a lack of cooperation from parents. The state of Virginia has developed a novel approach to this difficulty. In 1995, the state legislature passed a law requiring parents of public school students to sign a pledge "acknowledging the School Board's standards of student conduct and recognizing their responsibility to assist the school in disciplining their student." Under the law, a parent who "willfully and unreasonably" fails to sign the pledge can face a fine of $50.

Controversy erupted when the pledges went home with Virginia students at the beginning of the 1995–1996 school year. Within a month, the **Rutherford Institute,** a Virginia-based organization devoted to religious freedom, had filed suit on behalf of two parents who refused to sign the statement based on a religious belief that discipline is a parental concern. The **American Civil Liberties Union (ACLU)** also indicated an intent to file suit, claiming that the law forced speech, which violates the First Amendment. Faced with intense criticism, the state attorney general issued a letter mandating that parents not be asked to sign the pledge.

DISTRIBUTION OF RELIGIOUS MATERIALS When a public school student wishes to pass out religious literature such as tracts or personal testimonials, two important constitutional concepts conflict with each other. One is the student's First Amendment right to free expression [see **freedom of speech**]. The Supreme Court defined the extent of students' rights to free expression in ***Tinker v. Des Moines Independent School District,*** ruling that speech and symbolic expression that constitute neither a disruption of class work nor a violation of the rights of other students is protected under the Constitution. The other constitutional concept is the requirement that the school not run afoul of the establishment clause [see **establishment and free exercise clauses**], which prohibits the government and its agencies from promoting one religion over another. Courts apply the test set out in ***Lemon v. Kurtzman*** in determining whether a school policy restricting the distribution of religious materials abides by the spirit of the establishment clause. According to *Lemon,* the school policy must (1) have a secular, or nonreligious, legislative purpose, (2) have a primary effect that neither advances nor inhibits religion, and (3) not excessively entangle the government and religion.

In 1991, a federal court in Pennsylvania applied the *Lemon* test to a case in which high school students challenged a school district policy that required principals to screen materials students wished to distribute to cull out "unacceptable non-student written material(s)," which included "material(s) that proselytizes a particular religious or political belief." [*Slotterback v. Interboro Sch. Dist.,* 766 F. Supp. 280 (E.D. Pa. 1991)] The school district conceded that its policy was not content-neutral, but argued that such a policy would require district endorsement of religion in violation of the establishment clause. The court, however, held that a content-neutral policy would certainly pass the first step of the *Lemon* test by having a secular purpose: ensuring tolerance for all protected student-written speech.

The second prong of the *Lemon* test involves deciding whether an observer would perceive the policy as either an endorsement or disapproval of religion. In school cases the scrutiny given to this phase of the test varies with the impressionability of the students at different educational levels. In this case, the court adopted the language of the Supreme Court in the **Equal Access Act** case *Board of Education of Westside Community Schools v. Mergens* [496 U.S. 226 (1990)] that "secondary school students are mature enough . . . [to] understand that a school does not endorse or support student speech that it merely permits on a nondiscriminatory basis. . . . The proposition that schools do not endorse everything they fail to censor is not complicated." Accordingly, a school policy that permitted distribution of religious literature along with written materials on other topics would constitute neither promotion nor inhibition of religion.

The policy at issue in this case also failed the third prong of the *Lemon* test, which requires the government to avoid passing policies that entangle itself with religion. While a content-neutral policy that treated all materials equally regardless of viewpoint would pass, this policy failed because of the requirement that school officials entangle themselves with religion by scrutinizing written materials to weed out material that "proselytizes a particular religious or political belief." Based on the failure of the policy to meet the requirements of the *Lemon* test, the court declared the part of the policy targeting religious or political beliefs to be unconstitutional.

In 1993, a federal appellate court reached a similar conclusion regarding two school district policies. [*Hedges v. Wauconda Community United Sch. Dist.*, 9 F.3d 1295 (7th Cir. 1993)] The first policy lumped religious literature together with obscene or libelous material and prohibited the distribution of all such literature. The second policy forbade the distribution of literature expressing religious beliefs if the students would reasonably believe such beliefs to be endorsed by the school; limited distribution of materials written by nonstudents to ten copies; and restricted distribution of written materials to a table at the school entrance.

The court quickly concluded that the first policy was unconstitutional since it blatantly infringed on a legitimate First Amendment right. In analyzing the second policy, the court held that a school could remain religiously neutral by "reminding pupils and parents that it does not adopt the view of students who pass out religious literature before school. . . . Public belief that the government is partial does not permit the government to become partial. Students therefore may hand out literature even if the recipients would misunderstand its provenance. The school's proper response is to educate the audience rather than squelch the speaker." Although the court declared the prohibition against religious material to be unconstitutional, it upheld the other limitations set out in the policy as legitimate content-neutral exercises of the school district's power.

The same federal appellate court also heard arguments in 1993 in a case in which an atheist and his son protested a school district's policy that allowed the Boy Scouts of America (BSA) to distribute fliers during school hours. [*Sherman v. Community Consol. Sch. Dist.*, 8 F.3d 1160 (7th Cir. 1993)] The BSA had revoked the father's and son's memberships due to their objection to the provision in the Scout oath requiring a belief in God. The court held that because the religious message of the organization was "sufficiently divorced from the workings of the school," students would be unlikely to believe the school promoted the Scouts' message, and therefore no establishment clause violation existed.

DORMITORY SEARCHES

The issue sometimes arises as to whether Fourth Amendment protection against unreasonable searches and seizures applies to searches conducted by colleges and universities, particularly of their dormitories. Since the Constitution protects citizens only from actions of the state, not from the actions of other private individuals or institutions, such a search must be a state action in order for the Fourth Amendment to apply. If the college is a public institution, it is easier to find state action than if the school is private. Even where the school is private, however, state action may be found where the school acts as an agent of the police, either upon the request of the police or through its own actions in later involving the authorities.

For example, in a case involving a search by a maintenance person at a private university of a library locker (rather than a dorm room), a California court allowed into evidence a student's briefcase that was found to contain marijuana. [*California v. Lanthier*, 488 P.2d 625 (Cal. Ct. App. 1971)] The search had been initiated in response to complaints of a foul odor emanating from the locker. When the maintenance person found the marijuana, he turned it over to the campus police, who then alerted the sheriff. Since the search was initiated by the maintenance person for health reasons, the subsequent involvement of the police did not require suppression of the evidence.

The reason the search in question was initiated has played a key role in other decisions involving room searches. For example, where a routine cleanliness inspection turned up drugs sitting out in plain view, the drugs were allowed into evidence in the prosecution of the student, since the search had the disciplinary purpose of ensuring orderliness and safety in the dorm rooms. [*Arizona v. Kappes*, 550 P.2d 121 (1976)]

The Supreme Court examined the issue of dorm searches in 1981. In *Washington v. Chrisman* [455 U.S. 1 (1981)], a campus police officer arrested a student for possession of alcohol and accompanied the student to his room so the student could get his student identification. While in the room, the officer noticed drug evidence sitting in plain view on a desk. In the prosecution of the student's roommate on drug charges, the Washington court suppressed the evidence found by the campus police officer based on the Fourth Amendment. The Supreme Court, however, reversed this decision since "it was not unreasonable for an officer to monitor an arrestee's movements as his judgment dictates."

DRESS CODES Rules established by a school to restrict the wearing of inappropriate clothing by students. In the 1970s, some students challenged these rules as a violation of their Fourteenth Amendment rights. The Fourteenth Amendment holds that "no state shall make or enforce any law which shall . . . deprive any person of life, liberty, or property, without due process of law," and the Supreme Court has found personal appearance to be an interest in liberty. In order to prove infringement on such an interest, the government must show that the law it seeks to uphold has a rational basis related to a legitimate governmental interest. In 1970, a court proclaimed that a school could not prohibit the wearing of blue jeans where its interest was simply preventing the "relaxed attitude" that might come from wearing casual clothing. [*Bannister v. Paradis,* 316 F. Supp. 185 (D.N.H. 1970)] In 1972, another court held that while a school could prohibit very short skirts and tight pants because of their immodest and, therefore, disruptive nature, it could not restrict long skirts and tie-dyed clothing in an attempt to keep students from wearing "bizarre" clothing. [*Wallace v. Ford,* 346 F. Supp. 156 (E.D. Ark. 1972)]

Most recent challenges to dress codes, however, have used the argument that the codes violate the students' First Amendment right to free speech [see **freedom of speech**]. Clothing can constitute "speech" where it conveys a message through words (such as the writing on a T-shirt) or symbolically (such as certain **gang clothing**).

Of the three U.S. Supreme Court cases dealing with the free speech rights of students, two are important when dealing with clothing as speech. The first, ***Tinker v. Des Moines Independent School District,*** involved students who wore black armbands to protest the war in Vietnam. The Court held in favor of the students and said that nondisruptive speech that does not violate the rights of other students would be protected. The Court distinguished symbolic speech, such as the armbands, from other dress issues, such as skirt length and hair styles, which do not communicate a message and, therefore, do not constitute speech. In the second case, ***Bethel***

School District No. 403 v. Fraser, the Court held that a school could punish a student for making an offensive election speech at a school assembly, because the school was not trying to squelch the message but rather was censuring the sexual innuendo he chose to express the message. *Fraser* stands for the idea that "offensively lewd and indecent speech" by students will not be protected.

A number of challenges to dress codes have arisen over T-shirts. For example, in 1992, a school banned the wearing of T-shirts bearing the slogan "The best of the night's adventures are reserved for people with nothing planned," because the slogan was from an old advertisement for rum even though there was no other reference to liquor on the shirts. The court held that the prohibition was not allowable under *Tinker* because the shirts were not disruptive and there was no reason to believe they would be viewed as an endorsement of alcohol. [*McIntire v. Bethel Sch.*, 804 F. Supp. 1415 (W.D. Okla. 1992)] Another court held that a school could forbid a T-shirt expressing the sentiment that "Drugs Suck!" The court found that the use of the word "suck" was offensive, vulgar, and likely to be disruptive, which rendered it unprotected under *Fraser.* [*Broussard v. School Bd. of City of Norfolk,* 801 F. Supp. 1526 (E.D. Va. 1992)] Likewise, the next year yet another court allowed a school to bar students from wearing a T-shirt that said: "See Dick drink. See Dick drive. See Dick die. Don't be a Dick." The court found this language to be inappropriate for the school environment and held that its suppression was allowable since, as in *Fraser,* the school was not trying to suppress the message ("Don't drink and drive."), but rather the way in which it was conveyed. [*Pyle v. South Hadley Sch. Comm.*, 824 F. Supp. 7 (D. Mass. 1993)]

Not every dispute over T-shirts has wound up in the judicial system. In 1987, an Oregon high school found an innovative way to settle the controversy that arose when it banned T-shirts with messages relating to drugs and alcohol but allowed other T-shirts with messages of questionable taste. Students took their complaint—that the regulation was unconstitutionally vague in defining which shirts were restricted—to the **American Civil Liberties Union (ACLU),** which appointed an attorney to assist them. Rather than hashing it out in court, however, the school held a mock trial, complete with briefs and oral arguments, before a "court" composed of nine local attorneys. The court held in favor of the students, and the principal agreed to abide by its verdict.

T-shirt controversies, while plentiful, are not at the root of every recent dress code dispute. In 1992, a group of students was suspended for refusing to remove buttons worn in support of striking teachers. The appellate court held that the messages on the buttons ("I'm not listening, scab!" and "Do scabs bleed?") were not obscene, as in *Fraser,* and should therefore be judged in the lower court according to the *Tinker* standard. [*Chandler v. McMinnville Sch. Dist.*, 978 F.2d 524 (9th Cir. 1992)]

In deciding whether dress is protected speech, one must first determine whether the apparel is communicative or noncommunicative. Clothing must communicate a specific message that is likely to be understood by others in order to be given First Amendment protection. For example, in 1987, a court found that a T-shirt depicting caricatures of drunk school administrators did not communicate a message and was not protected. [*Gano v. School Dist.*, 674 F. Supp. 796 (D. Idaho 1987)] Likewise, in the *Pyle* case, the court also considered a student who had worn a T-shirt that said, "Coed Naked Band: Do It to the Rhythm." The court held that those words did not communicate any discernible message and could therefore be prohibited by the school administration.

DRIVERS LICENSES Faced with grim statistics regarding graduation rates, many states are looking for creative ways to encourage teens to stay in school. One such recent innovation is linking driving privileges to school attendance. In 1989, a congressmember introduced a bill that would cut federal highway funds by 5 percent to states that did not take away the drivers licenses of students under the age of 18 who dropped out of school. The bill, which contained a hardship provision for students who could show a clear need to drive, was defeated. A similar bill was introduced the next year, but it too died in committee. A number of states have taken the initiative in implementing their own policies even without pressure from the federal government.

By 1995, at least 13 states had statutes that allowed for the suspension of the licenses of students who withdrew from school. Some state legislators have even toyed with the idea of linking a student's driving privileges to passing a competency exam in order to motivate students who remain in school to work harder.

In 1990, a high school dropout challenged the constitutionality of West Virginia's statute, which provides for the revocation of the drivers license of anyone under the age of 18 who drops out of school and fails to enroll in a general educational development program. [*Means v. Sidiropolis,* 401 S.E.2d

447 (W. Va. 1990)] The statute contains an exemption for students who fail to meet these requirements due to circumstances beyond their control. The plaintiff in this case dropped out of school at age 17. When informed that his license would be suspended, he requested a hearing, which he finally had before a hearing examiner appointed by the commissioner of the Department of Motor Vehicles (DMV).

The plaintiff claimed that he needed to drive in order to get a job and to take his pregnant wife to the hospital. The examiner, however, held that only the school superintendent could authorize exemptions and ordered the license revoked. The plaintiff appealed to the circuit court judge, who upheld the revocation of his license, and then the Supreme Court of Appeals of West Virginia.

The appellate court looked to a couple of factors in examining the law's constitutionality. First, it said, the language of the statute's exemption granted for students who withdrew due to circumstances "beyond their control" did provide sufficient guidance over the discretion of the superintendent in granting such exemptions. The court imagined cases in which students withdrew from school due to physical disabilities or to support their families as being within the language of the statute. The court also found that the means of taking away driving privileges was reasonably related to the goal of the statute: to encourage school attendance. Therefore, the statute was constitutional.

In this particular case, however, the plaintiff's hearing was not in keeping with the requirements of the statute. Since only the superintendent or other appropriate school official could decide if an exemption should be granted, that would be the proper person to hold the hearing, rather than the delegate of the commissioner of the DMV. Accordingly, the court reversed that portion of the lower court's opinion. By the time this case reached the appellate level, however, the plaintiff had turned 18 and was able to get his drivers license in spite of the statute.

DRUG TESTING Prior to 1995, the U.S. Supreme Court had never considered a case dealing with drug testing of students. In cases dealing with the testing of other individuals, however, the Court has upheld the practice at least twice. For example, it found that testing of railway employees after accidents, even where drug or alcohol use was not specifically suspected, is allowable. Likewise, the Court upheld the testing of selected employees of the U.S. Customs Service to be a permissible intrusion on personal privacy, because the government's need outweighed the individual's right to privacy and because the program was an effective means of both detection and prevention.

In its landmark case concerning traditional searches of students, *New Jersey v. T.L.O.*, the Court held that while the Fourth Amendment requires police to have "probable cause" to conduct a search of an individual, a school official is required to have only "reasonable cause" to search a student. Most drug-testing cases that have gone through the judicial system, however, concern cases where a school has searched (by means of urinalysis) more than one student, thus giving rise to concern over whether widespread testing lacks the focus necessary to have reasonable cause.

Prior to the Court's 1995 decision in *Acton v. Vernonia School District* [115 S. Ct. 2386 (1995)], lower courts often reached different conclusions regarding the legality of testing students for drugs. In 1988, the Seventh Circuit examined a program requiring random urine checks of students who participated in school-sponsored athletics. [*Schaill v. Tippecanoe County Sch. Corp.*, 864 F.2d 1309 (7th Cir. 1988)] Rather than suspending or expelling a student who tested positive, the school would suspend the student from participating in sports for a certain amount of time. The student could shorten the length of his or her suspension by participating in counseling sessions. The court based its decision to uphold the program on several factors. First, the program was not aimed at the entire student body but rather at a particular group of students that had a responsibility to provide positive role models for their classmates and who were at an increased risk of injury if impaired by drugs. Also, the student athletes had a diminished expectation of privacy, since their participation required them to use communal locker rooms and showers and since they had already been given a urine test as part of their sports physicals. The court was also impressed by the fact that the test was conducted so as to preserve the privacy of the students to the extent possible. For example, the staff member who monitored collection of the urine specimens listened rather than watched. Finally, positive test results were not used punitively, but rather administratively to find students who needed drug counseling.

The Supreme Court case concerning student drug testing arose when a seventh-grade student who wanted to participate in his school's football program refused to submit to a urinalysis at the beginning of the season and to consent to surprise testing later. The school refused to allow him to play, since his refusal violated a district policy that had been passed in response to findings of widespread drug use among student athletes. The student and his parents lost at the trial level, but the decision was reversed by the court of appeals.

When the decision reached the Supreme Court, however, it was reversed again, this time in favor of the district. The Court declared that the compromise of the student's privacy interest by requiring him to take a drug test was minimal and reasonably related to the district's interest in deterring drug use among athletes, a group that had been found to be a substantial part of the drug-using population and that was at particular risk of injury for participating in sports while impaired.

All of these cases involved drug-testing policies that were established by individual school districts rather than mandated by the state. Some state legislators, however, are eager to see such testing programs implemented on a wide scale. For example, in 1995, a Virginia state senator tried unsuccessfully to attach a measure to a bill before the state senate that would allow school systems to give students random drug tests. The bill was defeated partly out of concern for taking away the power of local school boards to run their programs as they see fit.

DUE PROCESS Under the Fourteenth Amendment, a state may not arbitrarily deprive a citizen of "life, liberty, or property without due process of law." This mandate applies to employees of public schools, such as teachers and principals, since they are agents of the state.

Several times, the Court has found liberty interests to be at stake in education cases. In 1923, it held that **academic freedom**—the right of teachers to teach and students to learn—constitutes a liberty interest. [***Meyer v. Nebraska***] Two years later, the Court found a liberty interest on the part of parents "to direct the upbringing and education of children under their control." [***Pierce v. Society of Sisters***]

In 1975, the Court decided that disciplining a student by suspension [see **suspension and expulsion**] implicates both a liberty interest and a property interest. [***Goss v. Lopez***] The liberty interest at stake is the student's reputation, which could be damaged by an undeserved punishment. The property interest is the student's entitlement to a free, public education, which the state has created by offering such an education to its citizens. Accordingly, before the state can damage these interests, it must afford the student procedural due process. For a short-term suspension such as the one at issue in *Goss,* these procedures must include, at a minimum, notice of the charges and an informal hearing at which the student can tell his or her side of the story.

E

Educational Malpractice, Basic Skills and

Some would argue that just as professionals such as doctors and lawyers can be held legally liable for malpractice, teachers should also be held to performance at an acceptable standard. While a number of plaintiffs have brought cases alleging educational malpractice, such claims have generally not been successful.

In 1976, for example, a high school graduate who was unable to read beyond a fifth-grade level sued his school district for failing to provide him with basic academic instruction. [*Peter W. v. San Francisco Unified Sch. Dist.*, 131 Cal. Rptr. 854 (Cal. App. 1976)] The court found a number of reasons for denying his claim. First, the court held, there are no set standards for teachers, and any such standards should be set by schools, not by courts. Also, there are many factors that influence the success of a child's education, and the student in this case could not prove a sufficient connection between his injury and the performance of his teachers. Finally, educational grievances can be corrected through administrative channels and to recognize a legal cause of action for educational malpractice would open up a floodgate of similar cases and expose educational systems to overwhelming litigation.

A New York court heard a case in 1979 in which a student sued his school district for negligently promoting him from grade to grade without ever assessing his ability to learn. [*Donohue v. Copiague Union Free Sch. Dist.*, 391 N.E.2d 1354 (N.Y. 1979)] Because of this negligence, the student claimed to be unable to read. In this case, too, the court refused to judicially interfere in the educational system and held in favor of the school district. In 1993, however, another New York court held that while the state does not recognize a cause of action for educational malpractice, a student could bring a suit claiming that the principal intentionally changed his standardized test scores, resulting in denial of special-education opportunities in spite of his poor performance in the classroom. [*Helbig v. City of New York*, 597 N.Y.S.2d 585 (N.Y. Sup. 1993)]

A high school senior in Ohio filed suit when her failure of an elective psychology course prevented her from graduating with the rest of her class. She sued the teacher for malpractice, and the court agreed that the teacher's omissions did contribute to the student's problems with the class but held that the teacher's conduct was not the proximate cause of her failure. The court refused to interfere with the professional judgment of educators and held in favor of the teacher as a matter of public policy. [*Poe v. Hamilton*, 565 N.E.2d 887 (Ohio Ct. App. 1990)]

Private schools have also, on occasion, been the target of malpractice claims. In 1990, a student in Kentucky sued his private school for failing to readmit him for his junior year. The student claimed that his inability to perform to the school's standards stemmed from the school's failure to instruct him properly and to take into account his attention deficit disorder. The court found in favor of the school, holding that it was not required by the terms of its contract with the parents either to readmit the child or to establish a special program for him that would enable him to succeed. [*Rich v. Kentucky Country Day Sch.*, 793 S.W.2d 832 (Ky. Ct. App. 1990)]

Institutions of higher learning have not been immune from malpractice claims either. In 1992, a federal circuit court upheld a decision in favor of a university that had recruited a basketball player even though it knew he was not prepared to attend the school. In order to keep him eligible, the administration allowed him to take what he called "bonehead" courses like ceramics, marksmanship, and basketball theory. When his sports eligibility expired in four years, the student had only 96 of the required 128 credits, the reading skills of a seventh grader, and the language skills of a fourth grader. The trial court dismissed the action, denying the availability of educational malpractice as a viable cause of action. [*Ross v. Creighton Univ.*, 740 F. Supp. 1319 (N.D. Ill. 1990)] Although the decision was upheld on appeal, the appellate court found that the student did have a cause of action based on contract claims. The case eventually settled.

See **educational malpractice, special education and.**

EDUCATIONAL MALPRACTICE, SPECIAL EDUCATION AND Courts have historically been reluctant to allow lawsuits against school districts based on a theory of malpractice in failing to provide instruction in basic skills. Until recently this reluctance has carried over to prohibit suits where a school is negligent in the placement or removal of a student from a special-education program or in the misclassification of an educationally disabled student.

For example, a New York court heard a case in which a kindergartner had been placed in a class for the mentally retarded based on the results of a school-administered intelligence test. [*Hoffman v. Board of Educ. of the City of New York,* 400 N.E.2d 317 (N.Y. 1979)] The psychologist recommended that the child be retested in two years because of a speech impediment that made the reliability of the results questionable. No such retest was performed, however, until ten years later, at which time it was determined that the child was not retarded. The plaintiff sued the Board of Education for severe emotional detriment, lower intellectual attainment, and reduced future employment opportunities and won an award of $750,000 at trial. The decision of the trial court was reversed on appeal, however, for the public policy reason of avoiding judicial interference into matters that are better handled through administrative channels.

In 1982, however, a student prevailed in a case against the state of Montana. [*B.M. v. State,* 649 P.2d 425 (Mont. 1982)] The child had been negligently classified as retarded and then placed in a special-education program when she was six years old. The trial court initially entered judgment without trial in favor of Montana based on the finding that there was no special duty owed by the state to special-education students. The appellate court, however, disagreed and found that the case should proceed to a trial on its merits based on state constitutional provisions requiring education of all its citizens, compulsory attendance laws to achieve this goal, and administrative statutes outlining how special-education programs should be run in order to provide education for students with special needs.

Special-education students have also met with some success in claims grounded on a theory of medical, rather than educational, malpractice. In 1984, for example, a New York court upheld a judgment in favor of a student who had been confined to a state school for nine years on the belief that he was profoundly retarded despite certain statements in his records indicating that he was actually quite intelligent. [*Snow v. State,* 485 N.Y.S.2d 987 (N.Y. 1984)] The school had failed to discover that the child was, in fact, deaf. Likewise, another New York student succeeded in a claim against the Board of Education where the school had failed to notify the child's mother of severe psychological problems revealed in a psychological evaluation of the child performed by the school.

See **educational malpractice, basic skills and.**

ENGEL V. VITALE Early Supreme Court decision dealing with **prayer in the classroom.** [370 U.S. 421 (1962)]

A New York school district, on the advice of the state Board of Regents, required the following prayer to be read at the start of each school day:

> Almighty God, we acknowledge our dependence upon Thee, and we beg Thy blessings upon us, our parents, our teachers, and our country.

The parents of ten students filed suit, claiming that the prayer violated their freedom of religion as guaranteed in the **establishment and free exercise clauses** of the U.S. Constitution. The state court disagreed, holding that the prayer was permissible as long as no student was compelled to pray over his or her parents' objection.

The parents' appeal ultimately reached the U.S. Supreme Court in 1962, where the decision of the lower court was overturned. Due to the religious nature of the prayer and because it had been selected by school officials, the Court declared its daily reading in the public schools to be a violation of the establishment clause even though students could be excused from participating. In a footnote to the opinion, the Court said that while the Constitution bars religious exercises in the public schools, references to God found in the Declaration of Independence, other historical documents, and certain patriotic songs are acceptable for recitation by public school students.

See also ***School District of Abington Township v. Schempp*** and **prayer at school-sponsored events.**

ENGLISH LANGUAGE No one can provide an exact count of the number of U.S. students who are limited English proficient (LEP), but estimates have ranged from 3.4 million to over 6 million. While one might think that issues relating to the teaching of these students would pertain more to education theory than the law, they have been argued at great length in the legal and political arenas.

In 1974, the U.S. Supreme Court heard a class-action suit brought by parents of non–English-speaking Chinese students in the San Francisco public schools. The parents in *Lau v. Nichols* [414 U.S. 563 (1974)] sued for violation of their children's rights under Title VI of the Civil Rights Act of 1964 based on the failure of the school system to provide the children with English-language training. The defendants, on the other hand, argued that the non–English-speaking students had access to the exact same educational opportunities as all other students and that, therefore, they were treated equally. Although the parents lost at both the district court and circuit court level, the Supreme Court granted relief. In its opinion overturning the lower courts' decisions, the Court stated, "there is no equality of treatment merely by providing students with the same facilities, textbooks, teachers, and curriculum; for students who do not understand English are effectively foreclosed from any meaningful education."

Several months after the *Lau* case, the Department of Education's Office of Civil Rights published guidelines to assist school systems in "eliminating past educational practices ruled unlawful under *Lau v. Nichols.*" These guidelines, which favored bilingual education and multicultural curricula, were withdrawn under the Reagan administration as part of a campaign to restore discretion in the choice of programs to the local level.

Congress responded to *Lau* by amending the Bilingual Education Act of 1968 to increase grant money available to schools for bilingual educational programs. The statute was amended again in the 1980s to limit to three years the amount of time a student could spend in a bilingual program. The purpose of this limitation is to ensure that bilingual programs provide a transition for LEP students into regular programs, but it does not always work that way. For example, in 1995, one parents' organization in New York City filed suit against the state commissioner of education for allowing their children to "languish" for many years in bilingual education programs that were underfunded and of poor quality.

Congress also responded to the *Lau* decision by passing the Equal Education Opportunity Act (EEOA), which states that:

> No state shall deny equal educational opportunity to an individual on account of his or her race, color, sex, or national origin, by—
>
> . . .
>
> (f) the failure by an educational agency to take appropriate action to overcome language barriers that impede equal participation by its students in its instructional programs.

The EEOA is now the support most often relied upon in suits regarding language training. In 1981, the Fifth Circuit developed a framework for the analysis of claims under the EEOA, and many other districts have adopted this approach. [*Castaneda v. Pickard*, 648 F.2d 989 (5th Cir. 1981)] In deciding such a claim, the court must consider three questions:

1. How sound are the educational theories or principles upon which the challenged program is based?
2. Are the programs and practices actually used by a school system reasonably calculated to implement effectively the educational theories and principles adopted by the school?
3. What sort of results are being produced by the program?

Concerns over the English proficiency of students have been cited as a major reason for the passage of laws adopting English as the "official language" of a number of states. Florida, for example, passed an "Official English" amendment to its constitution in 1988. On a local level, Florida's Dade County passed an English-only ordinance in 1980 that was so restrictive that, as one scholar put it, "even zoo signs identifying an animal's name in Latin violated the law." That ordinance was repealed in 1993.

"Official language" laws have recently come into focus at the national level. In 1995, each house of Congress considered bills to make English the official language of the country. Republican Senator and presidential hopeful Bob Dole was particularly outspoken in his support of such a measure, proclaiming in one speech that "we must stop the practice of multilingual education as a means of instilling ethnic pride or as a therapy for low self-esteem or out of elitist guilt over a culture built on the traditions of the West." Opponents of such a law, however, argue that such rhetoric boils down to nothing more than simple prejudice against immigrants.

EQUAL ACCESS ACT

Federal statute passed by Congress in 1984 forbidding public high schools that receive federal money (virtually all public high schools) and have a "limited open forum" from refusing equal access to student groups based solely on their religious or political character. A school creates a limited open forum if it opens its facilities and resources for use by student organizations that do not have a **curriculum**-related purpose, such as a chess club or diving club. If a school chooses to allow such clubs, it may not refuse the same rights of access to **religious clubs.** Not only must religious clubs be allowed to hold meetings, they must also be given the same access to school resources, such as bulletin boards, school newspapers, and public address systems, that other clubs receive.

In 1994, the U.S. Supreme Court upheld the Equal Access Act as constitutional. [*Board of Educ. of Westside Community Sch. v. Mergens*, 496 U.S. 226 (1990)] More recently, students in Seattle, Washington, won $400,000 in attorneys fees for their successful defense under the act of their right to hold religious meetings, since their school allowed other types of clubs.

Some critics worry that if a student group with an unpopular viewpoint, such as a Nazi club, wanted to establish itself on the campus of a school with a limited open forum, the Equal Access Act would require the school to accommodate the organization. Two such controversies arose in 1996 in Utah. In the first case, students at a Salt Lake City high school wished to form a gay-straight student alliance. Rather than allow the students to start the club, the school district voted to ban all nonacademic clubs. In the second case, homosexual students who had been meeting informally for several years petitioned the school to become an official club. District officials proposed a new rule that would require parents to sign consent forms before their children could take part in clubs focusing on sex and other sensitive topics. The officials argued that such a rule would protect the rights of parents to direct the upbringing and education of their children. Critics, however, see the plan as a means of squelching participation in the club, since many gay students might be hesitant to address the matter with their parents. If so, the club could technically exist but not be a going concern. This would allow the school to continue to support its other extracurricular clubs without running afoul of the Equal Access Act.

The act applies only to student organizations; it does not apply to use of school property by religious organizations outside the school. Cases where such organizations wish to have access to school facilities are decided based on the 1993 Supreme Court decision *Lamb's Chapel v. Center Moriches Union Free School District*. [113 S. Ct. 2141 (1993)] In that case, a local church wanted to use school facilities after school hours to show a film dealing with family values from the church's perspective, but the school refused to grant the church permission. The Court sided with the church, since the school had allowed other community organizations to use school property to lecture about the same topic. Permitting the church to use school property as many others had done would not have violated the Constitution's establishment clause [see **establishment and free exercise clauses**], because the school would not be endorsing the content of the film. Not granting permission to the church because of the religious content of its message, however, did constitute viewpoint discrimination and a violation of the church's First Amendment right to free speech.

EQUAL PROTECTION The Fourteenth Amendment requires each state to give all persons located within its boundaries the "equal protection of the laws." Even so, states frequently pass laws that classify individuals in a number of ways.

Where a plaintiff claims a denial of equal protection, the court applies one of several levels of scrutiny in examining the law at issue. Strict scrutiny is the toughest level for the government to win. In those cases, the government must be able to prove that a law is necessary for achieving a compelling governmental interest. Strict scrutiny comes into play when a law either involves a fundamental interest or a suspect classification. The Supreme Court has held repeatedly that education is not a fundamental interest guaranteed by the Constitution. Strict scrutiny still applies in some education cases though, where the state passes a law that creates a suspect classification of students, such as by race or national origin, and treats that classification differently.

At the other end of the scrutiny spectrum is the rational basis test. Under this test, the person bringing the complaint bears the burden of proving that the law or action is not rationally related to a legitimate state interest. This level of scrutiny is applied where no fundamental interest is involved and where the classification involved is not suspect. For example, sometimes students challenge the laws setting out the criteria for how students should be assigned to particular schools. Such laws generally categorize students according to age and where they live. These classifications are not suspect, and since no fundamental right is involved, a court would apply the rational basis test. As long as the law is rationally related to a legitimate state interest (in this case, the orderly assignment of students to its schools), it will be upheld.

On the other hand, if a law directed that all white children go to one school and all black children to another—as was often the case before the ***Brown v. Board of Education of Topeka*** decisions set in motion the process of desegregation—it would be struck down as a violation of equal protection. Classifying the children by race creates a suspect class, and no compelling governmental interest is served by this classification scheme.

Between these two extremes lies a middle ground. At this level, a state must show that the classification is substantially related to an important state interest, which is more than the rational basis test but less than the strict scrutiny test. Cases alleging **sex discrimination** fall here. Where a public school treats male and female students differently, the policy must be substantially related to a legitimate state interest. For example, a school may not refuse to allow pregnant students to attend because such a policy is not substantially related to a legitimate state interest, such as ensuring that a proper moral atmosphere is maintained within the school.

One case that is interesting from an equal protection standpoint is *Plyler v. Doe* [458 U.S. 1131 (1982)], which dealt with a Texas statute allowing school districts to deny free, public educations to the children of **illegal aliens.** The Court declined to apply strict scrutiny, since illegal aliens are not a suspect class and since education is not a fundamental right. The Court also decided that the rational basis test would be inappropriate due to the important nature of education. Instead, the Court applied the midlevel scrutiny and held that the statute in question was not substantially related to any of the interests asserted by the state, such as discouraging immigrants from coming into the country illegally.

ESTABLISHMENT AND FREE EXERCISE CLAUSES

Clauses in the First Amendment of the Bill of Rights of the U.S. Constitution that protect religious liberty: "Congress shall make no law respecting an establishment of religion, or prohibiting the free exercise thereof. . . ." Thomas Jefferson explained that this was intended to build a "wall of separation between Church and State."

The Bill of Rights, and therefore the establishment and free exercise clauses, originally restricted only the actions of the federal government. Before the 1940s, most cases dealing with the mixing of education and religion were based on state laws and constitutions or on the Fourteenth Amendment of the federal Constitution, which restricts the actions of the state governments in infringing on the rights of the people. Then in 1940 and 1947, respectively, the U.S. Supreme Court incorporated the free exercise clause and the establishment clause, making these restrictions apply to the states directly as well as through the operation of the Fourteenth Amendment.

The free exercise clause means that all people are free to believe in the religion of their choice and to abide by its doctrines without interference from the government. The establishment clause, on the other hand, means that the government may not set up an "official" religion or act in such a way that favors one religion over another. Since public schools are part of the government, they are subject to the same restrictions.

Many schools try, whenever possible, to maintain a neutral stance on religious issues. Problems arise, however, when schools attempt to obey the free exercise clause and wind up violating the establishment clause, or the other way around. For example, a school that forbids student prayer could be accused of violating a student's right to free exercise of religion, while a school that allows or requires prayer or a moment of silence could be accused of promoting religion.

F

FINANCIAL AID While there is money available for higher education through scholarships and grants funded by private organizations, many college and university students rely, at least in part, on funds provided by the federal government through the **Department of Education.** The Department of Education provides financial assistance in a variety of ways—through grants, which do not have to be repaid; through loans, which do; and through work-study programs, in which the student exchanges a certain amount of labor (either for the school or for a designated organization or agency) in exchange for the award. In recent years, federal financial aid programs have been a source of political controversy for a number of reasons.

Take loans, for example. Many college students take out low-interest federal student loans, which are guaranteed by the government. This means that if the student fails to repay the loan, the government will step in and see that the bank gets its money.

In 1995, tuition loans taken out by college students (and nearly half of all college students had such a loan) totaled $24 billion. In the five preceding years, the percentage of default on federal loans fell from approximately 20 percent to nearly 12 percent. The Department of Education credited this decline to an aggressive crackdown on the part of the Clinton administration. Besides pursuing more debtors than before through the court system, the government also instituted a policy of garnishing federal tax refunds to compensate itself for money spent making good on delinquent loans.

As an alternative to the traditional plan in which students borrow from any of a number of banks with the federal government as a guarantor, the Department of Education launched a new plan called "direct lending." Under direct lending, students at certain schools can borrow money directly from the government instead of having to go through a bank. This program has proved popular with college financial aid offices, since it reduces the number of bureaucracies involved in loan transactions. Supporters of the program point out that it allows students much longer than the ten years usually offered by banks in which to repay their loans, which alleviates some of the pressure on graduates to take high-paying jobs instead of lower-paying jobs, such as teaching and social work. Critics, however, doubt the ability of the Department of Education to manage such a large program.

Over 100 schools participated in the program during its first year. That number jumped to over 1,300 schools the second year, with another 500 planning to join in the 1996–1997 school year.

Foreign Schools, Aid to

In 1991, a federal appellate court considered a constitutional issue that had never arisen before: does the Constitution's establishment clause [see **establishment and free exercise clauses**], which prohibits the government from favoring one religion over another and from founding an "official" state-sponsored religion, apply to government grants to religious institutions outside the United States?

Congress passed the Foreign Assistance Act in 1961 to help developing countries "acquire the knowledge and resources essential to development and to build the economic, political, and social institutions which will improve the quality of their lives." The act set up a number of foreign aid programs, one of which is the American Schools and Hospitals Abroad (ASHA) program, which authorizes the president "to furnish assistance . . . to schools . . . outside the United States founded or sponsored by United States citizens and serving as study and demonstration centers for ideas and practices of the United States." The U.S. sponsors receive grants that they, in turn, pass on to the overseas schools, which must meet a number of requirements. For instance, the schools "must be open to all persons regardless of race, religion, sex, color or national origin," and they must not use the ASHA grants "to train persons for religious pursuits or to construct buildings or other facilities intended for worship or religious instruction."

The plaintiffs in *Lamont v. Woods* [948 F.2d 825 (2d Cir. 1991)] challenged grants to 20 schools—9 Catholic schools in the Philippines, Egypt, Jamaica, Micronesia, and South Korea and 11 Jewish schools in Israel—whose U.S. sponsors were Catholic or Jewish. The plaintiffs argued that because of the sectarian nature of the schools, government assistance to them violated the establishment clause. The defendants, on the other hand, claimed that the establishment clause does not apply to the government's overseas activities. The federal trial court sent this issue to the Court of Appeals for consideration.

The appellate court declared that domestic concerns arise in a case such as this for several reasons. First, the actions that might be unconstitutional occur in the United States when the grants are given to the U.S. sponsors rather than overseas when the sponsors pass them on to the foreign schools. Also, providing aid to an institution that is affiliated with a major worldwide religion, such as Catholicism or Judaism, also strengthens that religion, which could potentially have an impact within the United States. Finally, if the grants do violate the establishment clause, every U.S. taxpayer suffers an injury, since government programs rely on funding through taxation.

Accordingly, the appellate court held that the establishment clause should apply to ASHA grants and that "once it has been determined that a particular ASHA grantee is pervasively sectarian, the government should be permitted to demonstrate some compelling reason why the usually unacceptable risk attendant on funding such an institution should, in the particular case, be borne." The court gave as an example of such a compelling reason "the fact that a particular grantee is, as a practical matter, the only channel for aid, or that a given country has no secular educational system at all" and returned the case to the trial court.

FRATERNITIES AND SORORITIES

Fraternities (for men) and sororities (for women) are private social organizations commonly established at colleges and universities but affiliated with a national organization. These clubs have been involved in an increasing number of lawsuits over the past several years for **hazing,** a practice in which new members are humiliated, tortured, and sometimes even accidentally killed as part of initiation rituals, and for injuries resulting from club-supplied alcohol.

While individual fraternity members tend to be directly responsible for the injuries that give rise to legal actions, plaintiffs commonly include the organization, its national leadership, and even the university among the defendants. These parties, after all, have more assets from which to recover a judgment than an individual college student would have.

Sometimes such suits meet with success under a theory of accomplice liability, in which the court examines the following factors set out by the Restatement (Second) of Torts:

> (a) the nature of the act encouraged; (b) the amount of assistance given by the defendant; (c) the defendant's presence or absence at the time of the tort; (d) the defendant's relation to the other tortfeasor; (e) the defendant's state of mind; (f) the foreseeability of the harm that occurred.

A federal court in Pennsylvania applied this theory in 1986 to a case in which the plaintiff had been paralyzed in a car accident. [*Fassett v. Delta Kappa Epsilon,* 807 F.2d 1150 (3d Cir. 1986)] The driver of the car was an 18 year old who had been drinking at a fraternity party. The court agreed with the plaintiff that the fraternity, which had used club funds to buy the alcohol, should be held liable for the accident even though, obviously, the fraternity was not directly behind the wheel of the car.

In 1987, parents of a 20-year-old fraternity member sued the local chapter and the fraternity's national leadership after their son died from alcohol poisoning following a drinking contest in the fraternity house. [*Andres v. Alpha Kappa Lambda Fraternity,* 730 S.W.2d 547 (Mo. 1987)] The contest occurred after a club-sponsored social function, and there was evidence that the son, who lived in the fraternity house, maintained his own supply of liquor. The Missouri Supreme Court found in this case in favor of the defendants under a theory set out in another Missouri case that a social host who furnishes alcohol is not liable for any accidents that might occur as a result, because a social host—unlike a bar or nightclub—does not stand to profit financially from encouraging drinking to excess. [*Harriman v. Smith,* 697 S.W.2d 219 (Mo. Ct. App. 1985)] Some critics of this opinion, however, argue that fraternities *do* profit financially, since the success of a fraternity's parties has a direct impact on the number of rushees (potential members) who choose to join its organization.

Sometimes a fraternity may be held liable for the actions of its members under an agency theory, in which a member is found to have acted on behalf of the organization. In a 1993 Alabama case, for example, an appellate court held that there was sufficient evidence of an agency relationship to preclude judgment in favor of the fraternity without a trial. [*Baker v. Pi Kappa Phi Fraternity,* 628 So. 2d 423 (Ala. 1993)] In that case, a fraternity member assaulted a party guest who became involved in an argument with the bartender. The evidence showed that another fraternity member had summoned the assailant, who had a reputation as a "bouncer figure," to break up the dispute and escort the plaintiff from the house. The court disagreed with the fraternity's argument that the assailant ceased operating on its behalf at "the point of physical contact."

Fraternities are not always defendants in legal actions; sometimes they are plaintiffs. In 1993, for example, one fraternity sued a public university in Virginia in federal court for the sanctions imposed on it by the university. [*IOTA XI Chapter v. George Mason Univ.*, 993 F.2d 386 (4th Cir. 1993)] Fraternity members had staged an "ugly woman contest" as part of their annual Derby Days event. The "contestants" were fraternity members dressed as women, including one who dressed as an offensive caricature of a black woman. He was painted black and wore stringy, black hair decorated with curlers, and his outfit was stuffed with pillows to exaggerate a woman's breasts and buttocks. He spoke in slang to parody African Americans.

Following many complaints from other students, the university placed the fraternity on social probation and required it to organize a program "addressing cultural differences, diversity, and the concerns of women." The fraternity sued, alleging that the actions of the university violated its First Amendment right to freedom of expression [see **freedom of speech**]. The court held in favor of the fraternity, pointing out that entertainment—anything from street performing to nude dancing—is expressive conduct deserving of constitutional protection. Since the university punished the fraternity for the message conveyed by its conduct—"that racial and sexual themes should be treated lightly"—the court found that the university had, in fact, violated the fraternity's right to expression, no matter how boorish and sophomoric that expression might be.

FREEDOM OF SPEECH

Controversies over when public schools can squelch the speech of students and parents began to erupt in force in the 1960s. In the landmark 1965 case dealing with the speech rights of students, the Supreme Court declared in ***Tinker v. Des Moines Independent School District*** that public school students do not "shed their constitutional rights to freedom of speech or expression at the schoolhouse gate," and that speech that does not (1) materially disrupt class work or (2) violate the rights of others will be protected. Twenty years later, the Court applied the *Tinker* standard in ***Bethel School District No. 403 v. Fraser*** in upholding the suspension of a high school student who gave a speech that was full of sexual innuendo at a school assembly. Two years after that, the Court distinguished *Tinker,* which dealt with when a school must tolerate student expression, from ***Hazelwood School District v. Kuhlmeier,*** which dealt with pulling potentially offensive articles from a school-sponsored newspaper and the issue of when a school must put its stamp of approval on student expression.

In the realm of higher education, the adoption of **hate-speech codes** by several universities has sparked debate in recent years. A court declared one such code at the University of Michigan to be void for vagueness for using words such as "stigmatize" and "victimize" in defining the prohibited speech, since such words are difficult to define concretely. [*Doe v. University of Mich.,* 721 F. Supp. 852 (E.D. Mich. 1989)] The court worried that the code could have a chilling effect on other types of speech if students were forced to censor themselves in hopes of not "stigmatizing" or "victimizing" anyone.

The issue of when a public school or university can retaliate against a teacher for speech, whether in or out of the classroom, raises arguments over **academic freedom** (the freedom to teach, research, and learn) and over the rights of government employees. In 1981, the Sixth Circuit upheld a school's decision to fire a white teacher who told two black school administrators at the all-black elementary school where she was employed that "I hate all black folks." [*Anderson v. Evans,* 660 F.2d 153 (6th Cir. 1981)] Six years later, that same circuit upheld the dismissal of a teacher who had been fired for showing the movie *Pink Floyd—The Wall* to two classes of teenage students on the last day of the school year. [*Fowler v. Board of Educ.,* 819 F.2d 657 (6th Cir. 1987)]

Such dismissals have also occurred for ideas expressed outside the classroom. For instance, in 1991, a philosophy professor at City College of the City University of New York successfully sued after the university created alternatives for his mandatory course for students who did not want to study under him. [*Levin v. Harleston,* 770 F. Supp. 895 (S.D.N.Y. 1991)] The students' desire to avoid him was based on remarks that he had made in articles denouncing "black criminals" and claiming that "on average, blacks are significantly less intelligent than whites."

Another professor at City College successfully sued after he was dismissed from his position as chairperson of the Black Studies Department for making various anti-Semitic and racist remarks in public speeches. [*Jeffries v. Harleston,* 21 F.3d 1238 (2d Cir. 1994)] In deciding cases such as these, courts generally follow this test: first, the court considers whether the topic of the teacher's speech is a matter of "public concern." If not, the court will usually end its analysis of the issue there, and the school will prevail. If the speech does involve such a matter, the court will go on to weigh the interests of the teacher, "as a citizen, in commenting upon matters of public interest and the interest of the State, as an employer, in promoting the efficiency of the public services it performs through its employees."

FUNDAMENTAL-INTEREST THEORY Test for determining whether a statute providing state aid to private religious schools [see **private schools, government money and**] is unconstitutional. Application of this theory requires courts to balance the extent to which the law furthers the fundamental interest of education against the benefit it gives to the religion. If the benefit to education does not significantly outweigh any incidental benefit to religion, the law does not pass. This test is seldom applied these days. Instead, a court facing such a situation would most likely apply the test set out in ***Lemon v. Kurtzman:*** (1) does the statute have a nonreligious (secular) purpose; (2) does it either advance or inhibit religion; and (3) does it involve excessive entanglement between the government and religion? If the answer to the first question is yes and the answers to the second and third are no, the statute would pass the test.

G

GANG CLOTHING

Gang Clothing In an effort to counter the influence and intimidation caused by the presence of gangs on campus, more and more schools are adding regulations to their **dress codes** that prohibit students from wearing clothing typically associated with gang membership. This generally includes such garments as baseball caps, bandannas, gang jewelry, and any other items reflecting the "colors" of a particular, local gang.

Such restrictions sometimes come under attack for violating the **freedom of speech** rights of the students. The Supreme Court, in ***Tinker v. Des Moines Independent School District,*** has held that students do not lose their First Amendment rights at the schoolhouse gate, although speech that is disruptive and violative of the rights of other students to an effective education will not be protected. Therefore, the first step in determining whether gang clothing is protected by the Constitution is to determine whether it does, in fact, constitute speech.

In order to constitute speech, a manner of dressing must communicate a specific message that others could reasonably be expected to understand. One could argue that students wear gang clothing to send a message of their affiliation with a particular gang and as a way to stake their claim to that gang's territory. Precisely for this reason, however, a challenge to a restriction on gang clothing could fail the exception to the rule established in *Tinker*: the intimidation inherent in the "message" of gang membership could be found to violate the rights of other students who do not belong to that particular gang.

Some opponents of such restrictions complain that they are enforced arbitrarily, with minority students receiving the most trouble. For example, some students in schools with restrictions on gang clothing have alleged that while the administration comes down hard on black students wearing banned items, such as baseball caps, white students wearing the same item are seldom hassled. Others complain that the regulations themselves are drawn in such a way as to single out gangs whose members are black, while ignoring white gangs. Some schools have found merit with this argument and redrawn their policies to include clothing and accessories indicative of neo-Nazi and skinhead gangs, such as combat boots, among the items prohibited.

Controversy can also arise when schools are not up to date on what gang members are wearing. A California school district, for example, implemented a policy prohibiting clothing that featured college and professional sports teams. Four students, ranging in age from elementary school to high school, sued the school district and the principals of the schools when the students were threatened with suspension for wearing sweatshirts and jackets of the University of California, the University of San Diego, the Chicago Bears, and the Los Angeles Lakers and Dodgers. [*Jeglin v. San Jacinto Unified Sch. Dist.*, 827 F. Supp. 1459 (C.D. Cal. 1993)] The appellate court pointed to reliable testimony offered at trial that the clothing banned by the dress code was not typical of that worn by gang members and that "this whole prohibition against wearing college or professional sports team logos or writings has affected only the regular kids who follow the rules. The gang kids are still wearing their plain white T-shirts and dickie pants." Even so, the court held that the policy was valid at the high school level, where the defendants were able to show a gang presence that could result in intimidation of the other students and faculty members, thus justifying infringing on the students' rights to free speech. At the elementary and middle school level, however, where the defendants were unable to show any gang presence justifying curtailment of the students' rights, the court found the regulation to be unconstitutional.

GOALS 2000 Legislation introduced by President George Bush in 1989 and finally passed by Congress and signed by President Bill Clinton in 1994 to appropriate federal money each year for states that adopt voluntary standards to meet new federal guidelines for student achievement.

The legislation encompasses eight main educational goals for the United States:

1. All children will start school ready to learn. This would be accomplished through greater emphasis on preschool programs, prenatal care, and health care and nutrition for preschoolers.

2. The high school graduation rate will increase to at least 90 percent. This encompasses not only reducing the dropout rate overall but also eliminating the disparity in graduation rates between minorities and nonminorities.
3. Students will leave grades four, eight, and twelve having proved competent in "challenging subject matter," such as English, math, and history. This goal also promotes access to physical and health education as well as training in a second language.
4. Teachers will have access to programs to improve their professional skills.
5. U.S. students will rank first in the world in math and science.
6. All adults in the United States will be literate and competitive in the global economy.
7. American schools will be free of drugs, violence, and weapons.
8. Parental involvement in U.S. schools will increase.

These goals are the ends; it is up to states who apply for funding under the act to determine the means to reach them. No state must apply for grants, but those that do will then make subgrants of the money to their Local Educational Agencies (LEAs).

The passage of Goals 2000 accomplished more than simply setting up a pool of money to be used for improving the educational system. It also affected other important legislation. For example, Goals 2000 amends the **Hatch Amendment,** which originally required schools to allow parents to inspect instructional materials used in research or in experimental or new programs and limited the use of psychological examination or treatment of students. As amended, the Hatch Amendment now requires schools to allow parents to inspect any instructional materials used in any programs funded in whole or in part by the **Department of Education** and requires parental consent for surveys connected to programs funded by the Department of Education that might reveal private information such as political or sexual attitudes. Goals 2000 also adds a requirement of notifying parents of their rights under the Hatch Amendment.

Goals 2000 also mandates smoke-free schools. Schools that refuse to comply by establishing and enforcing no-smoking policies can be fined $1,000 a day up to the amount of federal money they receive.

The directive in the act that caused perhaps the most controversy was the language regarding school prayer. As passed, the act provides that "no funds authorized to be appropriated under this act may be used by any State or LEA to adopt policies that prevent voluntary school prayer and meditation in public schools." North Carolina Senator Jesse Helms almost killed the bill by starting a filibuster because of the weakening of proposed language that would have denied funds to schools that deny voluntary, "constitutionally protected" student prayer.

Goals 2000 establishes two other acts that relate to curbing violence in U.S. schools, in promotion of Goal 7. The Gun Free Schools Act (not to be confused with the **Gun-Free School Zones Act**) forbids an LEA from receiving funds under Goals 2000 if it does not have a policy requiring the expulsion for one year of any student who brings a firearm to school. The Safe Schools Act, which is aimed at making schools peaceful and alcohol and drug free, establishes grants to be made by the secretary of education directly to LEAs that serve troubled areas, such as those with high juvenile homicide and crime rates or a high rate of suspensions and expulsions. The grants, which can amount up to $3 million a year for two years, can be used for a number of activities, such as conflict resolution training for school personnel, community education, peer counseling and mediation programs, the hiring of security guards, and the purchase of metal detectors.

The deadline for applying for Goals 2000 money was June 1995. By March 1995, six states still had not applied, probably due to what the governor of Virginia explained as a fear of losing local control over classroom matters to the federal government.

Goss v. Lopez Landmark Supreme Court case determining what amount of procedural **due process** must be given to public school students upon brief suspensions of less than ten days [see **suspension and expulsion**]. [419 U.S. 567 (1975)]

Ohio law provided for a free public education for the children of the state and required the compulsory attendance at school of eligible children. Additional laws gave the principals in the state the power to suspend unruly children for up to ten days or to expel them permanently. Following suspension or expulsion, the school administrators had 24 hours to notify the student's parents of the reasons for the punishment. The law also set forth an appeals process that included a hearing, but it applied only to children who had been expelled.

The plaintiffs in this case had been suspended for ten days for various disruptive acts. None of them had a hearing, either prior to the suspension or shortly afterward. They sued for a declaration that the law permitting suspension without a hearing unconstitutionally violated their Fourteenth Amendment rights to due process and sought to force the school to remove the suspensions from their permanent records.

The Fourteenth Amendment to the U.S. Constitution says that no state may "deprive any person of life, liberty, or property, without due process of law." The Supreme Court held that since the state had extended the right of education to its citizens, it could not arbitrarily withdraw that right—a student's entitlement to a public education falls within the property interests protected by the Fourteenth Amendment. Also, since the concept of liberty includes a person's reputation, and since charges of misconduct can damage one's reputation, the students had a liberty interest to protect.

Having decided that due process does, in fact, apply to suspension of school children, the Court faced the issue of "what process is due." It settled on the requirements of notice of the charges and a very informal hearing at which the student could present his or her side. The Court refused to extend the due process requirements to include a formal hearing or the rights to counsel and to call and examine witnesses but cautioned that the *Goss* decision applied only to suspensions of less than ten days. According to that ruling, "Longer suspensions or expulsions . . . may require more formal procedures."

GRADES While many legal challenges to grades involve situations in which a grade has been lowered as a punishment [see **academic sanctions**], in many other cases a student simply disagrees with the mark received—especially if the grade leads to further trouble, such as dismissal from a college program. Courts, however, are loathe to substitute their judgment for that of educators' and often refrain from finding that the awarded grade violated the student's rights. Such hesitancy on the part of courts to overturn purely academic decisions, however, does not stop students from bringing contests challenging either the grade itself or the appeals process provided by the school into the courts.

The most common argument offered in such cases is that the awarding of the grade violated the student's right to **due process** as guaranteed by the Fourteenth Amendment of the federal constitution and by the state constitutions. Such guarantees forbid the state and federal governments from denying any person life, liberty, or property without certain due process protections, such as notice and a hearing. Obviously, a grievance resulting from a grading dispute does not threaten the student's life; therefore, students generally argue that the grade threatens a property or liberty interest. One state university student, for example, argued that the school's catalogue gave him a property interest in his grades. [*Tobias v. University of Tex.*, 824 S.W.2d 201 (Tex. Ct. App. 1991)] Other students have argued that their liberty interest in finding employment upon completion of educational programs has been hurt. Courts have generally been reluctant to recognize these interests, but will sometimes assume that such interests do exist before going on to conclude that the appeal procedure provided by the school met the requirements of due process.

Remember that constitutional guarantees of due process protect the individual only from action of the government, not from that of private persons and entities. Accordingly, the due process arguments that a student at a public school or university might offer in court will not apply to a student at a private institution. Even so, private school students do occasionally bring judicial challenges to grades, most often under a contract theory. Under such an argument, the student alleges that his or her relationship with the school is contractual, with the student agreeing upon admittance to comply with the terms set out by the school and the school agreeing not to arbitrarily deny a degree to a student who meets its terms.

GUN-FREE SCHOOL ZONES ACT Federal law making it a federal offense to possess a gun within 1,000 feet of a school. The law was declared unconstitutional in *U.S. v. Lopez* [115 S. Ct. 1624 (1995)] as an impermissible exercise of Congress' power to regulate interstate commerce.

Statistics indicate that violent crime is an increasing problem in U.S. schools. For example, in one 1994 survey by the Centers for Disease Control nearly 8 percent of students surveyed admitted that they had carried a gun at least once in the preceding month. In an effort to address what one sponsor of the bill called "the devastating tide of firearm violence in our Nation's schools," Congress passed the Gun-Free School Zones Act in 1990. The bill was reluctantly signed into law by President George Bush, who stated, "Most egregiously, [this law] inappropriately overrides legitimate state firearms laws with a new and unnecessary Federal law. The policies reflected in these provisions could legitimately be adopted by the States, but they should not be imposed upon the States by Congress."

In order to understand Bush's opposition to the legislation, one must remember that powers that are not specifically delegated to the federal government by the Constitution belong to the states. Bush was pointing out that regulation of weapons is one such state power. Many scholars would argue that regulation of education is another.

One power that is constitutionally delegated to the federal government, however, is the power to regulate commerce. Under the commerce clause, Congress has the power "to regulate Commerce with foreign Nations, and among the several States, and with the Indian tribes." Prior to the 1930s, the Supreme Court applied a very narrow interpretation to this clause, striking down federal laws on labor issues such as wages, hours, and conditions, because of the indirect relation between these issues and interstate commerce.

In 1937, however, the Court broadened its interpretation to uphold the National Labor Relations Act, holding that Congress could regulate activities that did not cross state lines themselves but only where such activities had "such a close and substantial relation to interstate commerce that their control is essential or appropriate to protect that commerce from burdens and obstructions." [*NLRB v. Jones & Laughlin Steel Corp.*, 301 U.S. 1 (1937)] The Court upheld in 1942 a penalty assessed against a farmer under the Agricultural Adjustment Act of 1938 for harvesting 12 more acres of wheat than his allotment allowed, since this extra wheat was found to be substantially related to interstate commerce. [*Wickard v. Filburn*, 317 U.S. 111 (1942)] The Court was unimpressed with the farmer's argument that the extra wheat was for his own use and therefore had nothing to do with interstate commerce. The Court disagreed, saying of the wheat, "if we assume that it was never marketed, it supplies a need of the man who grew it which would otherwise be reflected by purchases in the open market. Home-grown wheat in this sense competes with wheat in commerce." Since the wheat case, the Supreme Court has consistently upheld federal legislation any time Congress can show any sort of connection between the regulated activity and interstate commerce.

The tide turned, however, in 1995, when the Court delivered its opinion in *U.S. v. Lopez*. In that case, Alfonso Lopez, a high school senior in Texas, was caught carrying a concealed .38-caliber handgun into his school. Officials initially charged Lopez under a state law making it a crime to carry a weapon on school property. The state charges were dropped, however, and

Lopez was charged under the Gun-Free School Zones Act instead. The district court found Lopez guilty and sentenced him to six months' imprisonment. Upon appeal, the Fifth Circuit reversed the conviction on the basis that the act exceeded Congress' power to legislate under the commerce clause. The United States petitioned for review by the Supreme Court.

The government argued to the Court that even though neither the act in question nor its legislative history contained any "express congressional findings regarding the effects upon interstate commerce of gun possession in a school zone," such possession is, in fact, an activity relating to commerce. It leads to violent crime, which has several effects on the national economy. First, insurance rates rise throughout the population to cover the cost of crime. Second, violent crime reduces people's willingness to travel to areas they perceive to be dangerous. Finally, according to the government argument, violent crime threatens "the educational process by threatening the learning environment. A handicapped educational process, in turn, will result in a less productive citizenry. That, in turn, would have an adverse effect on the Nation's economic well-being."

The Court, however, was not persuaded by any of these reasons. Lopez won, because in order for the Court to hold in favor of the government, it would have to "pile inference upon inference" in a manner that would "convert congressional authority under the commerce clause to a general police power of the sort retained by the States."

President Bill Clinton expressed disappointment at the Court's holding and ordered the Justice Department to find a way to draft similar legislation that would get around the ruling. One Justice Department attorney suggested two possible options for achieving the same effect as the Gun-Free School Zones Act without running into the commerce clause problem. On one hand, Congress could restrict application of the law to cases where the gun at issue has crossed state or national lines. As a practical matter, such a restriction would mean that the law would still apply to most cases, since most guns do cross borders at some point. On the other hand, Congress could use its spending power to cut off educational funds to states that do not pass their own versions of the act, "on the theory that federal education funds are more effectively spent in schools free from handgun violence."

The *Lopez* decision, which one legal scholar termed "the most important case of the decade," could have far-reaching ramifications in areas that have nothing to do with education. By narrowing its interpretation of the commerce clause, the Supreme Court weakened an argument used by Congress in passing a great deal of legislation, from the civil rights laws of the 1960s forbidding discrimination in restaurants and hotels to recent additions to the list of federal crimes, such as carjacking. Opponents of federal laws such as the ban on assault weapons and the rule against violence at abortion clinics could rely on *Lopez* in their efforts to challenge these statutes and others like them.

H

HAIR CODES Restrictions on hair length often found in school **dress codes.** Students have challenged such regulations since the early 1970s on a variety of grounds. Some have asserted that the right to wear one's hair as one wishes is a "liberty" to be afforded substantive **due process** protection under the Fourteenth Amendment of the Constitution. Others have claimed that Fourteenth Amendment procedural due process is violated where a long-haired student is punished through suspension or expulsion [see **suspension and expulsion**] without being given a hearing. Such arguments have met with mixed success in the courtroom.

Another popular argument is that long hair is a form of symbolic speech [see **freedom of speech**] deserving of First Amendment protection like the black armbands worn by high school war protesters in ***Tinker v. Des Moines Independent School District.*** Such claims are generally unsuccessful, because the Supreme Court specifically distinguished the communicative effect of the armbands worn in *Tinker* from long hair, which generally does not communicate any particular message that others would reasonably understand.

Finally, hair codes have been challenged under the equal protection clause of the Constitution [see **equal protection**], which requires that people enjoy the equal benefit of the law. Restrictions on hair length usually apply only to males, even though female students engage in most of the same activities, such as physical education classes. In such a case, a court might find an equal protection violation unless the school can demonstrate a reasonable basis for treating the sexes differently.

In 1993, a federal district court in Texas heard an unusual case involving all of the issues listed above. In *Alabama and Coushatta Tribes of Texas v. Big Sandy School District* [817 F. Supp. 1319 (E.D. Tex. 1993)], 12 Native American students, their parents, and their tribes filed suit against their school district over a regulation that stated: "Boys' hair should be of reasonable length and style so as not [to] interfere with the instructional program. Boys' hair should [be] no longer than the top of a standard dress collar." The school district's reasons for the regulation included creating a proper educational atmosphere, fostering respect for authority, and making certain the students reflected well upon the district and the community. Of the 12 students, some had been disciplined through suspension and "in-school suspension" for refusing to cut their hair, while others had given in to the demands of the school under the threat of punishment.

The court began by stating that the circuit court of appeals for that jurisdiction had held in 1972 that there is no constitutionally protected right to wear one's hair in a public high school in the length and style that suits the wearer. In this case, however, the long hair was an important part of the students' religious beliefs. The plaintiffs presented evidence that long hair is a tradition that their tribes have historically held to be sacred. Even after conversion to Christianity, many tribe members retained their tribal beliefs and rituals. The court held that the Native American Indian movement is a religion and is deserving of First Amendment protection if the beliefs are sincerely held.

Once the court ascertained that the plaintiffs' religious beliefs regarding long hair were in fact sincerely held, it turned its attention to the school's interest in regulating hair length. The court pointed out that "while freedom to believe in a particular religious creed or doctrine is absolute, freedom to act pursuant to one's religion is not" and may be regulated to protect society. Even so, the court held that the school failed to show that the regulation was a valid means of accomplishing the goals that inspired the restriction and that, therefore, plaintiffs' religious beliefs were unduly burdened.

The plaintiffs in *Big Sandy* also alleged that the regulation infringed on their First Amendment rights to free speech. The court agreed, saying that for Native Americans the wearing of long hair does have an expressive or communicative effect. Since the students' hair did not disrupt classes or violate the rights of other students, it was protected as symbolic speech under *Tinker.*

The parents claimed that the district's regulation interfered with their rights to direct the upbringing of their children. Such a right was upheld by the U.S. Supreme Court in 1972 in ***Wisconsin v. Yoder.*** The *Big Sandy* court agreed with the parents, even though the parents did not demand that their sons wear long hair but merely supported them in their religious pursuits.

Both substantive and procedural due process issues were brought out in *Big Sandy.* The court held that while there was no substantive due process violation, the lack of procedural safeguards given to the suspended students constituted procedural due process violations. For example, some plaintiffs were suspended for over a month without receiving the notice or hearing required by the Supreme Court in ***Goss v. Lopez.***

The court disagreed with the plaintiffs' final claim, that the enforcement of the rule violated their rights to equal protection. Since there was no evidence that the district intended a discriminatory purpose in implementing the rule, which was racially neutral, the court applied the rational basis test and upheld the rule as advancing the legitimate purpose of promoting order in the schools. Because of the arguments under which the plaintiffs prevailed, however, the court did issue an injunction to stop the district from enforcing the regulation against Native Americans.

HATCH AMENDMENT Federal legislation aimed at returning to the fundamentals of education. It requires public schools to allow parents to inspect certain classroom instructional materials used in experimental or new teaching programs. For example, one parent challenged the teaching of yoga in physical education classes.

The Hatch Amendment also requires schools to obtain parental consent before administering psychological examinations or treatments to students. Consent is required for any testing or activities that would require the student to divulge private information about his or her personal life, such as income, political preferences, or sexual practices. Many critics argue that these regulations are vague, which makes them useful weapons for anyone who opposes certain classroom activities. Some have even argued that this legislation could go so far as to prevent a teacher from asking a child how he or she feels. The watchgroup People for the American Way, which does an annual censorship study, reported in 1985 that over 25 percent of the previous year's attacks on instructional materials were based on claims that the material promoted the "religion" of secular humanism or that they violated the Hatch Amendment.

HATE-SPEECH CODES Regulations on prejudice-motivated speech sometimes adopted by colleges and universities in an attempt to foster tolerance and understanding. At government-sponsored institutions, such codes can amount to government censorship in violation of the students' First Amendment rights concerning free speech [see

freedom of speech]. Even at private universities, such regulations are often seen as a restriction on **academic freedom.**

The University of Michigan adopted a hate-speech code following a series of disturbing events during the winter of 1987. In January, a flier was distributed that declared "open season" on blacks. Then in February, the campus radio station broadcast racist jokes. When students staged a demonstration to protest these incidents, someone displayed a Ku Klux Klan uniform from a dormitory window. In response, the university adopted a policy that prohibited behavior that "stigmatizes or victimizes" individuals on the basis of "race, ethnicity, religion, sex, sexual orientation, creed, national origin, ancestry, age, marital status, handicap or Vietnam-era veteran status" and that involves a threat to the victim's "academic efforts, employment, [or] participation in University sponsored extra-curricular activities or personal safety."

In addition to issuing the policy in the fall of 1988, the university also distributed a guide entitled "What Students Should Know about Discrimination and Discriminatory Harassment by Students in the University Environment." The guide gave examples of conduct that could be punished under the policy, such as:

- A flyer containing racist threats distributed in a residence hall.
- Racist graffiti written on the door of an Asian student's study carrel.
- A male student makes remarks in class like "Women just aren't as good in this field as men," thus creating a hostile learning atmosphere for female classmates.
- Students in a residence hall have a floor party and invite everyone on their floor except one person because they think she might be a lesbian.
- A black student is confronted and racially insulted by two white students in a cafeteria.
- Male students leave pornographic pictures and jokes on the desk of a female graduate student.
- Two men demand that their roommate in the residence hall move out and be tested for AIDS.

The guide also contained a section entitled "You are a harasser when . . . " and gave the following examples:

- You exclude someone from a study group because that person is of a different race, sex, or ethnic origin than you are.
- You tell jokes about gay men and lesbians.
- Your student organization sponsors entertainment that includes a comedian who slurs Hispanics.
- You display a confederate flag on the door of your room in the residence hall.
- You laugh at a joke about someone in your class who stutters.
- You make obscene telephone calls or send racist notes or computer messages.
- You comment in a derogatory way about a particular person or group's physical appearance or sexual orientation, or their cultural origins, or religious beliefs.

An anonymous psychology graduate student challenged the policy in *Doe v. University of Michigan* [721 F. Supp. 852 (E.D. Mich. 1989)], claiming that it was unconstitutionally vague and overbroad. Doe had never been punished, or even charged, under the policy. Even so, he claimed that the policy chilled his right to discuss controversial theories in class for fear of being branded as sexist or racist. For example, Doe was interested in biopsychology, which is the study of biological reasons for certain psychological traits, and feared that he could be sanctioned for discussing the theory that men tend to outperform women at tasks involving spatial reasoning partly due to biological differences.

In holding in favor of Doe, the court first addressed the issue of overbreadth, pointing out that "statutes regulating First Amendment activities must be narrowly drawn to address only the specific evil at hand." A statute is overbroad if it not only prohibits that which may legitimately be regulated but also takes within its boundaries speech or conduct that is protected from regulation. The university argued that the policy was not used to regulate protected speech, but the court disagreed. It cited, for example, a case in which a graduate student was charged under the policy for expressing his view in a research class that homosexuality was a disease that could be cured.

After finding the policy to be overbroad, the court went on to consider the vagueness argument. Again, the court sided with the plaintiff, because the terms of the policy, such as use of the words "stigmatize" and "victimize," were susceptible to many definitions. "A statute is unconstitutionally vague," the court said, "when 'men of common intelligence must necessarily guess at its meaning.'" Because the university never set out a plan for distinguishing sanctionable speech from protected speech, the policy was deemed unconstitutionally vague.

The **American Civil Liberties Union (ACLU)**, which generally represents members of the groups that the University of Michigan sought to protect with its policy, supported the plaintiff in *Doe* and has also won against the universities of Connecticut and Wisconsin in similar cases. This is not the first time the ACLU has found itself taking on a position that at first seems odd considering the group's liberal outlook. In 1979 the ACLU defended the rights of neo-Nazis to march through predominately Jewish Skokie, Illinois. The Union's director, who had lost relatives in Hitler's concentration camps, declared that "Keeping a few Nazis off the streets of Skokie will serve Jews poorly if it means that the freedoms to speak, publish or assemble any place in the United States are thereby weakened."

The ACLU takes a similar position on university hate-speech codes, arguing that "More speech—not less—is the best revenge." The Union and other opponents of such speech codes suggest that instead of squelching offensive yet constitutionally protected speech, a university should fight fire with fire by speaking out against bigotry, raising awareness of students, and recruiting minorities to the faculty and student bodies. Also, opponents point out, some conduct that would be punishable under a speech code can legitimately be attacked under already existing statutes against harassment and trespass.

HAZELWOOD SCHOOL DISTRICT V. KUHLMEIER

Supreme Court case upholding the right of a school principal to remove potentially offensive material from a school-sponsored publication. [484 U.S. 260 (1988)]

When a high school principal ordered two pages of the school newspaper produced by the journalism class to be omitted from the paper before printing, a group of students in the class sued, claiming that the principal's actions violated their First Amendment right to free speech [see **freedom of speech**]. The pages that the principal deleted contained two objectionable articles. The first focused on three pregnant students at the school. Although the article used false names for the girls to protect their privacy, the principal worried that they were still identifiable through other characteristics in the piece and that the subject overall was unsuitable for younger students. The second article discussed the impact of divorce on children and quoted one student at length as to her father's shortcomings as a parent and husband. The principal felt that the father should have had an opportunity to respond to his daughter's allegations or even to consent to their publication.

The students lost at trial but won at the appellate level. The appellate court based its holding on the rule set out in the Supreme Court case ***Tinker v. Des Moines Independent School District*** for when student expression must be tolerated: when it does not (1) materially disrupt class work or (2) violate the rights of others.

However, in 1988, when the Supreme Court reviewed *Hazelwood,* it declared that the appellate court had made a mistake in applying the *Tinker* standard. While *Tinker* dealt with the issue of when school administrators are required to tolerate student expression with which they do not agree, *Hazelwood* concerned the issue of when school administrators are required to put the school's stamp of approval on student speech. The standard to be applied to cases such as *Hazelwood* is whether the school's reasons for its actions are reasonably related to educational concerns. The Court declared that in this case the principal did have valid reasons for exercising an editorial veto over the two articles because of his concern for the privacy of students and their parents and because he could reasonably believe that the students responsible for the articles had not absorbed the lessons in fair and accurate reporting taught in their journalism class.

The *Hazelwood* court was influenced by the fact that the school had consistently maintained control over the contents of the newspaper. If it had given control over to students or outsiders, the students' argument that the newspaper was a public forum might have carried more weight. The year after the Court issued its *Hazelwood* opinion, for example, a federal appeals court held that a school could not regulate career-day speakers in order to exclude peace activists, since it had opened up a topic for discussion by outsiders and could not suppress opinions with which it did not agree. [*Searcy v. Harris,* 888 F. Supp. 1314 (11th Cir. 1989)]

HAZING Rites of initiation into clubs such as fraternities [see **fraternities and sororities**], ranging from the absurd to the dangerous. Reports of hazing have included pledges (would-be members) being ridiculed, deprived of sleep, burned with matches, locked in car trunks, and forced to consume excessive amounts of alcohol.

Most lawsuits involving hazing have occurred at the college or university level, but this is not always so. In 1982, for example, the Florida Supreme Court found that a school principal was liable for injuries to a high school fraternity pledge because he should have foreseen the danger faced by the pledges based on the youthful age of the club membership and its reputation for hazing. [*Rupp v. Bryant*, 417 So. 2d 658 (Fla. 1982)]

The first U.S. antihazing criminal statute was passed by Congress in 1874 to outlaw harassment of first-year students, or plebes, at the U.S. Naval Academy. In 1901, Illinois became the first state to criminalize hazing. Since then, at least half the states have passed such statutes as well.

One potential problem with laws against hazing is vagueness. In order for a criminal law to withstand a constitutional challenge, it must clearly define the behavior that it seeks to prohibit. Otherwise, people might refrain from permissible conduct in an effort to obey the law. However, as one New York court pointed out: "It would have been an impossible task if the legislature had attempted to define hazing specifically. Fraternal organizations and associations have never suffered for ideas in contriving new forms of hazing."

State hazing laws are not uniform. In most states having such laws, hazing is a misdemeanor, or less serious crime. In at least four states, however, it can be a felony if the injury to the victim is serious enough. Because of this lack of uniformity, students who wish to engage in hazing and who are close to a border with another state sometimes cross state lines to escape the reach of their state's statute or to commit the crime in a state whose statute imposes less severe punishment. As of 1991, at least 19 states that had antihazing statutes shared a border with at least one state that had no such statute.

This does not mean that people who haze in a state without an antihazing statute are always beyond the reach of the law. Even in states without such statutes, other laws, such as ones outlawing assault and battery, would still apply. Certain forms of hazing, however, such as depriving pledges of sleep, ridiculing them, or requiring them to perform calisthenics would not be punishable.

Regardless of whether or not there is a criminal statute in place, an injured pledge still has the option of pursuing a civil case to recover money damages. In such cases, the pledge can often choose one or more of the following defendants: the individual fraternity members who inflicted the injury, the local chapter of the fraternity, the fraternity's national organization, or the college or university.

Such cases raise an interesting issue of consent or assumption of the risk as a defense. After all, in many cases the pledge, enticed by the benefits of fraternity membership, voluntarily submitted to the initiation ceremony. In cases involving excess consumption of alcohol, however, a number of courts have held that at some point the pledge became too intoxicated to have the capacity to consent or to understand the risk involved.

HENDRICK HUDSON BOARD OF EDUCATION V. ROWLEY Supreme Court decision interpreting the mandate under the **Individuals with Disabilities Education Act (IDEA)** that a disabled student receive a "free appropriate education." [458 U.S. 176 (1982)]

The IDEA (formerly known as the Education for All Handicapped Children Act) requires that in order for states to receive federal money under the act, each disabled child within the state must have access to a "free appropriate education" designed for that particular child in accordance with his or her **Individualized Educational Program (IEP).** In 1982, the U.S. Supreme Court defined the meaning of "appropriate" within the context of the statute.

In that case, the parents of Amy Rowley, a deaf first grader, requested a sign-language interpreter for their daughter's academic classes. Amy had been performing well at school, but the Rowleys believed that with the help of an interpreter she could do even better. The school denied the request, and the Rowleys fought the issue through administrative hearings, into the legal system, and ultimately to the Supreme Court.

The Court declared that the purpose of the act was not to guarantee any specific result in the outcome of the education of disabled children. Rather, it aimed to correct the unfair way in which the majority of disabled U.S. children had been totally excluded from the educational system. In pursuit of this goal, the act sets out very specific procedures that must be followed in planning an educational program for a disabled child. The role of the courts in cases such as these, the Supreme Court said, should be only to determine whether the procedures have been followed. If the school has followed the procedural requirements, and if the child's IEP is "reasonably calculated to enable the child to receive educational benefits," then the courts should not take it upon themselves to dictate to the school how to go about the business of education.

In Amy Rowley's case, the Court agreed with the school district that Amy was already receiving an "appropriate education." The school had followed the requirements of the act in setting up Amy's IEP, which was reasonably calculated to enable her to receive educational benefits, as shown by the fact that the special services she received allowed her to perform better than most of the other, nondisabled children in her class. Since the procedures had been followed, the Court declined to interfere in the techniques used in her education.

HOME SCHOOLS Educational setting where parents declare their home to be a private school for the education of their children. More and more parents are choosing to educate their children at home. Twenty years ago, there were only about 12,500 home schooled children in the United States. Some estimate the number now to be as high as 500,000. That number might actually be significantly higher, since in some states, such as California, there are umbrella schools that register as one school but represent many families.

Many parents who choose to home school are motivated by their religion. They might, for example, prefer the freedom to teach their children creationism instead of evolution [see **creationism and evolution**], as taught in the public schools. Many other parents who choose home schooling, however, do so for nonreligious reasons, such as a fear of drugs and **violence** in the public schools, or an inability to afford private schools.

The home school movement is not new, but it has only recently become commonly accepted as an alternative to traditional school settings. States used to view home schooling as a violation of the **compulsory attendance** laws and treated those children as truant [see **truancy**]. Now, however, home schooling is legal in every state. Over half the states have specific laws to regulate the practice and ensure some level of educational quality.

Critics of home schooling argue that educational quality suffers despite the existing laws. For example, most states do not require any particular level of education on the part of the parent to be qualified as a teacher. Some states do not require standardized testing of the students or the use of any particular educational materials. Sometimes parents argue that the state does not have authority to regulate and monitor home schools, but such claims generally do not succeed.

Controversy sometimes arises when parents are unable to agree on the value of home education. In several cases, noncustodial parents have sued to force the other parent to return the child to the public schools. In one case, an Arkansas court refused to allow a divorced mother to home school her children over the father's objections. [*Clark v. Reiss*, 831 S.W.2d 622 (Ark. Ct. App. 1992)] In another case, a Tennessee court declined to overrule a mother's decision to home school, since there was no evidence that home schooling was causing harm to the child. [*Rust v. Rust*, 864 S.W.2d 52 (Tenn. Ct. App. 1993)]

The national network of home schoolers had an opportunity in 1994 to demonstrate its lobbying powers. The House of Representatives was considering passage of the **Improving America's Schools Act** which reauthorizes the 1965 Elementary and Secondary Education Act. The bill contained an amendment that stated:

> Each State applying for funds under this title shall provide the Secretary [of Education] with the assurance that after July 1, 1998, it will require each local educational agency within the State to certify that each full time teacher in schools under the jurisdiction of the agency is certified to teach in the subject area to which he or she is assigned.

Concerned that this would mean requiring certification of teachers in private and home schools due to expansion of the definitions of "elementary school" and "secondary school," Representative Dick Armey offered the following amendment:

> Nothing in this Act shall be construed to permit, allow, encourage, or authorize any federal control over any aspect of any private, religious, or home school, whether or not a home school is treated as a private school or home school under state law. This section shall not be construed to bar private, religious, or home schools from participating in programs or services under the Act.

The Armey Amendment specifically stated that: "Nothing in this subsection shall be construed to require the certification or regulation of teachers in any private, religious, or home school."

Support for Armey's amendment was weak in the beginning. The Home School Legal Defense Fund Association (HSLDFA), however, distributed a letter to its entire membership warning against the original amendment of the 1965 act and posted a copy of the letter on Compuserve, a commercial online service. The HSLDFA also implemented an aggressive radio campaign.

The publicity worked. Concerned voters flooded Congress with phone calls and letters. One representative received over 800 calls in one day. When the bill finally came to a vote, an amendment removing the troublesome language passed 424 to 1, the lone holdout being the author of the original amendment. Armey's additional guarantees also passed with 374 votes to 53.

HOMELESS STUDENTS Children can be homeless in a variety of ways. Some are runaways and some have been abandoned by their families. Some literally live on the streets, while others live in shelters. Homeless children are, in theory, entitled to the same educational benefits as children with permanent homes, just as **illegal aliens** are entitled to the same education afforded legal aliens and citizens. In reality, however, many homeless students miss out on most educational opportunities.

Some students are unable to meet the administrative requirements for school enrollment. For instance, many school districts require that a child attending its schools be living with a parent or legal guardian. Some districts might require that a child enroll in the district in which he was living before he became homeless; in such situations, transportation might be unavailable. Homeless children may also have problems showing proof of **vaccinations,** as required by most public schools, and may also have difficulty obtaining and paying for the necessary shots. Many of these children also lack educational records from previous schools. These are just some of the hurdles homeless children face when trying to obtain an education.

In 1987, Congress passed the Stewart B. McKinney Homeless Assistance Act, which gives federal money to states "for the purpose of facilitating the enrollment, attendance, and success of homeless youths in schools." Critics of federal efforts to assist the homeless argue that McKinney grants are inadequately monitored by the government to ensure that they are used to assist those for whom they were originally intended. Many also claim that the act, with its emphasis on access to education, does little to ensure the effectiveness of that education, unlike other federal legislation, such as the **Individuals with Disabilities Education Act (IDEA),** which emphasizes providing supplemental services like transportation and counseling that help a child who qualifies under the act take advantage of the education to which he or she has access. In response to such criticisms, Congress amended the act in 1990 specifically to allow grant money to be spent on such supplemental services.

A number of states have taken it upon themselves to establish programs for reaching homeless children. A few, for example, have established branch schools at homeless shelters, which allows homeless children to attend without dealing with the frustrations of transportation between the shelter and school. Some activists argue that this separation further isolates homeless children from their more economically fortunate peers; others maintain that it saves these children from the teasing and taunting that they suffer in regular schools. Some school districts have simply increased their efforts to bend the regulations where necessary to assimilate homeless children into the student body, from waiving residency requirements to concealing the children's homeless status from the other students.

HOMEWORK

In recent years, the decision over whether or not students should be assigned work to be completed outside of the regular school day has been often made at the school administration level rather than at the classroom level. As a result, controversies have occasionally arisen in which critics find fault with a particular homework policy, arguing either that too much homework is expected or that not enough is given. In 1994, a trustee for a California school district received nationwide media attention for his proposal that the district abolish homework as a matter of policy. The trustee argued that giving homework cuts into valuable family time and tilts the scales in favor of upper-income children whose parents can afford home computers and time for tutoring. The proposal created such frenzy that the trustee ultimately pulled it from consideration. Even so, the board decided to form a committee to reconsider the homework policy, which had recently been revised to require anywhere from 30 minutes a day for younger students up to nine hours a week for older students.

Homework conflicts are not restricted to the public schools, however. For example, in 1986 parents of a New York first grader sued his private school for breach of contract for failing to assign homework as promised. The father tutored the child at home after school, and the parents eventually filed suit, asking for $2,700 to compensate them for the time spent tutoring and for tuition that they had paid. The parents also removed the child from the private school and placed him in a public elementary school where, interestingly enough, the policy disfavors giving homework to younger students.

HOMOSEXUALITY Statistics indicate that homosexual high school students face a number of overwhelming problems. They are frequently targets of violence by others—one study, for example, showed that 20 percent of gay students in New York schools had been attacked due to their sexual orientation. In 1989, the U.S. Department of Health and Human Services reported that homosexual teens are three times more likely to commit **suicide** than their heterosexual peers. Also, by some estimates, nearly one-third of all homosexual teens drop out of high school. Furthermore, acquired immune deficiency syndrome (AIDS) kills many teens each year, and many of the victims acquire the virus through unprotected sexual activity—homosexual as well as heterosexual.

The role of schools in combatting the problems faced by homosexual students starts out as a sociological issue. On one side are those who advocate solutions such as extending basic civil rights to cover homosexuals and expanding the **sex education** curriculum to include coverage of homosexual issues. The **National Education Association (NEA),** for example, issued a statement in 1992 that:

> The [NEA] believes that all persons, regardless of sexual orientation, should be afforded equal opportunity within the public educational system. The Association further believes that every school district should provide counseling by trained personnel for students who are struggling with their sexual/gender orientation.

On the other side are those who believe that homosexuality has no place in the public school system. Antigay groups and religious organizations often oppose efforts to include discussion of homosexuality in the school **curriculum,** believing that such inclusion wrongly promotes the idea that homosexuality is as morally acceptable as heterosexuality and gives the impression that the schools officially sanction homosexuality.

Legal issues quickly arise as each side resorts to the courts and state and federal legislatures in order to implement their desired solutions, and each position has met with some success. In 1994, for example, Congress twice refused to pass amendments to the **Improving America's Schools Act** (which reauthorizes the 1965 Elementary and Secondary Education Act). The amendments would have required the withholding of funding from public schools whose curriculums include homosexuality.A year earlier, the state of Massachusetts had passed a law banning discrimination against homosexual students in public schools. Besides giving gay and lesbian students who face harassment the right to sue the school district, the law also mandates that same-sex couples be allowed to attend high school proms and that schools support students in forming homosexual support groups and include homosexual issues in sex education classes. Those who oppose inclusion of homosexual issues have had other successes. For example, local clergy in Des Moines, Iowa, succeeded in pressuring the superintendent of schools to abandon a recommendation that would have extended tolerance in a number of ways, such as by highlighting historical contributions of homosexuals.

Ironically, one piece of federal legislation that was intended to further acceptance of religion by public schools has, in some instances, been used to support tolerance for homosexual support groups. The **Equal Access Act** forbids public schools that receive federal money and that have a "limited open forum," meaning they allow noncurriculum-related clubs to use their facilities, from discriminating against certain clubs based on their religious [see **religious clubs**] or political character. One California school, for example, decided in favor of allowing a homosexual support group to use school facilities after school rather than close its limited open forum, which would have meant excluding over 30 other clubs. On the other hand, the Salt Lake City school district voted to eliminate all noncurricular clubs rather than accept a gay-straight student alliance as an official school club.

Controversies surrounding how homosexual students should be treated have also reached into the world of higher education—especially where military programs are concerned. For example, a California university decided in 1995 to disband its Air Force Reserve Officers' Training Corps (ROTC) program because of the military's policy against homosexuality, which violates the school's nondiscrimination policy. In another case, a former student at the U.S. Naval Academy sued for reinstatement to the academy after he resigned in lieu of being discharged for confiding to a fellow student that he was homosexual. [*Steffan v. Perry*, 41 F.3d 677 (D.C. Cir. 1994)] A federal court initially ordered the academy to reinstate the student, since his discharge was based solely on his private thoughts, as opposed to any specific actions barred by the military judicial code. Later, however, the court vacated that decision and upheld as valid the academy regulations and Department of Defense Directives upon which the case against the student was based.

HONIG V. DOE Supreme Court decision requiring schools to keep disabled students in their current educational placements during hearings over any proposed changes. [484 U.S. 305 (1988)]

During the 1980 school year, a San Francisco developmental center for disabled children sought to expel two students who had committed certain disruptive acts, such as choking another student, kicking out a school window, stealing money, and making sexual comments to female classmates. While the hearings took place to determine whether or not the students should be expelled, the school proposed suspending them indefinitely.

The parents disagreed and took the matter to court, asking for an injunction against both the indefinite suspensions and the expulsions [see **suspension and expulsion**]. The lower court issued the injunctions based on the "stay put" provision of the Education of the Handicapped Act, later renamed the **Individuals with Disabilities Education Act (IDEA).** This provision requires that as long as it takes to complete the hearings and appeals relating to a proposed change in the educational placement of a disabled child, the child must remain in the placement specified in his or her **Individualized Educational Program (IEP),** unless the parents agree to an alternative arrangement.

The California Superintendent of Public Instruction appealed the decision through the court system and, ultimately, to the U.S. Supreme Court. The Supreme Court affirmed the lower courts' decision and pointed out that, in passing the IDEA, Congress had specifically included emotionally handicapped children in the definition of "handicapped" but had conspicuously left out any sort of exception for dangerous students to the "stay put" provision.

The Court cautioned that this ruling did not mean that educators were at the mercy of disruptive, disabled children. They were still free to use normal procedures, such as "use of study carrels, timeouts, detention, or the restriction of privileges," in dealing with these students. Also, in extreme cases where a student poses an immediate threat to others, the school may suspend him or her for up to ten school days. Such a suspension does not constitute a change in placement and, therefore, does not violate the act. During the suspension, the Court said, the school could appeal to the courts for relief, because the "stay put" provision was intended as a limit only on the power of schools to remove disabled children from the classroom over the objections of their parents; it did not limit the power of the courts to make such a decision.

However, in cases where a school appeals to a court to bar a disabled student from his or her current educational placement, a presumption arises in favor of that placement. The school can overcome this presumption only by showing "that maintaining the child in his or her current placement is substantially likely to result in injury either to himself or herself, or to others."

HONOR CODES Ethical standards promulgated by many colleges and universities. Many institutions that have such codes rely on other students to turn in offenders. This goal is often accomplished by inclusion in the code of a "nontoleration clause," as in the language found in the U.S. Military Academy Cadet Honor Code: "A cadet will not lie, cheat, or steal, *nor tolerate those who do*" (emphasis added). Such a clause means that a student who witnesses a violation of the code but who does not report it has, in fact, broken the code and may be punished accordingly.

One purpose served by an honor code is to put students on notice as to what is expected of them morally. In order to ensure that each student receives notice of his or her duties under the code, many institutions require students to sign a pledge at some point. Some institutions require a written pledge to uphold the honor code when a student is accepted for admission; others require that a student sign a pledge on each paper and test handed in.

When a student is accused of violating the honor code, the school generally conducts a hearing of some sort. Issues sometimes arise as to the amount of procedural due process to which the student is entitled—what sort of notice of the charges should be given, whether the right to cross-examine witnesses applies, whether he or she has a right to bring in an attorney, and so forth. As a general rule, private universities can get away with less due process than state schools can, since state schools must operate within the confines of the federal and state constitutions. Some would argue, however, that the line between public and private institutions has become blurred given the amount of government money that finds its way into private institutions in the form of scholarships and other sorts of **financial aid.**

When a student is found guilty of violating the honor code, the punishment meted out can be severe. In 1994, for example, a panel recommended the expulsion of 29 midshipmen from the U.S. Naval Academy for violating the academy's honor code against lying, cheating, and stealing. The students recommended for expulsion [see **suspension and expulsion**] had been involved in the worst cheating scandal in the academy's history in a variety of ways: some had sold copies of the test to classmates, while others had used the information from the copies to cheat on the exam and then lied when questioned about it.

I

ILLEGAL ALIENS Noncitizens who are in the United States without going through formal immigration procedures. Controversy surrounds the issue of whether or not illegal aliens constitute a drain on the resources of the country as a whole and on the resources of individual states with a large illegal population and, if so, what should be done about it. In 1994, Governor Lawton Chiles of Florida, the state of Florida, the Dade County Public Health Trust, and the School Board of Dade County sued the United States in federal court, charging that the federal government "has failed to properly enforce immigration policies, thereby causing the State of Florida to incur disproportionate and unfair expenses in educating and providing other public benefits to aliens." [*Chiles v. United States*, 874 F. Supp. 1334 (S.D. Fla. 1994)] Although this case was ultimately dismissed, it illustrates the desperation some states feel when it comes to the money spent on aliens.

This is especially true in the area of publicly funded education. In considering the Chiles lawsuit, the court cited a Department of Justice study that reported that Florida spent $424 million on illegal aliens enrolled in Florida public schools. In another case, taxpayers sued in a California court to prevent California State University from allowing illegal aliens to become California residents in order to pay the lower tuition paid by in-state students. [*American Ass'n of Women v. Board of Trustees of Cal. State Univ.*, 38 Cal. Rptr. 2d 15 (Cal. Ct. App. 1995)]

In 1982, the U.S. Supreme Court issued its opinion in the landmark case on the issue of illegal aliens and their rights to public education. In *Plyler v. Doe* [458 U.S. 1131 (1982)], a group of Mexican children living in Texas filed a class-action suit challenging a state statute that withheld state funds from local school districts for the education of children not "legally admitted" into the country and a county policy that allowed children of illegal aliens to enroll provided they could pay the "full tuition fee." The children prevailed at trial under the Constitution's equal protection clause [see **equal protection**], which provides that a state may not "deny any person within its jurisdiction the equal protection of the laws," but the defendants appealed the case, ultimately to the Supreme Court.

In its analysis of the situation, the Court first met the defendants' argument that the equal protection clause did not apply to illegal aliens. The Court flatly disagreed, holding that "an alien is surely a 'person,'" and even illegal aliens are entitled to protection by the Constitution based on their presence within the boundaries of the state.

Having answered that contention, the Court proceeded in its equal protection analysis. In determining a case like this under the equal protection clause, the Court must first decide if the group of people affected by the challenged law constitutes a "suspect classification" and if the law abridges a fundamental right. In *Plyler,* the Court conceded that illegal aliens are not a suspect classification and that education is not a fundamental right under the Constitution. It emphasized, however, the importance of education in terms of a person's potential for success and declared that this could not be taken away from the children of illegal aliens, who are, after all, in the country through no fault of their own and who are not free to leave on their own, unless it furthered a substantial state interest.

The defendants argued that the law furthered two substantial state interests. First, the state had an interest in stemming the tide of illegal immigrants swarming over its boundaries. Second, paying for the education of these children imposed a special burden on the quality of public education in the state of Texas. The Court, however, disagreed and affirmed the holding of the lower courts, pointing out that most illegal aliens are not drawn to the United States in search of a free, public education for their children—they come for jobs. Therefore, denying the children an education would do little or nothing to dissuade their parents from coming to the United States in the first place; it would merely ensure that the children be doomed to illiteracy.

Despite the holding of the Court in *Plyler,* states that have a large population of illegal aliens continue to fume about the aliens' impact on the state economies and to search for ways of getting around this problem. In 1994, California took the most drastic action in recent years against illegal aliens when 59 percent of its voters approved Proposition 187, which cut off public services, including education, to illegal aliens. Reaction to the passage of Proposition 187 was swift. A number of lawsuits were quickly filed and within several weeks, a federal court had issued a temporary injunction against all but two provisions of the new law: one against falsification of immigration documents and another prohibiting illegal immigrants from receiving public higher education. This second provision was also enjoined by a San Francisco Superior Court judge.

IMPACT FEES Fees imposed on a developer, as a condition to receiving a building permit, to cover the costs of public services required by the new development, such as water, sewerage, and schools. As of 1993, 20 states had statutes granting local governments the power to collect such fees.

Each state with such a statute also has a test for analyzing the fairness of fees collected and whether there is a sufficient connection between the fee and the need for the public service—a connection that could be assigned to the new development. North Carolina courts, for example, use a three-part analysis that a number of other state courts have adopted. In order to show this connection, a North Carolina local government must show that, first, a new public service (such as a school) needs to be built because of growing development. Second, the government must show that the fee collected from the developer does not burden the developer with more than a fair share of the cost of the new public facilities. Finally, the government must show that the new facilities will provide a sufficient benefit to the development.

Various issues occasionally arise in connection with impact fees. One question concerns how much time a local government has to build the facility funded by the fee. Most impact fee laws provide that the fees must be spent as intended within five or six years. If they are not spent within that time, the issue arises of what should be done with them. Often, the statute provides that fees not spent within the time allotted should be returned. The money is generally returned to the one who paid the fee in the first place, although the statute might provide for return of the fee to the current landowner if the original fee payer cannot be located.

If the public service funded by the impact fee is a new public school, a whole new issue can arise: should developers still be required to pay the impact fee if they can show that the development will not increase the population of school-age children? The Florida Supreme Court considered this issue in 1991 in a case involving a county impact fee ordinance that contained a section allowing a fee payer to avoid paying the impact fee to fund a new school if he or she could show that no children would be living in the unit subject to the fee. [*St. Johns County v. Northeast Fla. Builders Ass'n,*

583 So. 2d 635 (Fla. 1991)] The court agreed that under this section, "the impact fees have the potential of being user fees that will be paid primarily by those households that do contain public school children, thereby colliding with the constitutional requirement of free public schools."

IMPROVING AMERICA'S SCHOOLS ACT In 1965, as part of President Lyndon B. Johnson's "Great Society" initiative, Congress passed the Elementary and Secondary Education Act, which the **National Education Association (NEA)** has described as "the cornerstone of the nation's K–12 education policy." The main purpose of the act was to establish a number of programs for the benefit of U.S. education overall and especially to assist local educational agencies (LEAs) in the education of poor children. Since 1965, Congress has amended and changed the act's elements several times through reauthorization of the law every few years.

When the act was up for reauthorization in 1993, the proposal was renamed the Improving America's Schools Act (IASA). As passed, the IASA continues to emphasize financial support for schools with a high poverty level among their students. It also stresses the need for all students, disadvantaged or not, to reach certain standards that may be developed by the states either through participation in the **Goals 2000** program or independently. The IASA also deals with teachers meeting high professional standards and expands professional development programs provided for in the original act from just science and math to include other core academic subjects as well.

Through passage of the IASA, Congress hoped to improve the quality of education through new, sometimes controversial, approaches. For example, the act provides financial assistance to LEAs that wish to establish public **charter schools,** which operate without much of the bureaucracy that exists in the regular school systems. The act also aims to boost educational quality by improving the safety of U.S. schools; the IASA contains a provision requiring a one-year expulsion of students who bring guns to school.

A filibuster led by Senator Jesse Helms of North Carolina posed the biggest threat to passage of the IASA by Congress. Helms favored including a provision to withdraw federal financial assistance from school districts that forbid students from participating in constitutionally protected prayer. The school-prayer language that eventually was included allows for withdrawal of funding only from schools that violate court orders regarding student prayer. The filibuster was eventually defeated by 75 votes to 24, and President Bill Clinton signed the bill into law just two weeks later.

INDIVIDUALIZED EDUCATIONAL PROGRAM (IEP)

The **Individuals with Disabilities Education Act (IDEA)** requires that each disabled child have an Individualized Educational Program (IEP) drawn up to act as a blueprint for his or her education. A representative of the "local educational agency" (a public board of education or another agency having administrative control of public school matters), the child's teacher, the child's parents or guardian, and sometimes the child meet to design this blueprint.

Each child's IEP is tailor-made for his or her unique abilities and circumstances. The act requires that the IEP contain the following information: a statement of the current level of performance; a statement of annual educational goals; a statement of the specific educational services to be provided; a statement of "transition services" (outcome-oriented activities such as assistance with employment and independent living) to be provided if the child is at least 16 years old; an estimation of the date for beginning the educational and transition services and how long the services will last; and a means of evaluating whether the educational goals are being achieved. The IEP must be reviewed at least annually and revised as needed.

If the child's parents or guardian do not agree with the school officials concerning the IEP, they may first appeal to a local hearing officer appointed by the state board of education. If they are unsatisfied at the local level, they may have their case reviewed by an appeals officer. If they are still unsatisfied, they may file a civil action in either a state or federal court. From there, they are entitled to appeal an unfavorable decision up through the judicial system and even as high as the U.S. Supreme Court. See, for example, ***Hendrick Hudson Board of Education v. Rowley.***

INDIVIDUALS WITH DISABILITIES EDUCATION ACT (IDEA)

Originally entitled the Education for All Handicapped Children Act, this federal legislation sets out requirements for the public education of children with disabilities and allocates federal money to states that meet these requirements. Prior to the act's passage by Congress in

1975, half of the more than 8 million children with disabilities in the United States did not receive appropriate educational services. One million were entirely excluded from the public school systems. State and local authorities generally rationalized this situation as being due to a lack of funding for special programs. As a result, wealthy parents often paid out of pocket for special services that allowed their children to benefit educationally. The children of those who could not afford to pay were left out.

Congress stepped in and passed the IDEA to ensure that disabled children would have access to a free, appropriate education and related services designed to meet their special needs. It answered the states' argument that they were unable to pay for a variety of special programs, offering federal money to cover the costs. It also imposed on the states a number of mandatory procedures, such as giving parents notice of proposed changes in their child's educational placement and allowing the child to remain in his or her current placement while any hearings and appeals on the issue take place.

The act applies to children with a variety of disabilities, including mental retardation; impaired hearing, sight, or speech; serious emotional disturbances; impairments that prevent physical movement; and other chronic health problems that negatively affect a child's strength, vitality, or alertness. It also applies to children who have certain learning disabilities, such as dyslexia, an impairment of the ability to read. The IDEA requires the school to design an **Individualized Educational Program (IEP)** that specifically targets the disabled student's needs. Then, keeping in mind the IEP, the student must be provided with a free, appropriate education and related services (catheterization, for example, if a student requires it to take part in the educational process) at state expense. This education must be offered in the least restrictive learning environment possible. **Mainstreaming** into a regular classroom along with support services is regarded as the least restrictive environment and home instruction the most restrictive.

With the passage of the IDEA, classrooms and programs across the country opened up for children with disabilities. The **Department of Education** reported that in 1993 over 30 percent of disabled American children (many of whom had learning disabilities, as opposed to autism or mental retardation) were placed in regular classrooms.

Controversy arises, however, when people disagree on how to interpret the act. For example, in 1982, the U.S. Supreme Court was called upon in ***Hendrick Hudson Board of Education v. Rowley*** to rule on the meaning of "appropriate" in the phrase "free, appropriate education." In this case involving a deaf first grader, the Court rejected a lower court's interpretation in favor of the Rowleys that the state must "maximize the potential of handicapped children" and declared that the state meets the appropriateness requirement when it provides "personalized instruction with sufficient support services to permit the child to benefit educationally from that instruction.

Another controversial part of the IDEA is the "stay-put" provision, which mandates that a student not be removed from his or her placement against the will of the parents until after an impartial hearing. Unfortunately, the hearings and court battles often drag on for quite a while, all of which time the student may not be moved. The U.S. Supreme Court refused in ***Honig v. Doe*** to carve out an exception to the provision even in the case of violent, disruptive students.

This can lead to conflict when protecting the rights of a disabled student infringes on the rights of others. For example, when a California high school attempted to expel a student in compliance with a state law mandating expulsion of students who bring guns to school, the student's parents claimed that he had an attention deficit disorder. A federal judge ordered that the student not be expelled or sent to a different school until he was evaluated.

INGRAHAM V. WRIGHT Supreme Court decision holding that the Eighth Amendment prohibition against cruel and unusual punishment applies only to prisoners, not students. [430 U.S. 651 (1977)] Two junior high school students had received beatings from school officials due to such infractions as not answering the teacher quickly enough. The students required medical attention for their injuries, which included a hematoma (a blood-filled swelling) for one child and the loss of full use of one arm for a week for the other. The students filed suit against their school principal for these injuries and argued that their punishments violated two provisions of the U.S. Constitution: (1) the Eighth Amendment prohibition against cruel and unusual punishment and (2) the Fourteenth Amendment requirement giving procedural **due process,** such as notice of charges and a hearing, before depriving a person of "life, liberty, or property." The Court rejected their argument.

The Court concluded that the Eighth Amendment was meant to apply only to criminal cases involving prison inmates who had been tortured, mutilated, or killed by law enforcement officials. Schools, which are generally open places under the watchful eye of the community, are different from prisons, which tend to be closed environments where outsiders rarely know what is happening on the inside. Because of this difference, the Court held that students do not require the same constitutional protection as prisoners. Therefore, since students are not part of the class of people protected by the amendment, **corporal punishment** in schools, no matter how brutal or bizarre, does not fit the definition of cruel and unusual punishment and is not unconstitutional. (This does not, however, mean that it is not *illegal* under state or local laws.)

In examining the due process claim under the Fourteenth Amendment, the Court pointed out that teachers and other school officials have a historically recognized right to use force against students when it is reasonably necessary to maintain order in the schools. The Court reasoned that as long as a person who delivers corporal punishment is subject to civil or criminal penalties for using excessive force, the states satisfy procedural due process. Since any wrongdoing can supposedly be fixed in the court system later, schools are not required to provide a student with procedural due process before administering corporal punishment.

INTERNET CENSORSHIP More and more American students are gaining access through their schools to the Internet, a network of computer systems containing a vast array of information that can be reached in a variety of ways. Discussion groups, which consist of millions of postings on various topics, are popular among Internet users, and some of the most popular of these groups concern sex.

Carnegie Mellon University, a private university in Pittsburgh, was startled in the fall of 1994 when a researcher used the university network to access almost 100,000 sexual pictures—everything from basic nude shots to images of a bound woman being raped by a ski pole and men and women having sex with animals—and to track the number of times each picture was downloaded by users—a total of over 6 million times. Citing concerns over liability under a Pennsylvania statute making it illegal to distribute explicit, harmful, sexual materials to minors (even though most CMU students are 18 or older, many elementary and high school students have access to the network), the university announced that it would delete sex-related newsgroups from its computer network.

Controversy erupted over the decision. The **American Civil Liberties Union (ACLU)** sent a letter to CMU's president urging him to rethink his position, and students organized a "Protest for Freedom in Cyberspace." Arguments ranged from the belief that the university had misconstrued the Pennsylvania statute, which contains an exemption for "any library of any school, college or university," to the view that by blocking access to a newsgroup like "alt.sex," the school effectively blocked the students' access to its various branches, such as "alt.sex.safe_sex," which is a forum for discussing responsible sexual behavior. Many compared the university's decision to the removal of books from a library [see **library books**]. The university disagreed, pointing out that everything in the library was individually selected, unlike postings to newsgroups, which come in unedited. In the face of such strong opposition, however, the school retreated from its initial ruling that banned both graphic and textual files in favor of one that banned only graphics.

The relative newness of the Internet has opened up a number of legal issues that could have an impact on educational institutions and students. For example, in censorship cases such as the incident at CMU, rights of free speech [see **freedom of speech**] and **academic freedom** could go head to head with the liability a school might face for "distributing" obscene materials to students.

The very nature of the Internet could change the means by which courts decide what is obscene. The Supreme Court held in 1973 that obscenity issues should be judged by local community standards. The Internet, however, transcends local boundaries, reaching not only from city to city and state to state but also from country to country. The Internet makes it possible for a sixth grader in Kansas City to download files from a computer in San Francisco. In such situations, whose "local community standards" should apply? One federal court in Tennessee proposed an answer to that question in July 1994, when it convicted two California-based computer bulletin board operators for transmitting obscenity to Tennessee through interstate telephone lines. [*United States v. Thomas,* 74 F.3d 701 (6th Cir. 1996)] This was the first case tried in the state to which the obscene material was sent rather than in the state of origination.

Concern over the quality of material that is transmitted via the Internet has reached the realm of Congress. In the spring of 1995, a senator introduced a bill that would allow for criminal penalties, such as jail time and fines, for anyone who transmits "any comment, request, suggestion, proposal or other communication which is obscene, lewd, lascivious, filthy, or indecent." The goal of the bill is to protect minors who log onto computer networks, but critics protest that besides being almost impossible to enforce, such a measure could have the effect of reducing adults to reading only material that is fit for children.

IQ TESTS Tests that supposedly measure aptitude for learning have historically been a key factor in determining where each child is placed within the school system, whether the particular child is in need of special services mandated by the **Individuals with Disabilities Education Act (IDEA)** or whether the school district simply follows the practice of **tracking,** or grouping children according to ability levels. Controversies about the use of such tests hinge on the argument that they are biased in favor of middle-class whites. For example, a suit brought by a group of non–English-speaking students who had been wrongly labeled retarded and placed in a special-education class resulted in a settlement in which the school district agreed to reevaluate the affected students, correct the placement decisions where necessary, and change its procedures for testing in the future in order to remedy the cultural bias.

In one example of racial bias in IQ testing, each student was asked what he or she would do if sent on an errand to buy bread but the grocery store was out of bread. The testers had decided that the proper answer was "go to another store." Many black children from urban settings where grocery stores were not plentiful, however, chose the answer "go home." While this would be the correct answer in their real-life environments, it did not add points to their scores.

In the 1970s, a number of black children in California were mistakenly placed in classes for the mentally retarded based on tests containing such biases. In the ensuing trial, the federal district court judge was unimpressed with the state's argument that the racial imbalances that came from relying on the test scores were the result of a higher incidence of mild retardation among poor blacks because of poor nutrition and inadequate medical care. The judge ordered that every black student in the state who had been classified as retarded must be reevaluated. In 1974, the Ninth Circuit Court agreed and issued an injunction permanently barring California public schools from using IQ tests in determining the placement of blacks into special-education classes. [*Larry P. v. Riles*, 502 F.2d 963 (9th Cir. 1974)]

L

Lee v. Weisman Supreme Court decision holding that public school officials may not decide that a graduation speaker will offer a prayer and then assert control over the content of that prayer. [505 U.S. 577 (1992)]

After a rabbi was invited to deliver a prayer at a middle school graduation, the father of one of the graduates filed for an injunction to stop the school district's practice of including prayers at graduation ceremonies. The injunction was granted, and the school district appealed.

When the case reached the U.S. Supreme Court in 1992, the decision of the lower courts was affirmed. The Court found that because of the principal's actions, the school—and therefore the state—had controlled the content of the prayer to some extent. The principal decided to include an invocation as part of the ceremony, picked the speaker, gave him a book called *Guidelines for Civic Occasions,* and advised him that the prayer should be nonsectarian, or not associated with any particular religious denomination. This state control violated the establishment clause [see **establishment and free exercise clauses**] of the Constitution.

As in two earlier Supreme Court prayer cases, ***Engel v. Vitale*** and ***School District of Abington Township v. Schempp,*** students who objected to the prayer were not required to participate. In fact, they were not even technically required to attend the graduation exercises in order to receive their diplomas. However, the Court recognized the ceremony's role as "one of life's most significant occasions" and said that a student should not have to miss his or her graduation in order to "resist conformance to state-sponsored religious practice."

The following year, the Fifth Circuit heard the case of *Jones v. Clear Creek Independent School District* [977 F.2d 963 (5th Cir. 1992)], in which it approved graduation prayer where a majority of the students had asked for it and where the prayer was nonsectarian. Decisions of the Fifth Circuit apply only to the states of Texas, Louisiana, and Mississippi. Even so, opponents of school-sponsored religious activities view the *Jones* decision as a step backward in the line of cases since *Engel.* The **American Civil Liberties**

Union (ACLU), for example, says that the *Jones* decision "seriously misreads the Supreme Court's holding in *Lee*." The *Jones* court relied in part on the fact that the school reviewed the student prayers to make certain that they were nonsectarian. However, one could argue that this is precisely the kind of state involvement the Supreme Court rejected in *Lee*.

The *Jones* court also relied on the difference between the two cases, in that *Lee* dealt with school-initiated prayer and *Jones* with prayer requested by a majority of the graduating students. However, a majority of people cannot vote away the civil rights of others. According to the decision in the flag salute case of ***West Virginia State Board of Education v. Barnette:*** "One's right to life, liberty, and property, to free speech, a free press, freedom of worship and assembly, and other fundamental rights may not be submitted to vote; they depend on the outcome of no elections."

The Supreme Court denied *certiorari* to, or refused to review, *Jones*. Some who favor school prayer view this as approval of the decision. However, the Court agrees to review only a small fraction of the cases presented to it. Refusal to review a case does not reflect on the case's merits.

LEMON V. KURTZMAN

Supreme Court opinion setting out a test to be used in determining whether action by a state violates the First Amendment prohibitions set out in the Constitution's establishment clause or free exercise clause [see **establishment and free exercise clauses**]. The test comprises three parts: the activity or legislation must (1) have a nonreligious purpose; (2) neither advance nor inhibit religion; and (3) not involve excessive entanglement between the government and religion. [403 U.S. 602 (1971)]

In *Lemon*, the Court invalidated certain statutes of Rhode Island and Pennsylvania that provided financial aid to private schools [see **private schools, government money and**], many of which were affiliated with churches, as violative of the First Amendment. The Rhode Island law paid salary supplements directly to teachers of secular, or nonreligious, subjects in private schools. The Pennsylvania law allowed the state to refund to the private schools money that they spent for teachers' salaries, textbooks, and other instructional materials, where the money went to pay for the teaching of secular subjects. Both states implemented safeguards to ensure that the state money did not go to teaching religion, such as requiring the government to audit the financial records of the schools to determine how much of their money was spent on secular education and how much went toward religious instruction.

The Court found that although the purpose of the laws was not to advance religion but rather to "enhance the quality of the secular education in all schools covered by the **compulsory attendance** laws," the very procedures set up to guard against state promotion of religion actually constituted an impermissible level of government entanglement in religion. Requiring the state to analyze the financial records of the schools and the religious content of their curricula [see **curriculum**] fostered too intimate a relationship between church and state. Also, the Court pointed out, such a situation could have an impact on the state political systems, when supporters and opponents of religious education square off against each other in political campaigns. The Court restated that "political divisions along religious lines was one of the principal evils against which the First Amendment was intended to protect."

LIBRARY BOOKS The American Library Association's 14th annual *Banned Books Resource Guide* reported that in 1994 and 1995, at least 179 instances of book banning occurred in U.S. public schools. Over the years, school districts have banned everything from fairy tales to dictionaries for content that authorities found objectionable. Usually, the authorities object to the viewpoints expressed in the books on religion, sex, or even politics. One school board, for example, removed a book about the United States because it contained "funny pictures of Republicans and nicer pictures of Democrats."

The removal of books from public school libraries involves questions of free speech [see **freedom of speech**], because the right to receive expression goes hand in hand with the right to speak freely under the First Amendment of the Constitution. In analyzing free speech controversies, courts have traditionally looked to where the speech occurred and the reason given by the state for censoring it. For example, the government may prohibit only unprotected speech (such as obscenity and defamation) if it occurs in a public forum, such as a street or a park. On the other hand, if the speech occurs in a nonpublic forum, the government may infringe on the speaker's right to free speech for content reasons, as long as the restriction is viewpoint neutral. In other words, the government could restrict speech on an entire subject area, such as politics, but could not discriminate against any particular point of view on that subject.

Courts have historically deferred to the judgment of educators when their actions are challenged, as long as the challenged action is reasonably related to a legitimate government interest, such as the education or protection of students. For example, in 1980, a federal circuit court upheld the removal of books such as Patrick Mann's *Dog Day Afternoon* from a school library because the students failed to prove that removal of the controversial books subjected them to an "identifiable orthodoxy" of thought. [*Bicknell v. Vergennes Union High Sch. Bd. of Dirs.*, 638 F.2d 438 (2d Cir. 1980)] On the other hand, in 1976 another circuit court overturned the removal by school authorities of *Catch 22* by Joseph Heller and *Cat's Cradle* by Kurt Vonnegut from a school library because the fact that school authorities found the books "distasteful" was insufficient to justify infringing on the students' rights to receive information. [*Minarcini v. Strongsville City Sch. Dist.*, 541 F.2d 577 (6th Cir. 1976)]

In 1982, however, the Supreme Court provided some guidance for lower courts faced with library book removal cases when it delivered its opinion in ***Board of Education, Island Trees Union Free School District v. Pico.*** In *Pico,* the school board had removed 11 books from its school libraries based on a list of objectionable books provided by a conservative group. In banning the books, which the board described as "anti-American, anti-Christian, anti-Semitic, and just plain filthy," the board acted contrary to the advice of the superintendent, parents, and a committee created to study the issue. The Court held that the trial court had erred in granting summary judgment, or judgment without a trial, for the Board of Education, because there was evidence that the board's motivation made the removal unconstitutional.

Pico made two important distinctions. The first was between the acquisition of books (over which school officials enjoy almost limitless power) and the removal of books. When school officials remove a book from the library, they face the burden of proving, when challenged in court, that their motivation was not to unconstitutionally deny the students access to viewpoints offensive to the officials. The second distinction was between the school library (which has a "unique role" in exposing students to new ideas through their own voluntary reading) and the school **curriculum** (where school authorities retain greater control).

A 1990 case illustrates the application of this second distinction. A school ordered the Bible removed from its classrooms and library. The removal from the classrooms was upheld as a permissible use of school power. The court overturned the removal from the library, however, as an unconstitutional violation of the students' First Amendment rights. [*Roberts v. Madigan*, 921 F.2d 1047 (10th Cir. 1990)]

LOCKER SEARCHES Searches of students and their possessions by public school authorities are governed by the rule set out in ***New Jersey v. T.L.O.*** A search by school authorities that might be unconstitutional if conducted by a police officer of a private citizen will be upheld if it meets two requirements. First, rather than the probable cause required of a police officer, a school official's search is justified if he or she has "reasonable grounds for suspecting that the search will turn up evidence that the student has violated or is violating either the law or the rules of the school." Second, the scope of the area searched must reasonably relate "to the circumstances which justified the interference in the first place." The *T.L.O.* case dealt with the search of a student's purse, not with a locker, but courts still apply this test in deciding challenges to searches of school lockers by school authorities.

For example, a California court referred to the holding in *T.L.O.* in a 1995 case in which a minor who had been found delinquent by a court for carrying a loaded gun to school argued that the search that turned up the gun in the first place was unconstitutional and that, as a result, the evidence of the gun should have been excluded from his trial. [*In re Joseph G.*, 38 Cal. Rptr. 2d 902 (Cal. Ct. App. 1995)] In that case, a school official had received a call from another student's parent alerting him to the fact that the defendant had been seen with a pistol at a school football game the previous weekend. The official opened the defendant's locker but found only books. Several minutes later, however, the official saw the defendant put a backpack into his locker. When the locker was searched a second time, the official found the loaded gun inside the backpack.

The court began its analysis of the legality of the search by setting out the *T.L.O.* rule, but pointed out that the California Supreme Court has further elaborated the standard necessary to support such a search of a student. In California, that standard requires specific facts indicating that the student has broken or is breaking a school rule or the law. A search that is based on "mere curiosity, rumor, or hunch" will not pass the test. [*In re William G.*, 709 P.2d 1287 (Cal. 1985)] The court held that the facts in this case were sufficient to meet the standard, and that the trial court did not err in admitting the gun into evidence.

With the increased risk to students posed by drugs, alcohol, and weapons, and with the convenience provided by lockers in harboring such contraband, many school districts have begun looking for ways to combat the problem. Some have responded by removing lockers entirely; others, however, have instituted random searches. The problem with such searches is that they are not based on the individualized suspicion required by *T.L.O.* The Supreme Court, however, has upheld random drug tests of railway employees and border guards on the grounds of public safety concerns that outweigh the individuals' privacy interests. School officials would argue that the public safety interests put at risk by students concealing drugs and weapons in their lockers outweigh the privacy interest of individual students.

In such cases, a court must determine the extent of the individual's expectation of privacy in the area searched. Many states have found that students do have a legitimate expectation of privacy in their school lockers, which would usually prohibit school officials from searching unless they had an individualized suspicion that met the *T.L.O.* standard. At least one school system, however, has found a means of getting around this problem.

The policy handbook for Milwaukee, Wisconsin, schools specifically states:

> At no time does the Milwaukee school district relinquish its exclusive control of lockers provided for the convenience of students. Periodic general inspections of lockers may be conducted by school authorities for any reason at any time, without notice, without student consent, and without a search warrant.

In 1993, a Wisconsin state court heard a case in which a student charged with delinquency moved to suppress evidence of a gun and cocaine found in a coat in his locker during a random search. [*In re Isiah B.*, 500 N.W.2d 637 (Wis. 1993)] School officials initiated the search because of a number of recent incidents involving students with guns, but there was no individualized suspicion that the student charged had a gun; his locker was simply one of almost 100 searched. The court upheld admission of the gun and cocaine into evidence based on the school system's written policy.

LOTTERIES A lottery is a type of state-run gambling in which consumers try to pick a series of winning numbers in an effort to hit the "jackpot." By 1990, at least 34 states had lotteries whose profits were earmarked for public services like education.

Lotteries are frequently the subject of fierce criticism. Some authorities argue that lotteries constitute a form of a regressive tax in which poor people pay more than wealthy ones. Studies show this is because the poor spend a greater percentage of their income on lottery tickets than wealthy people do. This fact can be attributed to two reasons. First, simple mathematics dictate that a $1 ticket is a greater percentage of a $10,000 annual income than it is of a $100,000 income. Second, the needy have more motivation to try to strike it rich and are therefore more easily enticed into playing the lottery.

Supporters of lotteries, on the other hand, argue that the positive impact lotteries have on public services such as education more than outweigh any drawbacks. This may or may not be true.

The citizens of Florida, for example, voted overwhelmingly in favor of a lottery in 1986 in order to "enhance" education. Florida law dictates that 38 percent of lottery proceeds, which amounts to hundreds of millions of dollars each year, be given to local school districts. However, rather than adding that money to funds already raised through state taxes to support education, the state legislature has gradually allowed lottery profits to replace general education funds and has shifted money previously spent on education to other programs, such as prisons and health care for the poor.

This has led to a perception on the part of Florida voters that they were mislead. In an effort to correct this problem, proposals have come from several sources. For example, in the fall of 1995, the state education commissioner suggested a plan to replace lottery money that has found its way into the general budget with new tax dollars. This plan closely resembles a suggestion offered twice by the state governor and rejected twice by the legislature.

Another image problem faced by the Florida lottery is a lack of state control over how the funds are spent at the local level. Local school authorities can use the money for just about any expenditure to keep the system afloat rather than allocating the funds to programs that would actually improve the situation. The plan proposed by the education commissioner also includes a provision to mandate that lottery funds be used for specific items, such as prekindergarten programs and improvement of technological resources in schools. In some states, such as Georgia, lottery money is already specifically earmarked in that way.

M

Magnet Schools Schools that offer special programs in an attempt to attract students from different racial and economic backgrounds (hence the term "magnet"). Magnet schools serve a dual purpose by improving the quality of education through **desegregation** and innovation.

Magnet schools generally fall into one of two categories. In a full-site program, the entire school is part of the magnet program, and all students at the school take part in the special curriculum. In partial-site programs, a magnet program is established at a regular school—usually in an effort to pull white kids into formerly minority schools. While such programs may enhance integration of the overall school population, critics contend that they lead to segregation within the school in a manner similar to **tracking,** since the magnet transfer students are often carefully separated from the regular students.

Most magnet school programs share several key characteristics. First, each program offers something special, either a curriculum theme (like science, math, or performing arts) or a particular method of instruction (Montessori, for example). Second, students are enrolled voluntarily rather than being simply assigned to the program. And finally, a magnet school draws its student body from many attendance zones. Supporters of magnet schools point out that such programs entice white students into traditionally black schools. Desegregation tools such as **busing** or the redrawing of school district boundaries, on the other hand, seek to force students into the appropriate schools but often result instead in wealthier students transferring to private schools or even moving to a different school district.

In 1995, the U.S. Supreme Court heard *Missouri v. Jenkins* [115 S. Ct. 2038 (1995)], a case involving magnet schools as a remedy for segregation in Kansas City, Missouri. A federal district court had ordered the Kansas City school district to eliminate segregation within its schools by embarking on a "comprehensive magnet school and capital improvements plan." Under this plan, every senior high school and middle school and half of all elementary schools within the district became magnet schools funded by the state and the school district. Some of the improvements offered under the plan at an annual cost of $200 million included air conditioning, alarm systems, and computers in every high school classroom; a planetarium; green houses; a 25-acre farm; radio and television studios; and an art gallery. In effect, the plan turned the entire school district into what the Court called a "magnet district."

One reason behind the creation of this magnet district was the difficulty of desegregating schools in a school district whose enrollment was almost 70 percent black. By upgrading all facilities in such a dramatic fashion, the court hoped to attract nonminority students from other districts. The Supreme Court, however, held that such an "interdistrict remedy" (a remedy affecting more than the one school district at issue) would be appropriate only where there had been a showing of interdistrict segregation. In this case, the district court had exceeded its remedial authority.

MAINSTREAMING

Many schools in the United States excluded disabled children as a general practice until the 1970s. Those children who did receive educations were usually segregated from nondisabled students. Today, however, the preference is for mainstreaming, or including disabled children in regular classrooms, whenever possible.

Congress incorporated this preference into its **Individuals with Disabilities Education Act (IDEA),** which gives financial support to states that provide a "free appropriate education" to disabled children in accordance with the requirements of the act. One of these requirements is that this education be provided in regular classrooms with nondisabled classmates to the maximum extent appropriate.

The U.S. Supreme Court construed the "free appropriate education" clause of the IDEA in ***Hendrick Hudson Board of Education v. Rowley,*** but the child in that case was already mainstreamed into a regular classroom. Therefore, the Court did not have to determine what part mainstreaming plays in making an educational placement "appropriate." However, at least one federal appellate court has considered the issue.

The Eighth Circuit Court of Appeals heard a case in which a deaf child had spent three years as a student in a school for the deaf. When her parents moved, they decided to enroll her in their local school. The **Individualized Educational Program (IEP)** prepared for her by the school district, however, concluded that the most appropriate educational placement for her would be continued study at the school for the deaf. Her parents disputed the finding and appealed the case through administrative channels and into the judicial system. The court of appeals held that when faced with two educational alternatives, both of which are "appropriate," it is not necessary for the child to take the best alternative if the other offers a less restrictive environment. [*Springdale Sch. Dist. v. Grace,* 693 F.2d 41 (8th Cir. 1982)]

Not everyone favors across-the-board mainstreaming. Some argue that disabled children placed in regular classes take away time and energy that the teachers could invest in the rest of the class and thus interfere with the rights of nondisabled children to receive an education. Others contend that it is not necessarily in the best interest of every disabled child to be mainstreamed, because when a student is placed in a regular classroom based on a policy of mainstreaming rather than on his or her individual needs, his or her educational plan loses the individuality required by the IDEA.

METAL DETECTORS In an effort to crack down on armed students, more and more schools are using metal detectors to find weapons. Statistics show that the presence of guns and other weapons on school campuses is an enormous problem. For example, in 1990, the U.S. Department of Justice reported that 100,000 students carry guns to school every day.

Cases challenging the use of metal detectors in schools began appearing in the early 1990s. In 1991, a student moved to suppress as evidence the switchblade found in her book bag following a search with a hand-held metal detector. The school had posted signs warning that persons entering the premises were subject to such a search, but the student argued that the search was unreasonable and in violation of her Fourth Amendment rights. The court disagreed, however, and compared the search with those that have become common for security reasons at airports and courthouses nationwide. Even though students, unlike airline passengers and other citizens, are not free to leave school instead of submitting to a search, the court said such intrusion is not unconstitutional. [*People v. Dukes,* 580 N.Y.S.2d 850 (N.Y. City Crim. Ct. 1992)]

One interesting legal twist to the trend in favor of using metal detectors in schools is that their use could actually leave the school district open to additional liability. For example, in 1992, a $20 million suit was filed against the New York Board of Education following the fatal shooting of a student. Although the high school in question had metal detectors, they were not in use that day. In such cases, the presence of the detectors could be used as evidence to show that the school knew of the danger of shootings and yet failed in its duty to protect the students accordingly.

MEYER v. NEBRASKA Supreme Court decision affirming that although a state does have a legitimate interest in educating its children through **compulsory attendance** laws and regulation of the **curriculum** taught in the schools, it does not have unlimited power in this area. Parents and children also have rights that must be protected. [262 U.S. 390 (1923)]

In 1920, a teacher in a Nebraska private school taught a ten-year-old child to read in German. The teacher was convicted of violating a state statute passed in 1919 that forbade the teaching of school subjects in any language other than English [see **English language**] and allowed the teaching of modern foreign languages, such as German, French, and Italian, only to students who had already completed the eighth grade. The Nebraska Supreme Court upheld the conviction, saying the law was a valid exercise of the state's power in achieving the valid purpose of making English the "mother tongue" of all the children in the state, but the teacher appealed to the U.S. Supreme Court.

The Supreme Court reversed the judgment because the application of the law infringed on certain liberties protected by the **due process** guarantees of the Fourteenth Amendment of the U.S. Constitution. The Fourteenth Amendment commands that no state "may deny any person of life, liberty, or property without due process of law." The Court defined "liberty" as including:

> . . . the right of the individual to contract, to engage in any of the common occupations of life, to acquire useful knowledge, to marry, establish a home and bring up children, to worship God according to the dictates of his own conscience, and, generally, to enjoy those privileges long recognized at common law as essential to the orderly pursuit of happiness by freemen.

The Court pointed out that not only did the teacher have the right to teach languages in school as part of his lawful profession but that parents also have the right to hire teachers to instruct their children in foreign languages. Such liberties could not be interfered with by a law that had no reasonable relation to a purpose within the state's power. The Court acknowledged the desire of the state to create a uniform population, but held that prohibiting the teaching of foreign languages in order to achieve that goal exceeded the state's power.

Mills v. Board of Education of the District of Columbia Early federal case holding that disabled children have a right to be educated in states that have chosen to offer free, public educations to their citizens and that the financial limitations of the state's education budget does not excuse the state from educating these children. [318 F. Supp. 866 (D.D.C. 1972)]

During the 1972 school year, an estimated 18,000 "exceptional" children (children who are mentally retarded, emotionally disturbed, physically disabled, hyperactive, or suffering from other behavioral problems) in Washington, D.C., went without public education. Seven of these children sued the Board of Education of the District of Columbia for excluding them from the public schools and for denying them publicly supported education. The board admitted that it had a duty to educate the children and that it had not been fulfilling that duty. However, it argued, it simply did not have the financial resources to apply to the education of these children without taking money away from other educational services.

The federal district court agreed that the board had an interest in preserving its financial resources, but declared that this interest did not outweigh its interest in educating the excluded children. "If sufficient funds are not available to finance all of the services and programs that are needed and desirable in the system," the court said, "then the available funds must be expended equitably in such a manner that no child is entirely excluded from a publicly supported education consistent with his needs and ability to benefit therefrom." In other words, disabled children could not be made to bear the brunt of the school system's inadequate funding.

The district court went on to set out procedures to be followed, such as giving the parents notice and holding a fair hearing, in determining the proper educational placement for a disabled child. Many of these procedures, as well as those set out in ***P.A.R.C. v. Commonwealth of Pennsylvania,*** served as models for Congress when it enacted the Education for All Handicapped Children Act of 1975, later known as the **Individuals with Disabilities Education Act (IDEA).**

MINORITY SCHOLARSHIPS Financial aid sometimes offered by colleges and universities to attract minority students and remedy the effects of past segregation. Such scholarships are controversial because they utilize racial discrimination against nonminority students in an effort to counteract the damage caused by segregation.

A Fourth Circuit case received a great deal of attention in 1995 when the Supreme Court refused, without comment, to review the circuit court's decision. In that case, *Podberesky v. Kirwan* [38 F.3d 147 (4th Cir. 1994)], Podberesky, a Hispanic student at the University of Maryland at College Park, sued the university for maintaining a scholarship program that he claimed was unconstitutional.

The program at issue was the Benjamin Banneker Scholarship Program, which awarded at least 20 scholarships each year to high-achieving black students. The university had established the scholarship program as a partial remedy for the state's past discrimination in the area of higher education, in which black students were limited to attending one of its four "black colleges."

While Podberesky exceeded the minimum academic standards set for receipt of a Banneker Scholarship, he was not considered because he was not of African-American heritage. He was also ineligible for the university's other merit-based scholarship because his Scholastic Aptitude Test score and grade point average were not high enough to meet the higher standards of the other program.

Podberesky lost at the trial level. The federal district court, in considering his challenge, found four reasons justifying the program: (1) the university's poor reputation within the black community; (2) underrepresentation of blacks in the student body; (3) the low number of blacks enrolled at the university who stayed on to graduate; and (4) a campus atmosphere perceived as hostile to black students. Since the court found that the scholarship program was narrowly tailored to relieve these four effects of past discrimination, it granted summary judgment in favor of the university.

Podberesky, however, appealed the decision to the Fourth Circuit Court of Appeals. The circuit court began its analysis by pointing out that in order for the program to be upheld, the university had to overcome a presumption that it was unconstitutional, because "[r]acial and ethnic distinctions of any sort are inherently suspect and thus call for the most exacting judicial examination."

To begin with, the circuit court held, the first and fourth of the effects set out by the district court were insufficient to justify the program, because "mere knowledge of historical fact is not the kind of present effect that can justify a race-exclusive remedy" and because present-day racial discrimination within society at large was more to blame for the hostile campus climate than any acts of past discrimination on the part of the university. Furthermore, the court declared, the district court had erred in its statistical analysis of the second and third effects.

Even if the lower court's analysis of these points had been correct, however, the program still would have failed, since it was not narrowly drawn to remedy those problems. First of all, the university admitted that the goal of the scholarship was to attract high-achieving African Americans; high achievers of any race, however, are not the group that suffered discrimination at the hands of the university. Second, awarding Banneker scholarships to nonresidents of Maryland (and even to one Jamaican student in 1989) did not sufficiently correct the fact that, as asserted by the university, not enough qualified African-American students from Maryland attended school there. For these reasons and several others, the court held that the Banneker Program "more resembles outright racial balancing than a tailored remedy program." Accordingly, it reversed the district court's decision and demanded that the lower court enter judgment in favor of Podberesky and order the university to reconsider him for a Banneker Scholarship without consideration of his race.

The university appealed to the U.S. Supreme Court to consider its case. The Court, however, declined without comment in May 1995. Since the Court did not issue an opinion on the merits of the case, it is difficult to interpret from its refusal what its position would be on such an issue. Also, this refusal simply lets stand the Fourth Circuit Court's opinion, which is technically binding on only the states in the fourth circuit: Maryland, North Carolina, South Carolina, Virginia, and West Virginia; it does not create binding precedent for other jurisdictions.

Even so, the other circuits could certainly apply the Podberesky case as persuasive precedent in deciding similar cases. Some states, however, such as California, do not offer race-based scholarships in the first place. Other states are abandoning the practice as well. In 1996, the Colorado attorney general informed the state's public colleges and universities that they should no longer provide race-based scholarships.

N

National Education Association (NEA) Founded in 1857, the National Education Association (NEA) today represents over 2 million American educators, making it the largest education league in the United States. The NEA devotes much of its resources to informing its membership and the general public on education-related topics. For example, as part of its efforts to report progress made toward reaching the standards established under **Goals 2000,** the NEA publishes the "Daily Report Card." The association also works with The Learning Channel to produce a half-hour weekly show called "Teacher TV" that is designed to inspire teachers with ideas for improving education. In addition, the president of the NEA writes a biweekly newspaper column.

The NEA also devotes much time and attention to lobbying lawmakers at both the state and federal levels about legislation that has an effect on education. For example, in November 1995, NEA representatives spoke before a congressional subcommittee considering a push to make English the official national language [see **English language**]. In 1993, the NEA vice president testified before another congressional subcommittee on the issue of reauthorization of the Elementary and Secondary Education Act through the **Improving America's Schools Act.**

The NEA can be reached at 1201 Sixteenth Street NW, Washington, DC, 20036. It also maintains a home page on the World Wide Web (http://www.nea.org). Visitors to this site can find out more about the NEA and its local affiliates, find links to Web pages produced by U.S. schools, learn where certain politicians stand on educational issues, and read articles from the NEA's monthly publication *NEA Today.*

National Organization on Legal Problems of Education (NOLPE) Nonprofit organization founded in 1954 to promote interest in the legal system as it relates to education. NOLPE hosts an annual convention for its membership, which consists of attorneys, teachers, school administrators, and students. NOLPE members also receive the monthly *NOLPE Notes*, a loose-leaf publication providing information on the organization's activities and important developments in education law, and the *NOLPE School Law Reporter*, which gives citations and abstracts of state and federal cases dealing with education issues. Perhaps most valuable to someone with an interest in education law is NOLPE's *Yearbook of Education Law*, which has been published annually since 1933 and is devoted to analyzing new cases and legislation affecting schools.

NOLPE can be reached at 3601 Southwest 29th Street, Suite 223, Topeka, KS, 66614.

NATIONAL SCHOOL SAFETY CENTER (NSSC) Organization created in 1984 to act as a national clearinghouse of information relating to school safety and to help local school districts implement safety programs. It is operated as a joint effort of the **Department of Education,** the Department of Justice, and Pepperdine University.

The National School Safety Center (NSSC) offers a variety of resources for people interested in school safety issues. Besides its news journal, *School Safety*, which is distributed three times a year, and its newsletter, *School Safety Update*, which comes out six times a year, the NSSC offers a variety of other publications and resource papers dealing with school safety as well as a variety of videotapes and display posters.

The NSSC can be reached at 4165 Thousand Oaks Boulevard, Suite 290, Westlake Village, CA, 91362.

NATIVE AMERICAN EDUCATION Prior to the Civil War (1861–1865), most Native Americans who received formal educations were taught by missionaries who sought to "civilize" them and convert them to Christianity. Following the war, the federal government assumed greater responsibility for these indigenous people. At the same time, the role of missionaries in Native American education decreased, since the idea of churches fulfilling what was actually a governmental duty violated the constitutional prohibition against mixing church and state.

By the middle of the nineteenth century, the federal government had established boarding schools for the education of Native American youths. These schools shared at least one goal with the missionary educators—to civilize people commonly believed to be savages. In fact, the first superintendent of the Carlisle Indian School in Carlisle, Pennsylvania, has frequently been quoted as saying, "All the Indian there is in the race should be dead. Kill the Indian and save the man."

This practice of sending Native American children to school away from their tribes in an effort to assimilate them into mainstream U.S. culture continued into the early twentieth century. In the 1930s, the government began educating Native Americans in reservation schools.

Toward the middle of the twentieth century, however, the federal government implemented a policy designed to help it get out of supporting the native tribes. In fact, official recognition of some tribes was even terminated. Most members of these terminated tribes went to the cities, where they met with tough times due, in part, to their inadequate educations.

In 1970, this termination policy was reversed, but many educational problems remained. For example, in the late 1960s, Native American students had a 50 percent drop out rate and the unemployment rate among Native American adults was quite high, largely as a result of their deficient educational backgrounds. In response to problems like these, Congress passed such laws as the Education Act of 1975 and the Indian Controlled Community College Assistance Act of 1978.

Most issues relating to Native American education today revolve around a lack of cultural sensitivity within the educational system. Until recently, U.S. students who learned anything about Native Americans were generally taught to view them as savages to be conquered by the white man in the pursuit of westward expansion.

Native American students have also faced prejudice within the schools for their culturally based behaviors. In one case, a school punished male Native American students who refused to cut off their long hair as required by a district policy on the length of hair regarded as acceptable for male students [see **hair codes**]. Those students and several others who had given in to the school's demands sued the school district, claiming that the policy violated their rights to freedom of religion and expression. The court agreed and issued an injunction ordering the school district to stop enforcing the regulation against Native Americans.

NEW JERSEY V. T.L.O. Supreme Court decision establishing a test to be used by courts in determining the reasonableness of the search of a student by a school official. [469 U.S. 325 (1985)]

A high school teacher caught two students smoking in the restroom and took them to the principal's office. One student confessed immediately, but the other—identified in the court documents only by her initials, T.L.O.—steadfastly denied the accusation. The principal demanded to look inside her purse, where he found not only cigarettes but also a small amount of marijuana and assorted drug paraphernalia. He turned the evidence over to the police and T.L.O. was prosecuted in delinquency proceedings.

T.L.O. ultimately appealed her case to the Supreme Court based on the argument that the principal's actions violated her Fourth Amendment right to be free from unreasonable search and seizure. In 1985, the Court handed down its ruling, which is the landmark case concerning the Fourth Amendment rights of students in the public schools.

The Court began by stating that the Fourth Amendment prohibition against unreasonable searches and seizures extends to searches conducted by public school officials. Although students do have a legitimate expectation of privacy in their personal belongings at school (*T.L.O.* did not address the issue of privacy expectations in school property, such as lockers [see **locker searches**]), school officials also have a valid interest in maintaining a disciplined learning environment. These interests must be carefully balanced, and the search must be reasonable. (This is less than the probable cause required in police searches.) The *T.L.O.* court set out a two-part test for determining the reasonableness of a search by a school official: (1) was the search "justified at its inception" and (2) was the scope of the search reasonably related "to the circumstances which justified the interference in the first place"? In this case, the Court held that the evidence supported an affirmative answer to each question; therefore, the search was not unconstitutional.

NEWSPAPERS Public school students have asserted their rights to "freedom of the press" with varying degrees of success. A big factor in the outcome of such cases is whether or not the publication is school sponsored.

In cases involving school-sponsored but student-written newspapers, trial courts look to the 1988 Supreme Court decision in ***Hazelwood School District v. Kuhlmeier,*** which dealt with a decision by a school principal to pull two pieces from the newspaper produced by the journalism class. One article profiled several pregnant students at the school; in the other, a child of divorced parents described her father's personal shortcomings at great length. The Court declared that the principal's action was justified by a legitimate educational concern over the privacy of students and their parents and the question of whether the student-reporters had learned the basics of fair journalism.

The *Hazelwood* court was heavily influenced by the fact that the school had retained its right to editorial control over the paper. It is possible, however, for a school to surrender its rights of editorial control if it distances itself from the newspaper. For example, some school newspapers carry disclaimers stating that the contents do not reflect the views of the schools.

A 1991 circuit court opinion extended the *Hazelwood* ruling to cover advertising not written by students or teachers in school-sponsored forums. [*Planned Parenthood v. Clark County Sch. Dist.*, 941 F.2d 817 (9th Cir. 1991)] In that case, a school district refused to sell advertisement space in their yearbooks and newspapers to Planned Parenthood. The district's guidelines prohibited the advertising in school publications of certain things, like "X- or R-rated movies, gambling aids, tobacco products, liquor products, birth control products or information, drug paraphernalia and pornography." The schools had, however, sold advertising spots to casinos, bars, and political candidates. Even so, the court held that *Hazelwood* affirmed the power of the schools to control the advertisers accepted for their publications and that this school district had shown "an affirmative intent" to keep their school publications nonpublic and therefore subject to their editorial veto.

A student interested in protecting his or her right to free speech [see **freedom of speech**] in school publications can sometimes look to the state constitution for protection, since some state constitutions offer greater freedom of expression than that guarded by the federal Constitution. One New Jersey trial court, for instance, held that school authorities had violated the rights of a student under the state constitution, which offers greater protection for expression than does the federal Constitution, by refusing to publish in the school newspaper two movie reviews of R-rated films. On appeal, however, the higher courts still found in favor of the student, but based their determination on the fact that the actions by the school authorities had, in fact, violated the student's rights under the federal Constitution. [*Desilets v. Clearview Regional Bd. of Educ.*, 647 A.2d 150 (N.J. 1994)]

Courts have generally held that where the publication in question is not a school-sponsored publication, the school may set reasonable limitations on the time, place, and manner of its distribution. For example, a school could probably withstand judicial scrutiny of a decision to limit distribution of such newspapers to nonclass time or to restrict their distribution to a certain place, such as a table by the front door. Such limitations are reasonably related to maintaining a proper educational environment. If a school decided, however, to issue time, place, and manner restrictions that applied to publications based on their content (such as by severely restricting distribution of a nonschool newspaper expressing a very liberal or very conservative point of view), it would likely not hold up under a First Amendment challenge.

O

OPEN-MEETING LAWS Citizens have a right to see how their tax dollars are spent on the education of their children in the public schools. As a result, many states have laws requiring that school board meetings be accessible to all. In addition, many laws require that a school board not only allow citizens to attend its meetings, but that it also provide adequate notice of when meetings will be held and what business will be covered.

Most open-meeting laws do allow school boards to hold special closed meetings to discuss sensitive business. For example, it would be prudent for a board to consider privately issues such as a student disciplinary action or the efficiency of a teacher. In such instances, a closed meeting would protect the privacy of the person under review.

Besides closed meetings, board members are usually free to socialize with one another without granting notice to the public along with an open invitation. School boards must be careful, however, because courts generally will not hesitate to find a violation where a board has attempted to bend the rules. In one case a superintendent was found to have held impermissible closed meetings by meeting with each member individually and on a supposedly social basis but discussing board business and filling each member in on the views of the others. [*Blackford v. School Bd.*, 375 So. 2d 578 (Fla. Ct. App. 1979)]

School boards often attend retreats to help them work better as a group. This can be risky, since discussing official business—even in an informal setting—would transform the retreat into a closed meeting in violation of the open-meeting laws. Such retreats are allowable, however, provided that the members carefully avoid talking about anything resembling board business. One Missouri school board overcame a challenge in court by a newspaper that alleged the board had violated the state's open-meeting law by attending a weekend workshop to improve interpersonal communications within the group, which had a reputation for incompatibility. The court was impressed that the board had hired an attorney to attend the retreat to make certain that they did not inadvertently violate the law. [*Kansas City Star Co. v. Fulson*, 859 S.W.2d 934 (Mo. Ct. App. 1993)]

Even where a closed meeting technically does not violate the law, it can be a politically risky move. For instance, in January 1996 the school board members of Fairfax County, Virginia, were deadlocked on the issue of who should be their new chairperson. Tempers flared, and one contender for the position accused other board members of not supporting him based on racial bias. The board elected to go into a closed meeting under an exception in the Virginia Freedom of Information Act allowing such meetings for discussion of the performance of "specific public officers." Even though the closed meeting was legal, it was met with intense criticism for undermining public accountability of the board members.

P

P.A.R.C. v. Commonwealth of Pennsylvania

Federal case holding that disabled children are entitled to admittance into a state's educational system. [334 F. Supp. 1257 (E.D. Pa. 1971)]

In 1972 a federal district court reviewed a case in which the Pennsylvania Association for Retarded Children (PARC) sued Pennsylvania for excluding retarded children from its educational programs. Pennsylvania based its exclusion of the children on statutes that excused the state Board of Education from educating any child deemed "uneducable and untrainable" by a public school psychologist and that excused the parents of such uneducable children from compliance with the compulsory education laws.

The PARC relied on three arguments in attacking the application of these statutes: (1) the statutes violated the children's right to **due process** because they did not provide for notice or a hearing before a child could be barred from the education system or before a change could be made in his or her educational assignment; (2) the statutes violated **equal protection** because the underlying premise—that mentally retarded children are uneducable—lacks a rational basis in fact; and (3) the statutes denied a right specifically set out in the state Constitution—the right to an education for all children.

Eventually, the two sides worked out a compromise themselves. They agreed that since Pennsylvania had taken on the responsibility of providing its children with a free, public education, it also had the obligation "to place each mentally retarded child in a free, public program of education and training appropriate to the child's capacity."

This "consent agreement," which the federal district court issued as its order, set out a number of procedures to be followed in placing disabled children into an educational setting. For example, it established the principle that when choosing among the alternative programs, "placement in a regular public school class is preferable to placement in a special public school class and placement in a special public school class is preferable to placement in any other type of program of education and training."

The agreement also provided detailed procedural requirements before changes could be made in a mentally retarded child's educational placement. These procedures dictated exactly what sort of notice should be given to the child's parents or guardian and exactly how the hearing on the issue should be conducted. Many of the procedures originally spelled out in the *P.A.R.C.* decision (as well as those set out in ***Mills v. Board of Education of the District of Columbia***) were adopted in some form by Congress in 1975 when it enacted the Education for All Handicapped Children Act, later known as the **Individuals with Disabilities Education Act (IDEA).**

PIERCE V. SOCIETY OF SISTERS Supreme Court case upholding the rights of parents to direct the education of their children. [268 U.S. 510 (1925)]

The operators of Catholic orphanages and private schools together with the operators of a military academy sued to enjoin, or stop, the enforcement of an Oregon statute that required all children between the ages of 8 and 16 to attend public schools through the eighth grade. The Society of Sisters and the academy did not dispute the state's important interest in requiring its children to attend school and to regulate the quality of the education provided. This law, however, restrained the rights of parents to choose schools for their children that satisfied their intellectual and religious requirements.

Furthermore, the plaintiffs claimed, the law had caused the withdrawal of many children from their private schools, causing a decline in the schools' income. The plaintiffs asserted that application of this law denied them their property rights without **due process.** The U.S. Supreme Court agreed and held that although a business generally does not have a right to restrain the government's exercise of its proper powers in order to protect the business's clientele base, forcing all children to attend public schools in an effort to standardize the children is not a proper use of government power.

This case is still regarded as a landmark decision recognizing the rights of private schools and the rights of parents to choose them for their children. It represents a limitation on the power of the state to require the education of its children.

PLAGIARISM Misrepresenting the writing of another as one's own work. Whether a student has committed plagiarism may be decided on two different criteria. When faced with a student's paper that closely resembles someone else's work, a school may try to determine if the student specifically *intended* to steal the words or if the student simply failed, through oversight, to give appropriate credit to his or her source. This is a subjective standard and gives the student some benefit of the doubt. On the other hand, a school may simply look objectively at the paper and determine that plagiarism did occur based on striking similarities to another work and not even consider the student's subjective intent.

Several court cases have been brought in recent years by college students who have been disciplined for committing plagiarism. As a general rule (as in many cases involving education issues), however, courts are reluctant to replace the decisions of educators with the decisions of judges unless there is a compelling reason to do so. One New Jersey court upheld the decision of a university committee that a student had plagiarized a book when writing a paper. She had cited the source six times within the paper, but there were at least 30 other places where she had failed to give credit. In upholding this decision, the court validated the use of the objective standard for determining plagiarism and found that withholding the student's diploma for one year was a reasonable punishment. [*Napolitano v. Princeton Univ.*, 453 A.2d 263 (N.J. Ct. App. 1982)]

PLEDGE OF ALLEGIANCE A salute to the U.S. flag and the recitation of the Pledge of Allegiance have historically been part of daily opening exercises in many public and private schools. In fact, many school districts and states required all students to participate in the activities in an effort to impart patriotic values to the students.

A number of challenges to such requirements have focused on freedom of religion. Jehovah's Witnesses, for example, hold very strict beliefs against the worship of secular images, including flags. In 1940, the U.S. Supreme Court considered a case in which Jehovah's Witnesses challenged a school board's policy mandating a daily flag salute and held that the requirement was not unconstitutional, even though children faced expulsion [see **suspension and expulsion**] for refusing to take part in the activity. [*Minersville v. Gobitis,* 310 U.S. 586 (1940)] By 1943, however, the Court had changed its mind. In ***West Virginia State Board of Education v. Barnette,*** it struck down a West Virginia regulation that punished students for refusing to salute the flag. By implementing such a regulation, the Court said, the state Board of Education had gone beyond the limits placed on government by the Constitution and invaded the First Amendment religious rights of the students.

Other religious objections to the Pledge of Allegiance have centered around the language "one nation under God," which was added to the Pledge by Congress in 1954. In 1992, a federal appellate court heard a case in which an atheist challenged the following Illinois statute on behalf of his son: "The Pledge of Allegiance shall be recited each school day by pupils in elementary educational institutions supported or maintained in whole or in part by public funds." [*Sherman v. Community Consol. Sch. Dist.*, 980 F.2d 437 (7th Cir. 1992)] The court held that if all students were required to stand and recite the Pledge, the law would be unconstitutional under *Barnette.* However, since the law did not specify exactly which pupils should join in the recitation, the court construed the statute to mean "willing pupils," which saved the law from being declared invalid. The court also went on to hold that the words "under God" did not make the Pledge a prayer in violation of the establishment clause [see **establishment and free exercise clauses**].

Not all objections to the Pledge have been founded on religious objections. A number of students have won their rights to remain seated during the recitation of the Pledge based on political beliefs, such as disagreeing that "liberty and justice for all" really exist in the United States and that peace can come only through a one-world government. Numerous courts have held that, like students who object for religious reasons, students who object for other personal reasons may not be made to stand or leave the room during the Pledge.

Students are not the only ones who have protested the Pledge of Allegiance. In several cases, teachers have refused to lead their classes in the recitation as required by state statute or local rule. Several teachers have refused to take part to protest the "liberty and justice for all" language, and such action has generally been protected by the courts. While a teacher may abstain from leading the Pledge, however, he or she may still be required to adhere to a curriculum that teaches elements of patriotism.

PRAYER AT SCHOOL-SPONSORED EVENTS While state-mandated prayer in public school classrooms [see **prayer in the classroom**] has been forbidden on constitutional grounds since the early 1960s, a number of recent cases have involved prayer, either school or student sponsored, at events such as graduations and athletic meets.

For well over 20 years, courts have applied the *Lemon* test, which takes its name from the 1971 Supreme Court case ***Lemon v. Kurtzman,*** to school prayer cases. In order to pass the test for constitutionality, a state activity must meet three criteria: (1) it must have a nonreligious purpose; (2) it must neither advance nor inhibit religion; and (3) it must not involve excessive entanglement between the government and religion. However, when the Supreme Court examined the issue of prayer at high school graduations in 1992 in ***Lee v. Weisman,*** the Court did not emphasize the *Lemon* test. Instead, it pointed out that prayer at school-sponsored events carries a risk of coercion—students had either to protest or participate.

After the *Lee* decision, the Fifth Circuit, which includes Texas, Louisiana, and Mississippi, created controversy by holding in *Jones v. Clear Creek Independent School District* [977 F.2d 963 (5th Cir. 1992)] that nonsectarian prayer was allowable at graduation ceremonies if requested by a majority of the students. Since the *Jones* decision, however, other federal circuits have held that student-initiated prayer does violate the establishment clause [see **establishment and free exercise clauses**]. Even the Fifth Circuit, after its *Jones* decision, rejected prayers led by a coach before public high school basketball games, saying that *Lee* "is merely the most recent in a long line of cases carving out of the establishment clause what essentially amounts to a per se rule prohibiting public school-related or -initiated religious expression or indoctrination." [*Doe v. Duncanville Indep. Sch. Dist.,* 994 F.2d 160 (5th Cir. 1993)]

PRAYER IN THE CLASSROOM Before the 1950s, most attacks on prayer in public schools were heard in state courts, which generally upheld the practice. The issue first came into federal courts in the 1950s. In the 1962 case of ***Engel v. Vitale,*** the Supreme Court held that the daily reading in New York public schools of a prayer recommended by the state Board of Regents violated the establishment clause of the U.S. Constitution [see **establishment and free exercise clauses**], even though students who objected could be excused from participating. In 1963, the

Court heard the case of ***School District of Abington Township v. Schempp,*** which combined two cases dealing with daily opening exercises involving the recitation of Bible verses and the Lord's Prayer. Once again, participation was voluntary, but the Court struck down the practice.

Many states, in an effort to get prayer back into the classroom, enacted statutes that called for a "moment of silence" at the beginning of each school day. These statutes have generally been upheld as long as they are couched in terms of meditation and contemplation. A New Mexico statute, for example, that referred to a moment of silence to be used for "contemplation, meditation, or prayer" was declared unconstitutional, since it specifically referred to prayer.

In 1994, Georgia passed a law that required a moment of silence to start each day but specifically stated that the time "is not intended to be and shall not be conducted as a religious exercise." Some people, however, claim that the intent behind the law is to support unconstitutional school prayer. One high school social studies teacher was fired for refusing to abide by the required moment of silence and continuing his lecture.

Other attempts to restore prayer to the school day have been more conspicuous. A Mississippi school principal was fired in 1993 for allowing students to recite prayers over the intercom. His dismissal was later downgraded to suspension, and the state Supreme Court ordered him reinstated pending appeal of the decision by the school board. The Mississippi legislature passed a law in response to this controversy that would allow student-initiated school prayer. The **American Civil Liberties Union (ACLU)** and People for the American Way challenged the law on behalf of 14 students and parents, and a federal court held that the statute was unconstitutional because it was vague, since it did not instruct schools on administering the law and did not make provisions for students who did not wish to pray. [*Ingebretsen v. Jackson Pub. Sch. Dist.,* 864 F. Supp. 1473 (S.D. Miss. 1994)]

A number of students have worked to reinstate prayer in the public schools. At an annual program called "See You at the Pole," students across the nation congregate at their school flagpoles to pray outside of classroom hours. Over 2 million students took part in the 1994 rally. Such gatherings are generally considered valid exercises of free speech [see **freedom of speech**], since they avoid the limitations set out in ***Tinker v. Des Moines Independent School District:*** (1) they do not disrupt classes, and (2) participation is strictly voluntary.

The battle over school prayer has often reached the federal level. Members of Congress have tried repeatedly to insert some form of prayer into the nation's schools. For example, in 1994, the controversy over school prayer nearly killed passage by Congress of the **Goals 2000** legislation, which provides federal funds to schools that choose to participate in reform plans. Senator Jesse Helms started a filibuster in which like-minded senators made lengthy speeches in order to delay the vote, because a provision that would refuse federal money to schools that deny voluntary, "constitutionally protected" student prayer had been weakened in the compromise version of the bill. The new language merely states that federal money may not be used to adopt rules against voluntary prayer.

Following the extraordinary Republican victory in the 1994 congressional elections, plans were advanced to introduce a new amendment to the Constitution that would specifically protect organized school prayer. Amendments, however, are difficult to pass, requiring the approval of a two-thirds majority in both the House of Representatives and the Senate, followed by ratification of the proposal by three-fourths of the states' legislatures. In response to the potential constitutional initiative, President Bill Clinton said he would support a federal law allowing a moment of silence.

See also **prayer at school-sponsored events.**

PREGNANT STUDENTS Until as recently as 30 years ago, pregnant students were discouraged or forbidden from finishing high school with their classmates. In 1969, however, a federal district court held that a school district could not exclude students from school based solely on the grounds that they were unmarried mothers. The court explained that expelling a girl for either her pregnant status or her status as an unmarried mother denied her **equal protection** of the law under the Fourteenth Amendment unless the school could prove that she lacked the necessary moral fitness to be in school. [*Perry v. Grenada Mun. Separate Sch. Dist.*, 300 F. Supp. 748 (N.D. Miss. 1969)] Two years later, a federal court in Massachusetts held that forcing a pregnant student to stop attending classes violated the Civil Rights Act. [*Ordway v. Hargraves*, 323 F. Supp. 1155 (D. Mass. 1971)]

In 1972, Congress enacted Title IX of the Education Amendments, which mandates that: "No person in the United States shall, on the basis of sex, be excluded from participation in, be denied the benefits of, or be subjected to discrimination under any education program or activity receiving Federal financial assistance." The regulations implementing Title IX specifically include discrimination based on pregnancy, parental status, and marital status within the definition of the types of prohibited discrimination.

Under Title IX, a school may have a separate program for pregnant students and students with children so long as the instructional portion of the program is comparable to that offered in the regular classes. Participation in such programs must be completely voluntary, and schools may not deny a student a leave of absence for as long as her physician deems necessary.

In 1985, a federal appellate court considered a case in which a school district dismissed a pregnant student from the National Honor Society (NHS). The court held that the district's action violated both Title IX and the equal protection clause of the Fourteenth Amendment. [*Wort v. Vierling*, 778 F.2d 1233 (7th Cir. 1985)]

In 1990, however, another federal circuit court considered a case presenting similar facts. In *Pfeiffer v. Marion Center Area School District* [917 F.2d 779 (3d Cir. 1990)], the faculty council governing a high school's chapter of the NHS became aware that a senior who had been elected into the NHS was pregnant. They interviewed the student to determine whether the sexual activity leading to her pregnancy had been consensual. When she admitted that it was, the council voted to dismiss her from the society for "failure to uphold the high standards of leadership and character required for admission and maintenance of membership." The school board unanimously affirmed the council's decision, and the student later sued.

The trial court found that the student had not been dismissed based on her pregnancy, which would have been prohibited under Title IX, but rather for failing to uphold standards set by the NHS by engaging in premarital sexual intercourse. The appellate court affirmed the decision, holding that such a finding was not clearly erroneous, but was troubled by the exclusion at trial of certain testimony. One of Pfeiffer's male friends was prepared to testify on her behalf that two years after her dismissal from the society, he impregnated his girlfriend but was not asked to resign his membership or be forcibly dismissed. The appellate court held that excluding such testimony was a mistake, since it was relevant to the issue of whether the council members treated male and female students differently, and sent the case back to the trial level for consideration of the friend's testimony.

PREGNANT TEACHERS Until relatively recently, a teacher who found herself unmarried and pregnant could expect to be dismissed from her job. Due to the stigma surrounding an illegitimate pregnancy, many school districts believed such a pregnancy to be proof of moral unfitness.

In 1974, a federal district court found in favor of a teacher who had been dismissed based on her status as single and pregnant, since the school district had not shown any connection between her "claimed immorality" and her competency as a teacher. [*Drake v. Covington County Bd. of Educ.*, 371 F. Supp. 974 (M.D. Ala. 1974)] Not all courts have found in favor of the teacher, however. For example, another federal district court held that while the teacher had a right to become pregnant and have a child without being married, the school district acted within the bounds of its authority by transferring her elsewhere, since the transfer was motivated by the district's desire to protect her students from the negative publicity. [*Wardlaw v. Austin Sch. Dist.*, 10 F.E.P. 892 (W.D. Tex. 1975)] More recently, however, yet another district court held in favor of an unmarried pregnant teacher who had been dismissed. [*Eckman v. Bd. of Educ. of Hawthorne Sch. Dist.*, 636 F. Supp. 1214 (N.D. Ill. 1986)]

PRIVATE SCHOOLS, GOVERNMENT MONEY AND While public schools are financed through public funds (such as taxes) and private schools are financed through private sources (such as tuition), government money does at times find its way into private schools. Some states, for example, provide transportation for all students regardless of whether they attend public or private schools [see **private schools, transportation to**].

Controversies flare up when a private school that receives some form of government benefit has a sectarian, or religious, nature. This is because of the constitutional mandate for separation of church and state found in the **establishment and free exercise clauses** of the First Amendment. When a court considers a case challenging a statute that allows the use of public funds in a private, religious school, it usually applies the *Lemon* test, which was set out by the Supreme Court in ***Lemon v. Kurtzman.*** According to *Lemon*, the statute will be upheld if (1) it has a legitimate nonreligious purpose; (2) its primary effect neither promotes nor restricts religion; and (3) it does not lead to excessive entanglement between church and state.

For example, Chapter 1 of the Elementary and Secondary Education Act (reauthorized in 1994 as the **Improving America's Schools Act**) provides federal funds to be used for remedial educational services for educationally deprived children, with equal expenditures to be made on private and public school students. Until the mid-1980s, such services were generally provided to private school children in classrooms on the campuses of the private schools. In 1985, however, the Supreme Court held in *Aguilar v. Felton* [473 U.S. 402 (1985)] that such a practice violates the establishment clause of the Constitution when the private school is sectarian. Instead, students at sectarian schools have to be transported to public schools, or portable classrooms have to be leased off the property of the sectarian school. The extra costs incurred by this requirement are called "Felton costs."

The **Department of Education,** which administers Chapter 1, issued a regulation in response to *Felton* requiring such costs to be paid for "off-the-top" of the money granted to each local educational agency (LEA) before the money is divided into equal expenditures for public and private school students. Several suits were filed in the early 1990s by taxpayers who claimed that such an accounting arrangement lessened the amount of money available to assist public school students and had the effect of promoting religion in violation of the establishment clause. Under *Lemon,* however, the "off-the-top" accounting method set out by the Department of Education is usually deemed constitutional, because (1) it has the secular purpose of harmonizing the Supreme Court's holding in *Felton* with the congressional requirement of equal educational opportunity; (2) the funds are used strictly for secular, educational purposes, and the primary effect therefore neither advances nor inhibits religion; and (3) the regulation does not entangle government with religion.

In challenges to the use of government money in religious schools, it is important to distinguish who is the direct beneficiary of the spending and who has decided to use the money in a private, religious school. In 1993, the Court heard *Zobrest v. Catalina Foothills School District* [113 S. Ct. 2462 (1993)], in which the parents of a deaf student challenged the school district's denial of their request for a sign language interpreter for him. The child had been receiving this service as part of his **Individualized Educational Program (IEP)** under the **Individuals with Disabilities Education Act (IDEA)** for the three years he attended one of the district's public schools. When the parents decided to move him to a Catholic school in ninth grade, the school district refused to continue providing the interpreter based on the fear that providing services to a student in a religious school would violate the state and federal establishment clauses.

The parents sued, but the federal district court entered summary judgment in favor of the school district. The Ninth Circuit Court of Appeals affirmed this decision. The court agreed with the argument that giving the student an interpreter at state expense would fail the *Lemon* test by having a "primary effect" of giving the other students in the school the false perception that the state was a cosponsor, along with the school, of the school's religious activities.

The Supreme Court, however, disagreed and reversed the decision. Since the IDEA provides for benefits to be distributed to qualifying children without regard to whether they attend a public school or private school of any nature, parents of qualifying children have the freedom to choose which schools their children should attend. The only way a government employee could wind up working in a private, sectarian school would be if the parents of a disabled child decided to send their child to school there. As a result, the court declared that "because the IDEA creates no financial incentive for parents to choose a sectarian school, an interpreter's presence there cannot be attributed to state decisionmaking."

Under a situation like the one requested by the Zobrests for their son, the child benefits from the services of the interpreter and the interpreter continues to draw his or her salary from the state, but the private school receives no direct economic benefit. In fact, the Court decided, any argument that the school receives even an indirect benefit by having the disabled child attend is tenuous, since it relies on the assumptions that the school makes a profit on each child and that it would have been unable to find another student to fill the disabled child's slot had the child elected to go elsewhere in order to have an IDEA interpreter.

PRIVATE SCHOOLS, TRANSPORTATION TO A number of states provide transportation to private school students as well as to those attending public schools. Some people have worried that when a private school has a religious affiliation, giving its students transportation constitutes government promotion of religion in violation of the establishment clause [see **establishment and free exercise clauses**]. In 1947, however, the Supreme Court heard a case challenging a state statute that gave reimbursement for transportation costs to parents regardless of whether their children attended private or public schools. [*Everson v. Board of Educ.*, 330 U.S. 1 (1947)] The Court upheld the statute, saying the children were the ones who benefited from the statute rather than the private schools. The Court held, however, that while a state is free to provide transportation to private school students without running afoul of the Constitution, it certainly is not required to do so.

Most recent issues concerning transportation to private schools involve disagreements over whether state law is being correctly applied. For example, in 1992 an Ohio court dismissed an appeal brought by parents from a ruling upholding a decision by the Board of Education to stop providing transportation to private schools. [*Haig v. Ohio State Bd. of Educ.*, 584 N.E.2d 704 (Ohio 1992)] The parents lived on an island in Lake Erie, and air transportation was the only reliable means of getting the children to and from the mainland private schools. The costs had become too exorbitant to allow the practice to continue.

In 1991, a New Jersey court was called upon to interpret a state statute that provided transportation or a transportation allowance to private school students whose schools were no farther than 20 miles from their residences. [*Nelson v. Board of Educ.*, 587 A.2d 1327 (N.J. Sup. Ct. 1991)] The school district had determined that a particular student's school exceeded the 20-mile limit and refused to pay the allowance, so the student's father sued. The father claimed that the school exceeded the distance limit only if it were figured to include a private driveway of over three-quarters of a mile from the public highway to the school's entrance. The court held in favor of the district, pointing out that the statute required including the distance "from the door of the pupil's residence to the public way."

Plaintiffs in such transportation cases occasionally claim that the application of the statute violates the equal protection clause of the Constitution [see **equal protection**], which requires that all people enjoy the same benefits of the law. Such an argument was raised in a case brought against a district that refused to reimburse parents for the cost of their child's transportation to a private school that was more than 30 minutes from their house in accordance with a state statute. [*Novak v. Revere Local Sch. Dist.*, 583 N.E.2d 1358 (Ohio Ct. App. 1989)] The court pointed out that a class of children who attend private schools over 30 minutes from home is not a "suspect classification," such as certain minorities who have suffered a history of unequal treatment, and that there is no fundamental right to education and therefore no fundamental right to transportation to school. Had the court found either a suspect classification or a fundamental right, it would have applied a more stringent test in analyzing the application of the statute. In this case, however, the statute had to bear only a rational relationship to a legitimate state purpose to be upheld. The court found that the statute had the legitimate purpose of providing "means of access to education facilities for students while not unduly burdening the resources of the school district."

In another equal protection case, parents challenged a statute that provided for transportation to public schools and certain private schools within the district, even if the private schools had a religious affiliation. [*Fendele v. School Comm. of Westwood,* 587 N.E.2d 757 (Mass. 1992)] A private sectarian all-boys high school within the district was included among the approved private schools, but the district refused to provide transportation to the plaintiffs' daughter, who attended a private sectarian all-girls school outside the district. The court held that the statute was neutral with regard to both gender and religion and that its application did not deny the student equal protection based on her gender or her religion. It was simply a matter of location: had her school been located within the boundaries of the district, she would have been entitled to state-provided transportation.

A federal appellate court considered a case in 1992 in which a school district had been subsidizing the costs of transportation for students to attend a Lutheran school that the district eventually realized was located outside its boundaries. [*Healy v. Independent Sch. Dist. No. 625,* 962 F.2d 1304 (8th Cir. 1992)] When the district discovered its mistake, it refused to continue providing transportation benefits, and the parents sued. The statute controlling such situations required the district to provide transportation to the district boundary or reimbursement for transportation if there were no schools in the district with "the appropriate grades or departments," which could include a department of religion. The district based its decision on the location of the Lutheran school outside the district and the fact that there were five Lutheran schools within the district. The parents, however, argued that there are different branches of the Lutheran religion and that none of the schools within the district were sponsored by the Evangelical Lutheran Church of America.

The court found in favor of the district on several grounds. First, the parents asserted that the district's action violated their constitutional rights to free exercise of their religion. The court disagreed, pointing out that there is a difference between penalizing or prohibiting religious exercise and merely refusing to subsidize it. The court also disagreed with the parents' claim that the decision violated their **due process** rights, since the decision was not arbitrary or capricious, and declared that the alleged recognition of different types of Lutheran schools within the district did not give rise to an equal protection claim.

PRIVATIZATION OF PUBLIC SCHOOLS Turning over the management of certain public schools to private businesses in hopes of increasing efficiency and test scores at the same time. In 1992, the city of Baltimore, Maryland, granted a contract to a Minnesota corporation to take over management of a number of schools. Results were mixed: the company upgraded the physical plant and security of the buildings and attendance rates rose throughout the privatized schools, while test scores dropped slightly in some schools and rose slightly in others. Teachers' unions criticized the company for replacing many experienced (and unionized) teachers' aides with low-paid recent college graduates—one of the corporation's money-saving tactics.

Despite some of the poor reviews, other cities began considering the merit of letting a business run the business end of their schools. In 1994, Hartford, Connecticut, entered into a $200 million contract with the same company Baltimore had used to manage 32 city schools.

Critics of such programs maintain that private corporations should not be allowed to profit from public schools. Supporters, however, counter that many educational bureaucracies have proved themselves not quite equal to the task of efficiently managing their budgets and staffs. If a private management corporation fails to perform, it can be fired much more easily than government bureaucrats can be replaced.

This is exactly what happened in both Baltimore and Hartford. In 1995, Baltimore ended its relationship with the management company and Hartford followed suit in 1996. Both cities alleged financial concerns as their primary motivation in ending their privatization programs.

PROPERTY TAXES Taxes, sometimes called *ad valorem* taxes, assessed on real property. Money raised by such taxes has historically provided the foundation for public school finance.

When it comes to raising money through property taxes, school districts fall into one of two categories. Most school districts, such as those in Florida and Georgia, have been granted power by the states to assess property taxes themselves to pay for public schools. Others, such as those in Virginia and Pennsylvania, must rely on the local government, such as the city council, to collect the taxes and apportion them among the school boards.

One problem with reliance on property taxes to pay for public education is the difference in quality that results between schools in wealthy districts and those in poorer districts. Since property taxes are based on property values, and property values tend to be higher in more affluent areas, it stands to reason that wealthier school districts are able to raise more money to spend on education.

Sometimes parents in poorer districts challenge this inequality in court. In 1973, the Supreme Court heard just such a case, *San Antonio Independent School District v. Rodriguez* [411 U.S. 1 (1973)], which was brought by parents in Texas school districts with low tax bases. The parents claimed that the method of school finance in Texas violated their rights under the equal protection clause of the Constitution [see **equal protection**], since it led to less money being spent on students in poorer districts.

In an equal protection challenge, the Court generally applies one of two levels of review depending on certain factors. Strict scrutiny, under which it is relatively difficult for the government to win, applies in cases involving either unequal treatment of members of a suspect class (one based on race or gender) or the denial of a fundamental right (one found either explicitly or implicitly in the Constitution). In such cases, the state's action must serve a compelling government interest. If the case does not involve either of these factors, the Court applies a rational basis review, under which the state must show only that its action was reasonably related to a legitimate government interest.

The *Rodriguez* court held that strict scrutiny did not apply under the suspect class argument, since the parents were not part of a clearly defined group whose children were totally deprived of an education due to the state's actions. The Court pointed out that it might find a suspect class to exist in a case where a state assessed tuition against each student and excluded those students whose families could not afford the tuition. In such a case, the members of the suspect class would be easily identified. The Court also declined to apply strict scrutiny based on the fundamental right argument, since education—although important—is not a right guaranteed under the Constitution. Accordingly, the Court upheld the school financing scheme.

The *Rodriguez* decision did not stop challenges to school financing schemes that result in inequality based on wealth between districts. Now, however, most plaintiffs rely on the laws of the individual state rather than the equal protection clause, and sometimes they win. For example, in 1989 the Texas Supreme Court invalidated a school finance system where the value of property subject to taxation in the most affluent school districts was 700 times as valuable as taxable property in the poorest districts and where spending per student ranged from $2,000 in the poorer districts to almost $20,000 in the wealthier districts. The court held that this system violated the state constitution and ordered the legislature to come up with a better, more equal plan for public school finance. [*Edgewood Indep. Sch. Dist. v. Kirby*, 777 S.W.2d 391 (Tex. 1989)]

In 1993, the state of California also grappled with issues arising from the use of property taxes to finance its public schools. California law requires a two-thirds "super majority" for the passage of local school **bonds.** Under such a system, two "no" votes equal one "yes" vote, which makes the passage of such issues incredibly difficult. In fact, between 1986 and 1993, voters defeated 145 bond issues, even though 123 were approved by a simple majority. In 1993, California voters considered Proposition 170, which would have reduced the number of voters needed to pass a local school bond measure to a simple majority and would have capped **impact fees** charged on new development. Opponents of Proposition 170 argued that since school bonds are usually paid back with tax money, the real result of Proposition 170 would have been to make it easier to raise taxes. Apparently, the majority of voters agreed and Proposition 170 was defeated.

R

Racial Discrimination The United States has a long, unfortunate history of racial discrimination in its public schools. Prior to 1954, black children attended public schools that were supposedly "separate but equal" to the schools attended by white children. In 1954, however, the Supreme Court recognized the impossibility of separate schools actually being equal and, in ***Brown v. Board of Education of Topeka,*** issued an opinion that set in motion the process of **desegregation.**

Over the next 50 years, racial discrimination remained a fact of life in many schools, although many cases of such discrimination have taken on a more surreptitious nature and are not always easy to spot. For example, some studies have shown that minority children are subjected to certain forms of **discipline,** such as **suspension and expulsion** and **corporal punishment,** more frequently than their white classmates.

Not all cases of discrimination are so carefully concealed, however. In 1994, a nationwide furor erupted after a high school principal in Weedowee, Alabama, threatened at a school assembly to cancel the prom if any interracial couples attended. When one mixed-race student stood up and asked what race her date should be, Principal Hulond Humphries allegedly said, "Your mommy and daddy made a mistake, and I'm going to see to it that no other mistakes like that are made." The student sued both the principal and the school board for intentional infliction of emotional distress and violation of her civil rights, but settled out of court for $25,000.

As the case played out before the media, it came to light that the **Department of Education**'s Office of Civil Rights had investigated Humphries in 1989. At that time, there were allegations that he made black students and white students ride separate buses to vocational classes and that he had a record of disciplining blacks more often and more harshly than whites.

The school board suspended Humphries but voted to reinstate him two weeks later. The U.S. Justice Department, however, sent in officials who filed suit in federal district court requesting that he be fired on the grounds that his words and actions contributed to a racially hostile environment, violating a 1970 desegregation order on Alabama schools. Three days before the hearing, the board voted unanimously to reassign Humphries to an office job, and the hearing was canceled.

Some schools have gone on the offensive to eradicate racial discrimination, but such efforts have not always been upheld by the courts. The University of Michigan issued a regulation forbidding hate speech [see **hate-speech codes**] based on a number of factors, including race. A court, however, held that the policy was both too broad and too vague and that it hampered speech protected by the First Amendment of the Constitution. [*Doe v. University of Mich.*, 721 F. Supp. 852 (E.D. Mich. 1989)] Other universities, including public universities, have offered **minority scholarships** in an effort to make amends for past discrimination. At least one federal court, however, has invalidated such a scholarship program that it found smacked of impermissible "outright racial balancing." [*Podberesky v. Kirwan*, 38 F.3d 147 (4th Cir. 1994)]

REDUCTION IN FORCE (RIF) In recent years, declining enrollment in public schools, inadequate financing, reorganization of schools, and the elimination of certain programs and classes have left many local school boards with more teachers and school employees than they need or can afford to pay. As a result, many boards have been forced to pare down their work forces. Dismissal under a reduction in force (RIF) does not carry the stigma attached to dismissal for a reason such as incompetency or immorality. It does, however, mean the loss of jobs and thus is a sensitive subject.

Often, boards that implement an RIF go by a policy of dismissing teachers and workers with tenure or seniority only as a last resort (although these longtime employees do not necessarily have guaranteed job security). Some critics of such a method argue, however, that in some schools women and minorities have fought long, hard battles for their employment within the system. Getting rid of these workers first, the argument goes, serves to turn back the clock on the rights of these newer employees.

On the other hand, school boards occasionally decide to give preference to women or minorities in an effort to maintain or enhance the school's diversity. For example, one county in North Carolina recognizes in its RIF policy the "need or desire to take affirmative action to retain a diverse faculty by race, sex, age, national origin and handicap" as a legitimate reason for not getting rid of certain workers who otherwise would be dismissed under a RIF.

This approach can be controversial, especially in schools that do not have a past history of discrimination for which to make amends. For example, in 1989 a New Jersey school board faced the challenge of deciding which of two business teachers to let go. Both teachers had been hired on the same day 14 years earlier and had both received tenure at the same time. One, however, was black and one was white. Although there had never been allegations of **racial discrimination** at the school, the board decided to dismiss the white teacher in order to promote the faculty's racial diversity. The white teacher filed suit and won $144,000 in damages for the violation of her civil rights. [*United States v. Board of Educ.*, 832 F. Supp. 836 (D.N.J. 1993)]

REHABILITATION ACT Legislation passed by Congress in 1973 to prohibit the exclusion of "otherwise qualified handicapped individuals" from participating in or benefitting from "any program or activity receiving federal financial assistance." In the arena of education, this law gives rights to disabled students, teachers, and other employees in public schools.

The act defines a "handicapped individual" as one who has an impairment (physical or mental) that substantially limits the person's performance of major life activities, such as walking or seeing. Besides obvious disabilities, such as blindness or missing limbs, courts have held that attention deficit hyperactivity disorder, epilepsy, and even certain communicable diseases such as tuberculosis are qualifying disorders giving rise to rights under the act. On the other hand, a federal court held in 1991 that the **Department of Education** was not liable under the Rehabilitation Act for refusing to give an employee an extended leave of absence to care for her adopted child, where the employee was unable to have children as a result of suffering polio early in her life. The court said the relationship between her disability and her decision to adopt was too diluted to qualify. [*McWright v. Alexander*, 771 F. Supp. 256 (N.D. Ill. 1991)]

In order to be an "otherwise qualified handicapped individual," the person must be able to meet the requirements of the job or program despite his or her disabilities. For example, one who seeks a job as a bus driver must be capable of driving safely despite a disability. If a person is disabled by a communicable disease, he or she is not "otherwise qualified" if there is a significant risk of passing the disease on to others. In the case of students infected with the human immunodeficiency virus (HIV), which causes acquired immune deficiency syndrome (AIDS) [see **AIDS, students with**], a number of courts have held that such children qualify as disabled under the act. Since other students are not at risk of contracting HIV through normal classroom contact, an infected child may not be excluded from a public school based solely on his or her HIV status.

The act does, however, require making "reasonable accommodations" for disabled persons unless doing so would impose an undue hardship on the operation of the program. For example, requiring a school to provide an interpreter at home for every hearing-impaired student might constitute such a hardship. One federal court held that special provisions made on the National Teacher Examination for a teacher who was disabled by test anxiety and difficulty processing auditory information, such as by giving her extra time on the communications part of the test and allowing her to read a script of the material rather than just listening to it, were reasonable even though she continued to fail that part of the exam. [*Pandazides v. Virginia Bd. of Educ.*, 804 F. Supp. 794 (E.D. Va. 1992)]

In 1990, Congress passed the **Americans with Disabilities Act (ADA),** which incorporates most of the regulations of the Rehabilitation Act and makes them applicable to all employers, public and private. The ADA also adds remedies that were not available under the Rehabilitation Act, such as damages for future monetary losses, emotional pain, suffering, mental anguish, inconvenience, and loss of enjoyment of life.

RELEASED-TIME PROGRAMS Programs in which public school children are excused from their studies to receive religious training. In the 1948 case *McCollum v. Board of Education* [333 U.S. 203 (1948)], the U.S. Supreme Court examined a released-time program in which Catholic, Jewish, and Protestant clergymembers came into the public school classrooms and gave religious instruction to students with their parents' permission. The children who did not take part in the religious classes left their classrooms and went elsewhere to continue their secular (nonreligious) studies. The state did not pay the salaries of the clergymembers, but the school did keep records of who attended the religion lessons. The Court rejected the plan, saying the state must remain neutral in religious matters. The use of tax-supported public school buildings for religious ministries, as well as the state's compulsory education laws to help provide pupils with the religious instruction, constituted an impermissible mixing of church and state matters.

The Supreme Court considered another type of released-time program four years later in *Zorach v. Clauson.* [343 U.S. 306 (1952)] In that program, children whose parents requested it left school during the day and went to a church for religious training. As in *McCollum,* the churches offering the classes paid the teachers' salaries; attendance records were kept and returned to the public schools to ensure that those students released from their regular classes were attending the special program. The Court upheld this program as a reasonable schedule accommodation of the church by the state. Such reasonable accomodations are necessary, the Court pointed out, because without any cooperation between church and state, a city fire department would not be permitted to come to the aid of a burning church. Since the churches did not benefit from the use of public buildings or the compulsory education laws, the program was not a promotion of religion by the state.

No state today forbids released-time programs like the one upheld in *Zorach,* where the students leave the school property for religious training. In fact, over half the states have specific statutes or regulations setting out the details of these programs. California, for example, allows public schools to release students from their regular classes for up to four hours a month to take part in religious instruction. Such an arrangement came under attack in 1991 when a school district excused students to take part in religion classes but prohibited the public school teachers from introducing new material or giving exams to students who chose not to participate. Teachers and administrators complained that this restriction interfered with the school day for the rest of the children, but supporters of the policy worried that if the released students had to make up missed class work, fewer would be inclined to participate in the program.

In the fall of 1994, the superintendent of schools in Lincoln County, Nevada, declared that students who left school property during the day to attend religious instruction would be considered truant [see **truancy**] and referred to the juvenile court. Students were allowed to complete the first quarter, but the program was then suspended until a committee could investigate and recommend a workable alternative.

In 1979, a federal court examined a Utah released-time program, which was held off campus. [*Lanner v. Wimmer,* 463 F. Supp. 867 (D. Utah 1978)] Ninety-five percent of the participants were enrolled in a Latter Day Saints program for one hour per day, in which they took classes on the Old and New Testaments, the Book of Mormon, and church history and doctrine. The high school gave elective credit toward graduation for the classes on the Old and New Testament but not for the others.

The court held that while the program itself was not unconstitutional, the practice of giving school credit for participation could not pass one of three elements set out in ***Lemon v. Kurtzman*** for determining when state action violates the First Amendment prohibition against the mixing of church and state. In order to pass the *Lemon* test, the action must (1) have a secular purpose, (2) neither advance nor inhibit religion, and (3) avoid excessive entanglement between the government and religion. According to the court, giving credit advanced the cause of religion because the courses were "geared toward reinforcing [Latter Day Saints] beliefs."

RELIGIOUS ART

Paintings with religious themes have hung in public schools for many years, but such paintings have come under attack in the court system recently as being in violation of the establishment clause [see **establishment and free exercise clauses**]. In 1990, a federal trial court in New York considered a case in which a student had created a 10-by-12-foot painting on the wall of the school's auditorium in 1965. [*Joki v. Board of Educ. of Schuylerville Cent. Sch. Dist.*, 745 F. Supp. 823 (N.D.N.Y. 1990)] The painting depicted 21 figures, most of which were unidentifiable, 6 of which could reasonably represent various biblical figures, and 1 that the court held was clearly Christ on the cross. The school argued that the painting's theme was not religious but rather depicted man's inhumanity to man. Parents who were raising their children in the Jewish faith, on the other hand, maintained that the painting had a primary effect of endorsing Christianity and, therefore, failed the second prong of the test set out in ***Lemon v. Kurtzman:*** that in order to be constitutional, a government activity, such as a school's endorsement of a painting, must neither advance nor inhibit religion.

The court agreed with the parents, since the painting "prominently displays a figure whom the average observer would believe to be Jesus Christ at his crucifixion." The imposing size of the painting when compared to two others also hanging in the auditorium as well as two nonfunctioning spotlights aimed at the painting supported the parents' argument that the school failed to negate or neutralize the religious message. Accordingly, the court ordered the painting removed.

Four years later, a federal appellate court upheld a similar order in a case in which a high school senior challenged the presence of a painting entitled *Head of Christ*, which had hung in the hallway outside the principal's office for 30 years. [*Washegesic v. Bloomingdale Pub. Schs.*, 33 F.3d 679 (6th Cir. 1994)] The court of appeals agreed with the lower court's decision that the hanging of the painting in a public school failed all three elements of the *Lemon* test: (1) It had no secular, or nonreligious, purpose; (2) it advanced religion; and (3) it entangled government with religion.

The court pointed out that an opposite finding could have been reached if the circumstances had been different—if, for example, the school had placed the painting of Christ in a display of "representative symbols of many of the world's great religions on a common wall." The lone portrait of Christ, however, had a "proselytizing, affirming effect that some nonbelievers find deeply offensive."

One judge wrote a concurring opinion in this case in which he agreed that *Lemon* required removal of the painting. He worried, however, that cases such as this establish "a class of 'eggshell' plaintiffs of a delicacy never before known to the law," and that people who are "offended" by something are not necessarily "injured" and deserving of judicial action. He urged that such issues should be resolved within the forum of the school:

> In this age, this picture hanging alone might reflect some insensitivity to the diversity that is now the United States. But let us tackle the problem with some good old Yankee ingenuity—lobby for a course in comparative religions; put a picture of Martin Luther King on the wall; form a Zen Buddhist club; wear a T-shirt proclaiming the virtues of agnosticism; but, if I am permitted to use the expression, for heaven's sake, stay out of the courthouse and quit trivializing the Constitution!

RELIGIOUS CLUBS The prohibition against state establishment of religion has made many schools hesitant to allow religious clubs access to school facilities. However, in their efforts to abide by the principles of church-state separation, many wind up instead violating students' rights to free religious exercise and free speech [see **freedom of speech**].

In the 1990 case *Board of Education of Westside Community Schools v. Mergens* [496 U.S. 226 (1990)], the U.S. Supreme Court held that if a high school sponsors extracurricular activities it may not ban student prayer groups. The *Mergens* case upheld the constitutionality of the **Equal Access Act,** a federal statute passed by Congress in 1984 that forbids public high schools that receive federal money and have a "limited open forum" from refusing equal access to student groups based solely on their religious or political character. According to the Court, if a public school offers resources such as classrooms for meetings and bulletin boards for member recruitment and information to student organizations whose focus is on topics other than school subjects, such as a chess club or service club, it has created a limited open forum for expression and does not unconstitutionally endorse religion by giving the same privileges to religious clubs that it gives to nonreligious clubs.

This does not, however, mean that schools receiving federal money are required to accommodate clubs at all. A school may certainly choose to have no clubs or organizations that are not curriculum related. In that case, the school is not required to give access to religious clubs either.

RELIGIOUS DRESS

The wearing of clothing and accessories pertaining to one's religious faith.

Around the beginning of the twentieth century, some public school systems began to employ nuns as teachers. Some people were disturbed when the nuns' wore their traditional garments, called habits, in the classrooms, and went to court to challenge the wearing of these garments. These early challenges were overruled on the theory that the schools knew how to run religiously neutral organizations and that if they thought they could accomplish this by hiring nuns in religiously distinctive dress, their judgment should be honored. The dissatisfied objectors took their arguments to their respective state legislatures, which began to pass laws against public school teachers wearing religious garb. When these laws faced challenges in the courts, the courts tended to uphold them as valid exercises of the states' power to create regulations for religiously neutral public schools.

Most recent cases challenging these laws have been brought by adherents of religions that seem "foreign" to the largely Judeo-Christian U.S. society, much as the habits of Roman Catholic nuns appeared strange in turn-of-the-century Protestant schools. For example, in the late 1980s, a teacher who had converted to the Sikh religion and came to school wearing a white dress and turban went to court to challenge an Oregon state law against public school teachers wearing religious dress on the job. Her victory in the lower court was eventually overturned by the Oregon Supreme Court, which upheld the law as a protection of religious neutrality. [*Cooper v. Eugene Sch. Dist.*, 723 P.2d 298 (Or. Sup. Ct. 1986)]

In a 1990 case, a Pennsylvania substitute teacher converted to Islam and began dressing accordingly, even at work. When three schools turned her away as a substitute because her manner of dress violated the state statute prohibiting the wearing of religious garb by public school teachers, she sued the Board of Education, claiming violation of her civil rights through employment discrimination based on her religion. The court held in favor of the board, because the board could not accommodate her religious observances without undue hardship in light of the state law prohibiting such apparel for public school teachers. [*United States v. Board of Educ. for the Sch. Dist. of Philadelphia*, 911 F.2d 882 (3d Cir. 1990)]

In a similar case, a Mississippi court upheld the dismissal of a teacher who wore a head wrap for religious reasons but held that the teacher was entitled to unemployment benefits because the head wrap was a "form of both religious and cultural expression." [*Mississippi Employment Sec. Comm'n v. McGlothin*, 556 So. 2d 324 (Miss. 1990)] However, a later case in federal court held that the school district had not violated her constitutional rights by not accommodating her hairstyles and headwraps, which the court found to be more reflective of the African culture than of any particular religion. [*McGlothin v. Jackson Mun. Separate Sch. Dist.*, 829 F. Supp. 853 (S.D. Miss. 1992)]

RELIGIOUS HOLIDAYS Controversies regarding the celebration of religious holidays in the public schools usually center around Christmas, since it has perhaps the greatest impact on school activities because of vacation, special programs, etc. What is true for Christmas, however, can generally be applied to other holidays as well.

Students may exercise their rights to free speech [see **freedom of speech**] in celebrating the holidays of their choice as long as they comply with the guidelines set out in ***Tinker v. Des Moines Independent School District.*** They may, for example, exchange Christmas cards and wish each other "Merry Christmas" or "Happy Hanukkah" outside the classroom.

It can be more difficult to figure out how far the school itself is permitted to go in recognizing holidays that have religious significance.

For example, when the father of a kindergartner complained about the emphasis on religion in his child's Christmas program, the school board adopted rules for future programs. Rather than solving the problem, the rules themselves were challenged in court in *Florey v. Sioux Falls School District* [464 F. Supp. 911 (D.S.D. 1979)]. Of particular concern were the rules that stated: (1) that schools could observe holidays that had both a religious and a secular (or nonreligious) significance, such as Christmas and Easter; (2) that school-sponsored activities and programs could incorporate religious music, art, literature, and drama, if the religious elements were presented objectively as a "traditional part of the cultural and religious heritage of the particular holiday;" and (3) that religious symbols such as crosses, menorahs, and the Star of David could be used as teaching aids or in displays if they were used to show the cultural and religious history of the holiday and if they were temporary. The trial court held that although the content of the original program that sparked the controversy was impermissibly religious in nature, the rules set out by the school board, if properly applied, would not be unconstitutional. This decision was upheld by the Eighth Circuit in 1980.

Two famous U.S. Supreme Court cases dealing with state-sponsored religious holiday observances do not deal with school settings, but actions by public schools would likely be scrutinized in accordance with those holdings. In 1984, in *Lynch v. Donnely* [465 U.S. 668 (1984)], the Court heard a case in which a Rhode Island city sponsored a holiday display in a private park in the city's shopping district. Along with a crèche, which showed the biblical scene of the birth of Jesus, the display also included colored lights, a banner proclaiming "SEASON'S GREETINGS," Santa Claus and reindeer pulling his sleigh, a Christmas tree, carolers, and figures of a clown, an elephant, and a teddy bear. City residents and members of the **American Civil Liberties Union (ACLU)** sued to enjoin, or stop, the city from including the crèche in the display.

The trial court found that inclusion of the crèche violated the establishment clause [see **establishment and free exercise clauses**]. An appellate court affirmed the decision, but the U.S. Supreme Court applied the test set out in ***Lemon v. Kurtzman*** and reversed. The *Lemon* test is a three-part test for determining whether state action is allowable under the First Amendment: it must (1) have a secular purpose; (2) neither advance nor inhibit religion; and (3) not involve excessive entanglement between the government and religion. The Court held that the crèche, when viewed in the context of the holiday season, passed the test: (1) it had the secular purpose of showing the origins of the Christmas holiday; (2) it provided no greater benefit to religion than a number of other accommodations that the Court had upheld in previous cases, such as tax exemptions for church property, Sunday closing laws, and **released-time programs** for the religious training of public school students; and (3) there was no administrative entanglement between the city and religion, since the city did not pay for maintenance of the crèche and no church had any influence over the content of the display.

Five years later, however, the Court enjoined the display of a crèche in a county courthouse in *Allegheny County v. American Civil Liberties Union, Greater Pittsburgh Chapter* [492 U.S. 573 (1989)]. In that case the nativity scene was the focus of the courthouse holiday display. The Court held that since there was nothing else to detract from the religious symbolism of the crèche and its banner announcing "Glory to God in the Highest," it sent a clear message that the local government promoted the Christian religion.

In the same case, however, the Court refused to enjoin inclusion of a menorah in a holiday display in front of a city-county building. That display consisted of a 45-foot-tall Christmas tree, an 18-foot-tall menorah, and a message from the mayor stating: "During this holiday season, the city of Pittsburgh salutes liberty. Let these festive lights remind us that we are the keepers of the flame of liberty and our legacy of freedom." The Court found that the theme of light expressed in the sign and common to both Christmas and Hanukkah as winter festivals showed merely a secular recognition of diversity rather than a promotion of the religious aspects of the holidays. The Court held that the Christmas tree was a secular symbol of Christmas and pointed out that while the menorah was both a religious and nonreligious symbol of Hanukkah, there was no Jewish equivalent of the Christmas tree to show only the secular significance of Hanukkah.

RUTHERFORD INSTITUTE Civil liberties organization founded in 1982 by John Whitehead to provide legal assistance to people facing religious discrimination. Although much of the institute's staff is evangelical Christian and many of their cases deal with supporting the right *to* religion rather than the right to be free *from* religion, one of its clients was a person who sued for the right to put the word "ATHEIST" on his car's license plate.

The Rutherford Institute is actively interested in the religious rights of students and their families and will send out legal briefs on request dealing with issues such as the teaching of creationism [see **creationism and evolution**], student prayer [see **prayer at school-sponsored events** and **prayer in the classroom**], and the right of parents to educate their children in **home schools.** In addition, the institute publishes such booklets as "Your Rights in the Public Schools" and "Modern Parental Rights: Issues and Limits."

The Rutherford Institute may be reached on the Internet at http://www.rutherford.org., or by mail at P.O. Box 7482, Charlottesville, VA, 22906-7482.

S

School Calendar It is up to local school boards to determine the length of the school day and year. However, if the state has set out certain requirements, the local government must set its standards consistent with them. Sometimes the state requirements have an unfair impact on a certain segment of the student population. For example, until 1994, the legislature of Virginia supported the "King's Dominion law," which took its name from a popular amusement park near Richmond. The King's Dominion law prohibited all schools from opening for the year until after Labor Day in order to assure a large teenage labor force at the state's famous eastern amusement parks over the busy holiday weekend. Many students in the east benefitted from this law, because it allowed them to continue their summer jobs for a while longer. Students in the west, however, suffered, because not only did they not have access to the jobs, but they also usually had to make up snow days at the end of the year, which kept them in classes later into the summer. Eventually, the General Assembly exempted western districts from the law and allowed them to set their own schedules to take into account possible bad weather.

Employment issues sometimes arise regarding the setting of the school calendar. For example, setting the calendar may be a subject for collective bargaining with the teachers' unions. The issue of when teachers are required to make up missed days, such as for bad weather or teacher strikes, is generally covered by the teachers' contracts.

School Choice Faced with orders to desegregate [see **desegregation**], some school systems in the 1960s instituted programs of freedom of choice in which students were allowed to decide for themselves which public schools they wished to attend on the theory that this was a racially neutral means of handling school assignments. In 1968, the Supreme Court examined such programs as a desegregation tool and held that, if they worked, they did not violate constitutional principles. In one case, however, the Court disapproved a plan that had, in three years of operation, resulted in no white children requesting admission to the all-black school and only 15 percent of the black children being reassigned to the white school. [*Green v. County Sch. Bd.*, 391 U.S. 430 (1968)]

Today, integration is still one motivation behind adoption of school choice plans. Some districts, for example, are setting up **magnet schools** to attract white students to traditionally minority-dominated areas. Others are establishing majority-to-minority programs, which allow a student who is in the majority race at his or her old school to transfer to a new school in which he or she will be part of the minority.

An incentive that is receiving even more attention is the idea that if schools are forced to compete for students (and therefore dollars), they will be forced also to improve their quality. There are a variety of school choice plans being implemented throughout the nation; some involve choice only among public schools, while others open up the choices to include private schools.

In the traditional method of assigning a child to a school, the child enrolls in the school that serves his or her district. At the opposite end of the spectrum are open enrollment plans, where a child may opt to attend any public school in the state. Somewhere in the middle lie plans allowing for intradistrict and interdistrict transfers, which limit the student's choice to schools that are either in his resident district or within participating districts.

Some districts establish **alternative schools** that cater to students with particular interests, such as performing arts or science, or that offer a second chance to students who have not succeeded at their regular schools. Other schools let students take part in special programs that allow them to attend college classes for either high school or college credit.

Among school choice vehicles that expand the field of options to include private schools are **vouchers** and tuition tax credits. Vouchers are educational coupons that the state gives to parents to "spend" at the school of their choice, including a private school, instead of giving the money directly to the public school to which the student would be assigned under a traditional plan. Tax credits, on the other hand, allow parents to deduct the cost of tuition (up to the amount of the credit) from their taxable income.

When public funds are spent at private institutions [see **private schools, government money and**], controversy sometimes arises as to whether or not it is constitutional to cover religion-affiliated schools. Some would argue that this amounts to state promotion of religion in violation of the establishment clause [see **establishment and free exercise clauses**], while others contend that it merely opens up opportunities to an entire class of citizens that, for economic reasons, would otherwise be left out. The first voucher plan that included private schools, established in Milwaukee, Wisconsin, resolved this issue by limiting participation to nonsectarian schools.

SCHOOL DISTRICT OF ABINGTON TOWNSHIP V. SCHEMPP

Supreme Court decision holding that morning prayers and recitation of Bible verses in the public schools violated the **establishment and free exercise clauses** of the Constitution. [374 U.S. 203 (1963)]

In 1963, one year after it struck down the use of a state-composed prayer in public classrooms, the U.S. Supreme Court heard two more prayer cases, each dealing with daily opening exercises in which students heard Bible verses and recited the Lord's Prayer. The two cases were consolidated into one: *School District of Abington Township v. Schempp.*

In the first case covered by *Schempp,* Pennsylvania required the reading of ten Bible verses [see **Bible reading and distribution**] at the beginning of each school day. Students in the radio and television workshop broadcast the verses throughout the school over the public address system. The radio and television students also broadcast the Lord's Prayer and children in their classrooms were asked to join in. Although the statute allowed children whose parents objected to be excused, one set of parents, the Schempps, sued to enjoin, or stop, the school district from continuing the morning ceremonies because some of the readings conflicted with their religious beliefs as members of the Unitarian faith.

The now well-known atheist Madalyn Murray O'Hare and her son sued to stop the Baltimore, Maryland, schools from starting the day with a reading from the Bible and recitation of the Lord's Prayer in the companion case in the *Schempp* opinion. The Murrays claimed that this practice violated their rights to freedom of religion because it placed "a premium on belief as against non-belief."

Once again, participation in each of the exercises was voluntary, but the Court struck down the practice, holding that the ability of students to opt out is not a defense to a violation of the Constitution's establishment clause. Furthermore, the Court disputed the schools' claim that forbidding the morning ceremonies would conflict with the right of the majority to free exercise of their religion, because "while the free exercise clause clearly prohibits the use of state action to deny the rights of free exercise to *anyone,* it has never meant that a majority could use the machinery of the State to practice its beliefs."

SCHOOL FEES In order to supplement their budgets, a number of schools impose fees on students to cover the cost of certain items and activities. Such fees may include, for example, uniform fees for students involved in activities such as band or sports, supply fees for art classes and science labs, and even fees for textbooks. Public school students and their parents have occasionally challenged such fees as violating the right of the student to a free public education.

In 1988, the Supreme Court considered a case in which parents challenged a North Dakota statute allowing school districts to charge for school bus transportation. [*Kadrmas v. Dickinson Pub. Sch.*, 487 U.S. 450 (1988)] The parents argued that this amounted to a "user fee" that violated the **equal protection** rights of poor students. The Court upheld the statute, pointing out that education is not a fundamental right guaranteed by the U.S. Constitution and that the child in question was able to find alternative transportation to school and was, therefore, not totally deprived of an education. One Maryland school board proposed county legislation in 1996 that, if passed, would allow for collection of a $50 annual fee from students who used schoolbus transportation. Critics of the proposal claimed that it infringed on the right of children in Maryland to a free public education.

Challenges to school fees that have been fought in the state courts have had mixed results. Since the 1970s, a number of state courts used one of two analyses in deciding such cases: the historical approach or the plain meaning approach. Under the historical approach, a court looks at the language in the state's constitution granting free public education to the state's citizens and imposes the meaning given to the language at the time the constitution was adopted. The question becomes whether the document's framers intended to include the particular item or activity as part of a free education, and the educational value of the item or activity is irrelevant. For example, the Illinois Supreme Court used this approach in 1970 to uphold a textbook fee, stating that the constitution provided only for a "schoolhouse and teachers at public expense." [*Hamer v. Board of Educ.*, 265 N.E.2d 616 (Ill. Ct. App. 1978)]

Courts that follow the plain meaning approach, on the other hand, consider the educational value of the item or activity in question. This approach has been used to restrict fees charged for textbooks and other classroom supplies but has generally allowed for fees on extracurricular activities, which "by definition fall outside a district's educational program." In 1984, however, the Supreme Court of California applied the plain meaning approach and struck down extracurricular activity fees. [*Hartzell v. Connell*, 679 P.2d 35 (Cal. 1984)] The court based its decision on the argument that extracurricular activities are an "integral component of public education," as shown by the importance other courts have placed upon them in deciding other school-related issues, such as **desegregation.**

Controversy surrounding school fees has not been restricted to the elementary and high school level, nor to the issue of whether they violate a student's right to education. In 1993, the Supreme Court of California considered a case in which students at the University of California at Berkeley challenged the authority of the regents of the University of California to impose a mandatory student activity fee. [*Smith v. Regents of Univ. of Cal.*, 844 P.2d 500 (Cal. 1993)] The regents gave most of the monies collected to the Associated Students of the University of California (ASUC), which in turn passed on funds to student activity groups. The plaintiffs objected to the use of their fees to support certain groups that pursued "frankly political or ideological goals," such as Amnesty International, the Campus Abortion Rights Action League, the Gay and Lesbian League, and Greenpeace Berkeley. The court decided that collection of the fees was clearly within the power of the regents under the state Constitution. Financial contributions, however, are a form of speech and are protected by the First Amendment [see **freedom of speech**]. The regents could not, therefore, use the fees to finance organizations whose educational value was merely incidental to their mission of furthering their political and ideological interests. Such use constituted coerced speech, which violated the rights of the students.

When the Supreme Court decided that the University of Virginia must provide funding to an evangelical Christian student magazine in the same manner in which it subsidized other student publications [*Rosenberger v. Rector and Visitors of Univ. of Va.*, 115 S. Ct. 2510 (1995)], the university faced a dilemma. On one hand, it was required to honor the judgment of the Court. On the other hand, it wanted to avoid challenges such as the one faced by the University of California in *Smith* from students who opposed supporting a religious activity through their $28 annual student activity fees. As a compromise, the university decided to allow students to identify organizations with which they disagreed and receive a refund of a proportionate part of their fees.

SCHOOL MEALS Congress passed the National School Lunch Act in 1946 to help protect the health of students by ensuring that they received proper nutrition at school. One important part of this legislation is the provision for free and reduced-cost lunches served by local school districts to needy students and reimbursed by the federal government. In 1966, Congress added the National School Breakfast Act, which made similar provisions for breakfast programs.

School meal programs are administered by the U.S. Department of Agriculture (USDA) through its Food and Consumer Service. According to USDA reports, 25 million children take part in the National School Lunch Program, with over half of them receiving free or reduced-cost meals. Over 5 million children take part in the School Breakfast Program, and over 80 percent of these children receive their breakfasts for free.

Despite the number of children participating in the meals programs, some critics allege that the programs are not as successful as they could be. One problem is the application process. Schools have traditionally sent application forms home with students, trusting that the students would safely deliver them to their parents and then back to the schools. In 1989, Congress amended the National School Lunch Act to take into account the fallibility of this application system. Under the amendment, a school district may cross-check a list of families within its jurisdiction who receive food stamps or Aid to Families with Dependent Children against a list of students in its schools and declare children appearing on both lists automatically eligible for free meals. The district then sends a letter home with each eligible student and adds each student to its list of free meal recipients unless the parents choose not to take part in the program.

Once the students are properly enrolled in the program, however, a new problem arises. Many students dislike the stigma associated with receiving the free or reduced-cost meals. As a result, many who are enrolled do not take advantage of the program. The Philadelphia School District implemented a pilot program in 1991 to solve this problem in some of its schools that have a majority of students eligible for free or reduced-cost lunches. The district picked up the tab for the students who were not eligible and received federal money from the USDA to cover the cost of the lunches for those who did qualify for the assistance. Unfortunately, such a program would be financially feasible only in schools where most students meet the family-income requirements for free or discounted meals. In that case, however, one could argue that the **welfare** stigma is not as great as it would be in a more affluent school where only a minority of students qualify.

In the case of discounted breakfasts, an additional problem in some schools is a lack of time for eating the meal. Many students simply do not arrive early enough to have breakfast. One possible solution to this problem is to have a set breakfast period added on to the daily schedule. This, however, brings with it more financial problems, since it would usually mean changing bus schedules and hiring extra people to supervise the students during this additional time.

Even if all students who qualify are properly enrolled in the programs and are at school in time to take part, there is the problem of actually getting them to eat the meals. For many years, school cafeterias have been the target of jokes about "mystery meat" and other unpalatable culinary creations. In an attempt to decrease the amount of food that winds up in its schools' garbage cans, the state of Rhode Island privatized its school meal programs in 1995. Under the new program, school districts receive their reimbursements directly from the federal government rather than having the money passed through the state government. Hiring private contractors has led to tastier meals that more students are buying and eating at a lower cost to the government. While some critics worry that the privately prepared meals will not be as nutritious as those prepared by the state, many of the meals actually exceed the minimum standards set by the USDA.

With school lunch programs opening up at many schools in which private companies provide all or part of the menu, many restaurants have been eager to cash in on this previously untapped market. For example, McDonald's, Subway, Taco Bell, and Kentucky Fried Chicken are all present to some extent in a number of schools, and some of these companies have even built food courts right in school cafeterias. Restaurants that provide fresh meat pizzas, however, faced some problems getting into the game. USDA regulations under the Federal Meat Inspection Act required department inspection of meat products sold to third parties (such as schools) other than their ultimate consumers (such as students). In November 1992, however, Congress passed the "Pizza Hut Amendment" (named in honor of the chain's lobbying efforts) to the 1990 farm bill, which changed the law to allow pizza restaurants to sell fresh meat pizzas to school students without the additional inspections.

In 1995, the USDA unveiled a $20 million plan designed to breathe new life into the school meal programs. The new program is called "Team Nutrition," and its mission is "to improve the health and education of children by creating innovative public and private partnerships that promote food choices for a healthful diet through the media, schools, families, and the community." Some critics, however, have taken issue with the means by which the USDA hopes to accomplish this end. For example, some have questioned the wisdom of paying Walt Disney Studios $400,000 to use two characters from *The Lion King*, the meerkat Timon and his warthog sidekick Pumbaa, as "spokestoons" in television and poster promotions.

Another USDA innovation has been the setting of new standards for the nutrition content of school meals, which should be in place for the 1996 school year. However, in 1995, the entire federal school meals program appeared to be on shaky ground. The House of Representatives approved a measure as part of its "Contract with America" that would dismantle the federal program and turn control over to the states through the use of block grants. However, this drastic measure was dropped from the welfare reform bill passed in August 1996.

SCHOOL UNIFORMS School uniforms have traditionally been a requirement of private school students, but in recent years a number of public schools have begun experimenting with policies that favor students wearing identical clothing. Many believe that uniforms cut down on tension and **violence** among students because they take away the issue of clothing as a status symbol and because students no longer have to worry about causing problems by inadvertently wearing colors or accessories associated with gangs [see **gang clothing**].

More and more school districts are allowing each school within their boundaries to make an individual decision regarding the use of uniforms. In the District of Columbia, for example, over 30 schools have students in uniform.

In 1994, Long Beach, California, became the first district *requiring* students to wear the same colors. The Long Beach policy allows parents to opt out of dressing their children in uniforms and does not allow for the punishment of students who come to school in regular street clothes. Even so, some critics argue that the policy infringes on the students' freedom of expression, just like the policy forbidding the wearing of black armbands in ***Tinker v. Des Moines Independent School District.*** In fact, the **American Civil Liberties Union (ACLU)** sued the school district, claiming that the policy places unjust financial burdens on poor families and that students who opt out are harassed. Supporters of the policy, on the other hand, point out that since the uniform policy was implemented, fighting among students has dropped by 50 percent.

A local ACLU chapter in Phoenix, Arizona, assisted an attorney in representing two students and their families who challenged a school policy requiring school uniforms (with no provision for students to opt out of the requirement) but allowing students to wear buttons bearing political, religious, and other statements. In 1996, the local trial court found in favor of the school's policy and issued a restraining order telling the students to stay off the school's campus and to transfer to another school where uniforms are not required.

SCHOOLYARD STATUTE In a 1984 effort to create drug-free zones around schools, Congress passed legislation that doubled prison sentences for drug dealers caught within 1,000 feet of any school, from the elementary to university level. The same punishment applies to dealers caught operating within 100 feet of certain other areas that are popular with children, such as playgrounds, youth centers, public swimming pools, parks, and video arcades. A second conviction could result in a sentence of life imprisonment.

Under the Schoolyard Statute, dealers bear the burden of determining whether or not they are operating within a drug-free zone; ignorance is not an acceptable excuse.

Courts have zealously embraced the Schoolyard Statute and construed its terms broadly in order to apply it to as many defendants as possible. For example, courts have used the statute to punish dealers caught after school hours. Also, courts have generally interpreted the 1,000-foot and 100-foot zones to be "as the crow flies" rather than up and down actual routes of access to the school. One woman punished under the law was caught smuggling drugs in a pair of sneakers into a jail located within 1,000 feet of a high school. Another defendant was deemed to fall within the terms of the statute because his car happened to be pulled over by police in front of a school.

Some critics of the statute have pointed out that in urban areas, where there are many schools and other facilities that fall within the terms of the statute, an entire city could become one big "drug-free zone" due to many overlapping zones. For example, one defendant introduced evidence to show that up to 80 percent of Spokane, Washington, would qualify as a drug-free zone. [*United States v. Pitts*, 908 F.2d 458 (9th Cir. 1990)] Some critics worry that this could have a negative effect on the statute's deterrence effect. After all, they ask, what incentive would a dealer have to remove his or her operation from near a school if there were practically no areas in the city where the act would not apply?

SCOPES V. STATE Famous case against John Scopes, a Tennessee high school biology teacher, for violating the Butler Act, a state law against teaching evolution [see **creationism and evolution**] in the public schools. [289 S.W. 363 (Tenn. 1927)] A circus-like atmosphere surrounded the trial, which came to be popularly known as the "Scopes Monkey Trial" because Scopes had been teaching the evolutionary theory that mankind descended from a lower order of animals, such as apes. The trial court found Scopes guilty and fined him $100. The trial brought even greater fame to the lawyers involved—Williams Jennings Bryan for the state and Clarence Darrow for the defense—and was eventually made into a play and film called *Inherit the Wind.*

When the case reached the Supreme Court of Tennessee in 1927, the court reversed Scopes's conviction based on a minor technicality concerning the imposition of the fine. Before addressing that point, however, the court took great pains to address the constitutionality of the Butler Act.

The court held that the law against teaching evolution did not violate Scopes's right to liberty because the statute applied to him only in his capacity as an employee of the state. The state, the court reasoned, had a right to place limits on its employees' professional conduct, and the law did not restrict Scopes's freedom to believe in evolution and teach it elsewhere other than in his classroom. The court also rejected the argument that forbidding the teaching of evolution impermissibly favored any particular religion in violation of the **establishment and free exercise clauses** of the U.S. Constitution because members of the same faith often disagree on the fine points of creation. It would be, therefore, impossible to link one theory with any particular religion. Furthermore, the court explained, the law did not require teaching any particular theory—it merely prohibited the teaching of evolution.

The Butler Act remained the law of Tennessee until it was repealed in 1967. By 1970, no state had such a law on its books anymore. Controversies still arise, however, when creationists attempt to reinsert creation science into the curriculum. Some teachers who believe in creationism claim that forbidding the teaching of their beliefs infringes on their religious rights; others claim that such a prohibition meddles with their rights to **academic freedom.**

SEX DISCRIMINATION Since the 1960s, inequitable treatment of students based on gender has received increasing attention in the field of education law. In 1972, Congress passed the Education Act Amendments, including Title IX, which prohibits denying anyone the benefits of an educational program on the basis of sex if that program receives federal funds. The power of Title IX is monetary, since federal funds can be terminated for an institution that elects to engage in discrimination. A 1984 Supreme Court decision held that funds could be terminated only for the specific programs that discriminated and not for the entire institution, which meant that a school could discriminate through a program, such as athletics, that did not receive any federal money without having to worry about losing its other federal financial assistance. [*Grove City College v. Bell*, 465 U.S. 555 (1984)] Three years later Congress amended Title IX to specifically overrule that decision. Title IX now mandates that an institution that indulges in sex discrimination can lose all of its federal funding, even if the program through which the discrimination takes place never received government money in the first place.

Courts have also held that Title IX permits a private cause of action, meaning that one who suffers sex discrimination is not limited to waiting for the federal government to take action by investigating and terminating funding. Instead, he or she may file suit against the institution directly. One benefit of such action is that plaintiffs can seek remedies that are more appropriate to redressing their injuries than a termination of funds, which hurts the institution but does nothing to help the plaintiff specifically. In earlier cases, courts were more likely to award only injunctive relief, such as ordering that a student be admitted to a program to which he or she sought entrance, than to give monetary damages. In 1992, however, the Supreme Court upheld a decision awarding monetary damages to a female student whose school discouraged her from pressing charges against a coach for **sexual harassment.** [*Franklin v. Gwinnett County Pub. Sch.*, 112 S. Ct. 1028 (1992)]

Plaintiffs also sometimes sue for sex discrimination under the equal protection clause in the Fourteenth Amendment of the U.S. Constitution [see **equal protection**]. When a court examines a sex-based discrimination claim brought under this clause, it will uphold a classification treating males and females differently only if it serves a substantial (which in legal jargon means more than merely "rational") governmental interest.

Sex discrimination issues arise in nearly every facet of education. Many cases have been brought, for example, challenging admission policies at single-sex schools, and not all of those have been brought by women. In perhaps the most important such case, a man brought an equal protection challenge against the Mississippi University for Women, which did not allow men into its nursing program. The case reached the U.S. Supreme Court, which declared in 1982 that excluding men did not achieve a substantial state purpose. The school tried to argue that the provision of compensatory education to women was that substantial state purpose, but the Court disagreed. Nursing, it explained, has traditionally been a female-dominated discipline, which undermined the state's argument that the policy of admitting only women compensated women for past discrimination. [*Mississippi Univ. for Women v. Hogan*, 458 U.S. 718 (1982)]

Students have also brought gender discrimination claims to challenge **dress codes** and **hair codes.** Since 1970, when a federal circuit court held that a school had to satisfy a "burden of substantial justification" in order to exclude a long-haired male student [*Crew v. Cloncs*, 432 F.2d 1259 (7th Cir. 1970)], such claims have not met with much success. In 1992, however, a state appellate court held that a lower court could not reject without a trial the discrimination claim filed by a mother on behalf of her third-grade son, who had been confined to a small room away from other students because he refused to cut a thin ponytail that violated the school's rule regarding hair length on boys. [*Toungate v. Bastrop Indep. Sch. Dist.*, 842 S.W.2d 823 (Tex. Ct. App. 1992)]

See also **pregnant students** and **athletics, sex discrimination and.**

SEX EDUCATION

Like most issues concerning what should be taught in a public school's **curriculum,** the questions of whether or not to provide sex education and, if so, what aspects of sexuality to cover, are legal and political in nature since they are generally not decided in each individual classroom. Instead, local boards of education and state legislatures usually determine the answers. In the mid-1980s, only Maryland and New Jersey required the teaching of sex education in their public schools. By 1993, however, 47 states had passed laws either requiring or suggesting coverage of the topic.

Even once it has been determined that the subject will be offered, however, controversies tend to continue over the question of how much should be taught. In choosing a program, school boards must decide whether to offer simply a clinical, nuts-and-bolts approach or delve into more controversial topics such as AIDS [see **AIDS education**], homosexuality, abortion, and birth control. Either way, someone winds up unhappy.

Some critics of more comprehensive programs believe that by giving teenagers information on contraceptives, the schools are giving their stamp of approval to premarital sex. Some parents are offended by classroom activities such as blowing up **condoms** like balloons and role-playing in sexually suggestive scenarios. These parents often say that such activities interfere with the free exercise of their religion, which is guaranteed by the free exercise clause [see **establishment and free exercise clauses**] of the First Amendment. On the other hand, critics of abstinence-based programs argue that withholding information on other methods of birth control and the use of condoms to prevent the transmission of the human immunodeficiency virus (HIV), which causes acquired immune deficiency syndrome (AIDS), is unrealistic in the face of statistics about sexual activity, pregnancy, and AIDS among teenagers. Furthermore, they argue, abstinence-based programs generally reflect religious beliefs; therefore, their presence in a public school system goes against the First Amendment prohibition against the promotion of any particular religion by the government. In California, for example, a group of parents backed by Planned Parenthood filed suit in 1994 against a school district that had adopted Sex Respect, an abstinence-based course that the parents claimed reflects conservative Christian theology through such assertions as calling AIDS "nature's comment on sexual behavior."

Some courts will uphold a sex education program that has been challenged for violating the right to free exercise of religion based on the idea that the state has an interest in the health of its youth and that sex education classes are a proper means of protecting that interest, similar to classes in physical education. Other courts have upheld sex education where parents are given the option of keeping their children out of such classes.

In 1987, Virginia passed a law requiring local school systems to offer appropriate training for its students in "family living and community relationships, the value of postponing sexual activity, human sexuality, human reproduction, and the etiology, prevention and effects of sexually transmitted diseases." Most programs offered the classes to all students unless their parents returned a form "opting out." Approximately 2 percent of parents chose to exercise this option each year. Seven years later, however, the governor launched a campaign to change this procedure. Under Governor George Allen's plan, local school boards would still be permitted to offer such classes, but they could only offer them to students whose parents returned a form "opting in." The passage of this plan would give Virginia one of the most conservative sex education policies nationwide and would impose a tremendous administrative burden on local schools if the number of parents choosing sex education for their children remained the same, since the schools would now have to process forms sent in by a majority of parents rather than a relatively small number.

The fallout over how a proper sex education program should work has been felt at the national level as well. In 1994, President Bill Clinton fired Surgeon General Joycelyn Elders after remarks she made at a World AIDS Day conference concerning masturbation. While Elders defended her statements as reflecting her position that masturbation should be taught as "a part of human sexuality," not that schools teach technique, her handling of this taboo topic prompted the president to declare, "She must resign."

SEXUAL HARASSMENT

Recognition of sexual harassment as a problem affecting school students grew out of the increased awareness in the 1960s and 1970s of **sex discrimination** and harassment in the workplace. Title VII of the Civil Rights Act of 1964, which was originally intended to protect black workers from discrimination, was eventually expanded to cover sex discrimination in the workplace, and in 1980 guidelines were issued declaring sexual harassment to be a type of discrimination.

In the 1980s, a number of college students brought cases in federal courts claiming harassment by professors. It was not until 1992, however, that the Supreme Court finally heard a case brought by a high school student against a teacher. In *Franklin v. Gwinnett County Public Schools* [112 S. Ct. 1028 (1992)], the plaintiff alleged that a sports coach began harassing her during her sophomore year. Franklin complained that the teacher engaged her in sexually oriented discussions, forcibly kissed her on the mouth in the school parking lot, and telephoned her at home asking her to meet him. The next year, on three occasions the coach requested that other teachers excuse the student from class, took her to a private office, and raped her. When teachers and administrators became aware of what was happening, they took no action to stop it and even discouraged the student from pressing charges.

Franklin eventually sued the school district for monetary damages under Title IX of the Education Act Amendments of 1972, which provides that "no person in the United States shall, on the basis of sex, be excluded from participation in, be denied the benefits of, or be subjected to discrimination under any education program or activity receiving federal financial assistance." The trial court held that Title IX does not authorize an award of damages, and the appellate court affirmed this decision. The Supreme Court, however, reversed, saying that an award was proper under these circumstances.

Recent attention has focused on the high incidence of sexual harassment that is committed against students by other students. In a 1993 survey of public school students by the American Association of University Women, 85 percent of girls and 76 percent of boys reported experiencing harassment. Only 18 percent of those students, however, had been victimized by an adult—in the rest of the cases the perpetrators were other students.

In the first reported federal decision concerning peer sexual harassment [*Doe v. Petaluma City Sch. Dist.*, 830 F. Supp. 1560 (N.D. Cal. 1993)], a junior high school student identified only as Jane Doe was forced to transfer to a private school to escape taunts by both male and female students that she was a "hot dog," "hot dog bitch," "slut," and "hoe." Despite repeated requests by her parents that the school do something to stop the taunting as well as the graffiti on the walls of the school bathrooms, the school counselor concluded that the problem was not very important and that "boys will be boys."

Doe and her parents sued the school district, the principal, and the counselor on several claims. First, they requested damages under Title IX. That request was denied, however, because the court held that the Does showed mere negligence on the part of the school district instead of the intentional discrimination necessary to support such an award. The Does also filed a claim under section 1983 of the 1871 Civil Rights Act, which prohibits the deprivation of constitutional rights "under color of state law." This claim, too, was unsuccessful. Finally, the Does asserted violation of state laws, but the court declared the facts insufficient to support such a finding.

Two students in Minnesota had better success with state law claims heard before the Minnesota Department of Human Rights. In the first case, school officials in Duluth failed to remove sexually explicit graffiti concerning a particular student from the bathroom walls after the student complained. The department held that under the Minnesota Human Rights Statute, the school had a duty to respond quickly and aggressively to such harassment. The settlement between the victim and the school district consisted of $15,000 to compensate the victim for her mental anguish and adoption by the district of a sexual harassment policy.

In the second Minnesota case, a high school student complained of several episodes of harassment—in one incident male students circulated a list in which they rated how "f——able" 25 female students were. When the student's mother asked the dean what was being done, the dean replied, "Nothing, we don't want to make a big deal out of this." The list was thrown away, but the Department of Human Rights held that throwing away the list and the "hush-hush" attitude of the administration did not go far enough in educating students that such harassment would not be tolerated.

SHARED-TIME PROGRAMS

SHARED-TIME PROGRAMS Programs in which a private school student is admitted into a public school on a part-time basis to take a class not offered in the private school. The reverse are called a **released-time programs,** in which public school students are released from their classrooms to take part in religious instruction off school grounds.

The constitutionality of such programs has been upheld, but local school boards have discretion over whether or not to sponsor them. For example, in 1983, a Michigan court held that a public school was not required to admit a sixth grader from a religious school into its band class, since the public school allowed only full-time students to take part in band. Although the school board certainly could institute a different policy, it was not required to. The court suggested that students who wish to take part in a shared-time program work toward electing school board members who would be sympathetic to their desires. [*Snyder v. Charlotte Pub. Sch. Dist.*, 333 N.W.2d 542 (Mich. Ct. App. 1983)]

Sometimes financial and contractual controversies arise over shared-time programs. Suppose, for example, that the school district receives state funding for the private school students for the portion of the day that these students are in the public schools. The parents of these students have also paid tuition to the private schools as required by their contracts with them. If no partial refund of tuition is given, parents may wonder why they should be charged full tuition at the private school when their children were not there full time.

SINGLE-SEX SCHOOLS

While the rights of private schools to operate as gender-segregated institutions is largely uncontested, legal issues arise when public schools attempt to cater to only one gender. For example, several innercity school systems have proposed a new solution to the overwhelming problems facing African-American males as they grow up, including unemployment, homicide, and school dropout rates that far exceed those of other groups. The proposed solution: male-only schools that focus on the needs of black youth.

Detroit, Michigan, announced a plan in 1991 to open three all-male (but not all-black) elementary schools that would offer an **Afrocentric curriculum** focusing on male responsibility. The **American Civil Liberties Union (ACLU)** and the National Organization for Women filed suit on behalf of several girls enrolled in Detroit public schools, claiming that the arrangement violated the girls' **equal protection** rights, as well as Title IX of the Education Act Amendments of 1972 and the Equal Educational Opportunities Act.

In order to pass a constitutional challenge, a classification by gender must serve "important governmental objectives," and the means employed must be "substantially related to the achievement of those objectives." While it could be said that combating the problems facing urban males is an important governmental objective, the court concluded that the all-male schools failed the test because "there is no evidence that the educational system is failing urban males because females attend schools with males." Based on this finding and the finding that the federal statutes cited by the plaintiffs barred public schools that receive federal money from discriminating among students on the basis of gender, the court granted the injunction to prevent the boys' schools from opening. [*Garrett v. Board of Educ.*, 775 F. Supp. 1004 (E.D. Mich. 1991)]

The debate over government-funded single-sex schools has even reached the realm of higher education. In the mid-1970s, women were first admitted to the nation's military academies, such as West Point. Controversy has been brewing for several years, however, at the last two state-supported all-male military academies: the Virginia Military Institute (VMI) and the Citadel. In order to see past the furor caused by these cases, one must keep in mind that the central issue is not whether all-male military academies are more effective than they would be if they admitted women. The central issue is whether schools that receive government financing should be allowed to exclude potential students based on gender.

In the late 1980s, the Justice Department sued VMI for its policy against admitting women. As a compromise, VMI proposed setting up military programs for women at Mary Baldwin College, a private school near the Institute. The Fourth Circuit upheld the constitutionality of the plan, but said it must be revised in order to be an acceptable alternative to VMI. In January 1996, the case was argued before the Supreme Court, which declared VMI's policy of excluding women to be unconstitutional. [*United States v. Virginia,* 116 S. Ct. 2264 (1996)]

In 1993, Shannon Faulkner, a young woman who had been admitted to the Citadel but denied admission when the school found out her gender, also filed suit. A federal judge ordered the school to admit her to the corps of cadets. [*Faulkner v. Jones,* 51 F.3d 440 (4th Cir. 1995)] Faulkner's admission sparked controversy over whether or not she would be required, like the male cadets, to shave her head. The judge ruled in favor of the haircut, but Department of Defense officials worried that such action would constitute **sexual harassment** and become grounds to withdraw federal support from the school. The haircut was delayed when an appeals court granted the school a stay of any action on the lower court's decision until the hearing of the school's appeal. Faulkner was admitted to the corps of cadets in the fall of 1995. However, she (along with a number of male cadets) dropped out within a matter of days.

Supporters of an all-male Citadel reacted enthusiastically to VMI's plan to establish a separate program for women. Critics of such a plan argue that separate schools for women could never equal the prestige and opportunities afforded a graduate of an established, all-male institution. The issue became moot, however, when the Supreme Court handed down its VMI decision and the Citadel quickly announced its intention to begin admitting women.

SNIFF SEARCHES

Searches in which trained dogs are brought into schools to detect the presence of contraband, such as drugs.

The Fourth Amendment to the U.S. Constitution sets out the right of the people, including students, to be free from unreasonable searches and seizures by state officials. Public school officials such as teachers and administrators are state employees, but they have not been held to the same standard as police officers regarding when a search is reasonable or unreasonable. In fact, the U.S. Supreme Court held in the 1985 case ***New Jersey v. T.L.O.*** that while a police officer must have probable cause to search a person, a school official need only have reasonable cause to search a student—an easier burden to meet.

T.L.O., however, dealt with a search by a principal of a student's purse for drugs and did not involve the use of dogs. Since the Supreme Court has yet to hear a case involving a sniff search, it is necessary to examine lower court opinions that consider the issue. In one of the earliest sniff cases, *Doe v. Renfrow* [631 F.2d 91 (7th Cir. 1980)], a school contacted a private agency that handled drug-detecting dogs for help in combating its drug problem. The agency brought the dogs to the school and sent them up and down the aisles of the classrooms. If a dog reacted to a student, the student was asked to put his or her personal items on the desk. If the dog reacted again, school officials would search the student. One 13-year-old girl, who was strip-searched despite her protests that she did not have any drugs, sued. The court held that while the strip search [see **strip searches**] was outrageous and therefore not protected, the use of dogs was allowable as a means of establishing reasonable suspicion.

At least one other court, however, has limited the situations in which the use of dogs is permissible. A federal court in Texas held in *Jones v. Latexo Independent School District* [499 F. Supp. 223 (E.D. Tex. 1980)] that a school official must have reasonable cause to believe that a particular student is carrying drugs, not just a generalized suspicion. To use dogs to locate the guilty person amounts to a "fishing expedition" and disregards the requirement of individualized suspicion.

Other courts have drawn distinctions between permissible and impermissible use of dogs based on the area searched. For example, at least one court has held that there is a greater personal intrusion where a dog sniffs the students, as in *Jones*, than where the dogs are used to search automobiles and lockers [see **locker searches**]. Courts have also been swayed by the track record of the individual dog: a search conducted with a dog that has had a high number of false alarms might not be deemed as worthy for establishing reasonable cause as a dog with an excellent record of reliability.

SPECIAL EDUCATION Before the 1970s, special education in the United States was poorly funded and many disabled children were either not provided with educations at all or received ineffective ones. Congress attempted to address this issue in 1966 when it amended the Elementary and Secondary Education Act of 1965 to establish a grant program "for the purpose of assisting the States in the initiation, expansion, and improvement of programs and projects . . . for the education of handicapped children." This program was replaced in 1970 by one established through the Education of the Handicapped Act. Neither program, however, provided specific guidelines for the use of the grant money, and the majority of disabled children continued to fall through the cracks.

In the early 1970s, two major federal district court decisions, ***P.A.R.C. v. Commonwealth of Pennsylvania*** and ***Mills v. Board of Education of the District of Columbia,*** declared that disabled students had a right to receive public educations. Inspired at least in part by these two decisions, Congress enacted the Education for All Handicapped Children Act in 1974 to give financial assistance to states that provide disabled children with free public educations in accordance with the strict procedural requirements of the act.

Passage of the act opened the doors of U.S. classrooms to an estimated 1 million disabled children who until then had been entirely excluded from the educational system. It also helped to improve the educations of some 4 million children who had been languishing in inappropriate educational programs. The act was later renamed the **Individuals with Disabilities Education Act (IDEA)** and continues to be the most important piece of federal legislation dealing with education of the disabled.

STRIP SEARCHES Searches in which students are made to remove some or all of their clothing. The Supreme Court case that covers searches of public school students, ***New Jersey v. T.L.O.,*** requires that rather than have probable cause, a school official need only have reasonable cause to search a student. Based on *T.L.O.*, a search will be upheld if it is reasonable in its inception, or beginning, and reasonable in its scope.

In 1993, school officials ordered a student they believed to be "crotching" drugs (concealing them in his underwear) to change into a gym suit while they watched. Once he changed into the gym suit, they searched his street clothes but found nothing. The court held that the search was reasonable in its inception—because the student had made remarks about "crotching," a bus driver smelled marijuana on him, and other students said he had carried drugs in the past—and reasonable in its scope, since it was the least intrusive way to find out whether the student had drugs and was conducted in private in the boys' locker room without any touching. [*Cornfield v. Consolidated High Sch. Dist. No. 230*, 991 F.2d 1316 (7th Cir. 1993)]

In another strip-search case, a student was caught in a school parking lot cutting class. A school official searched her purse and then made her take off her jeans and bend over so the official could examine the contents of her bra. There was no touching, but the court held that this search was not reasonable in its inception, because the student's behavior "could have indicated that she was truant, or that she was stealing hubcaps, or that she had left class to meet a boyfriend." The court went on to say that the school administration has the burden of establishing that a student's behavior created a reasonable suspicion that a specific rule had been violated and that a search could reasonably be expected to yield proof of that violation. In this case, proof of the student's infraction could not reasonably be expected to be found in her jeans or her bra. [*Cales v. Howell Pub. Sch.*, 635 F. Supp. 454 (E.D. Mich. 1985)]

Courts emphasize that under the *T.L.O.* standard a search must not be "excessively intrusive in light of the age and sex of the child." Logically, this means that the searcher should be of the same sex as the student. Also, some courts have found that a very young child does not have the same ability as an older student to understand the search and to give meaningful consent.

Applying *T.L.O.* to search cases, it is apparent that greater justification is needed for an intrusion as large as a strip search. For example, in 1993, a West Virginia court examined a case in which $100 was stolen from a teacher's purse and found in the back of the underwear of a student who had been alone in the room and who had a criminal record. The court held that this search was justified in its inception because the officials had a legitimate reason to suspect that particular student. The search was not, however, justified in its scope, because theft, unlike possession of drugs or weapons, does not pose enough of an immediate danger to justify a warrantless strip search. [*State v. Mark Anthony B.*, 433 S.E.2d 41 (W. Va. 1993)]

SUICIDE The intentional taking of one's own life. Until relatively recently, suicide among young people was a rare tragedy. Today, approximately 5,000 teens kill themselves each year. Teen suicide can raise issues of school liability when a school has reason to know of a student's intentions.

One of the earliest cases in which parents of a suicide victim sued the child's school occurred in 1960 in Wisconsin. Parents sued a college counselor for negligently terminating counseling with their daughter and for failing to notify them of the termination and of their daughter's precarious mental and emotional state. (Their daughter had killed herself six weeks after the termination.) The court, however, refused to hold the counselor liable, saying liability is only proper "where the wrongful act produces a rage or frenzy or uncontrollable impulse, during which state self-destruction takes place." [*Bogust v. Iverson,* 102 N.W.2d 228 (Wis. 1960)]

Another Wisconsin court relied on this case as precedent 30 years later when parents of a teenage suicide victim sued the public school district. Their son was an emotionally disabled student who attended counseling sessions off-campus to deal with his alcohol and drug problems. The counseling center sent progress records to the school, some of which noted that he had expressed suicidal thoughts. When the son was suspended for marijuana use, school officials attempted to notify his parents by telephone. Because the parents could not be reached, the principal gave a copy of the written notice to the student, mailed the original to his parents, and sent him home. Both parents interacted briefly with their son during the time between his suspension and his suicide one to three days later, but he never mentioned the suspension. The court relied on the 1960 case in granting summary judgment for the school board, because "a delayed suicide under circumstances similar to those that occurred here is not sufficiently connected to any negligence so as to permit recovery." [*Lenzer v. Shawano-Gresham Sch. Dist.,* 458 N.W.2d 388 (Wis. Ct. App. 1990)]

Other courts, however, have imposed liability on school officials for the suicide of a student. In a 1991 Maryland case, students told two counselors that one of their friends had made suicidal remarks. The counselors called the suicidal student in for questioning, but she denied having made the statements. The counselors let the matter drop and did not inform either the parents or the school administrators. The court held that in a case like this, where the suicide is foreseeable, "school counselors have a duty to use reasonable means to attempt to prevent a suicide when they are on notice of a child or adolescent student's suicidal intent." [*Eisel v. Board of Educ.*, 597 A.2d 447 (Md. 1991)]

SUSPENSION AND EXPULSION Two disciplinary methods in which students lose their privilege of attending class for various behavioral offenses. Suspensions are generally shorter in nature, usually less than ten days, while expulsions tend to be longer in duration, such as for the remainder of the term. Students are often suspended for offenses like cheating or smoking, while expulsion is usually reserved for more serious offenses, such as drug use or carrying a weapon on school property. Many schools have recently embraced the concept of in-school suspension, in which students do their school work in an alternative setting on the school grounds rather than being sent home.

Occasionally, a student who disagrees with his or her suspension or expulsion will file suit against the school district. As a general rule, courts do not like to substitute their judgment on educational matters for the judgment of the educators. For example, in 1992, an Ohio appellate court heard a case brought by a high school student who had been suspended for ten days for stealing a copy of an algebra test from a teacher's filing cabinet and using it to cheat on the test. The lower court agreed with the student that it was unfair to suspend him in addition to giving him an "F" in the class when other students who had cheated using the stolen test merely received the "F." Accordingly, the lower court reversed the decision of the school district. On appeal, however, the appellate court pointed out that a court should alter an administrative decision only if the decision is "unconstitutional, illegal, arbitrary, capricious, unreasonable, or unsupported by the preponderance of substantial, reliable, and probative evidence on the whole record." [*Reed v. Vermilion Loc. Sch. Dist.*, 614 N.E.2d 1101 (Ohio Ct. App. 1992)]

Despite judicial distaste for tampering with the decisions of school officials regarding suspensions and expulsions, courts will do so in certain circumstances. For example, in 1975, the Supreme Court heard ***Goss v. Lopez,*** in which a group of high school students filed suit after they were suspended from school without any sort of hearing. The Court held that the suspensions had a potential impact on certain rights protected under the Fourteenth Amendment: property rights in the education the state had extended to them and liberty rights in damage to their reputations. Since substantive rights were implicated, the Court set out certain procedures that a school must follow before it may deny a student those rights. Before suspending a student for more than ten days, the Court declared, a school must give the student notice of the charges and some sort of informal hearing.

Since *Goss,* most states have set out statutes detailing what procedures must be followed in the suspension or expulsion of students. This does not mean, however, that the procedures are always followed. For example, in 1987, a Florida high school student successfully sued the Polk County School Board after his principal removed him from school and transferred him to the Polk School's Opportunity Center for a "major infraction of the School Board's code of conduct." The board argued that this reassignment amounted to a transfer and was therefore not covered by Florida laws requiring notification of parents before a student may be suspended. The court, however, disagreed and found in favor of the student. [*W.A.N. v. School Bd. of Polk County,* 504 So. 2d 529 (Fla. Ct. App. 1987)]

In recent years, suspension and expulsion have come under fire as disciplinary techniques due to the disproportionately large number of minority students, especially males, affected by such punishments. According to the **Department of Education**'s Office of Civil Rights, black children comprised over 20 percent of the U.S. student body but accounted for nearly 40 percent of the suspensions in 1988. That same year, males made up nearly three-quarters of all suspensions. In a number of instances, black students have won in cases brought against school districts for racial unfairness [see **racial discrimination**] in the administration of punishment where black students were disciplined for conduct that was tolerated from white students.

T

TEACHER CERTIFICATION Each state sets out in its statutes the minimum qualifications one must possess to be certified to teach in the state's schools. For example, it is common to require potential teachers to possess at least a bachelor's degree with a specified number of credits in certain subjects. Once a teacher has been certified by the state, he or she is often required to complete continuing education classes to keep his or her skills current.

As a means of enhancing **accountability** for student successes and failures, just about every state now also requires teachers to take and pass competency tests in order to be certified. For new teachers entering the profession, this is just one more requirement they must meet before entering their chosen field. For practicing teachers who are suddenly required to pass tests in order to continue their careers, however, certification is a touchy issue.

The matter is made worse by the fact that, in general, minorities tend to fail these standardized tests in greater numbers than their white counterparts, raising questions of **racial discrimination.** For example, when the state of Georgia began requiring practicing teachers to take competency exams in the 1980s, nearly all the teachers who failed were black.

When a teacher who loses his or her certification and job for failing these tests brings suit, he or she has several arguments on which to rely. For example, a tenured faculty member [see **tenure**] might argue that he or she was unconstitutionally deprived of a property interest in continued employment. Or a group of minority teachers who have lost their jobs for failing these tests might allege that they have been discriminated against as a class, in violation of the equal protection clause of the Fourteenth Amendment [see **equal protection**]. The problem with this argument, however, is that the teachers must prove that the state had an intent to discriminate against them. As a starting point, this intent can be inferred from a disparate, or unequal, impact on minorities, but ultimately it is difficult to prove.

Teachers who find themselves in this position might have more success with an action brought under Title VII of the Civil Rights Act of

1964, which forbids employment discrimination based on race, sex, or national origin. In a Title VII suit, the teachers need only prove that the test has a disparate impact on minorities. Once this is proved, the state has the burden of proving the validity of the tests as related to the job of teaching. In 1986, a teacher's union brought a Title VII class action against the state of Georgia on behalf of the minority teachers who failed the newly required competency tests and were dismissed. The state settled out of court for several million dollars. In 1993, a federal judge certified a class of black, Hispanic, and Asian-American teachers who had failed California's competency test. The teachers claimed that the low passage rate of minorities when compared to the 80 percent passage rate for whites showed a disparate impact.

Another issue surrounding teacher certification that has cropped up in recent years is the question of whether parents who choose to educate their children at home should be required to meet the same standards for certification that the state requires of teachers in its schools. With the increasing popularity of home schooling [see **home schools**], most states now allow parents who are not state certified to teach their own children. One of the last holdouts on this issue is the state of Michigan, which requires all students to be taught by a certified teacher.

Critics of the Michigan law argue that the requirements for certification (including a bachelor's degree, many hours of supervised teaching, and a request for certification within five years of completing the requirements) impose a significant burden on parents who have decided to take on the responsibility of educating their children. Furthermore, many argue, many home schoolers are motivated by religious beliefs. As a result, they must sometimes choose between disobeying their religious principles or breaking the law and suffering the resulting fines and imprisonment.

The Michigan Supreme Court considered a case in 1989 in which the parents relied on the latter argument. In that case, the mother's beliefs allowed her to delegate her responsibility to a teacher, so there was only a minimal burden on her. The father, however, believed that it was "a sin to submit to state authority and to employ certificated teachers;" therefore, the greater burden fell on him. Even so, the court upheld the conviction of the parents for violating the state **compulsory attendance** law, since the parents had an unlimited right to believe whatever they wished but only a limited right to act upon those beliefs. [*People v. DeJonge*, 449 N.W.2d 899 (Mich. 1989)]

TEACHER STRIKES Sometimes, when teachers' unions negotiate with school boards regarding contracts and benefits and the negotiations reach a stalemate, the teachers will refuse to work. Some would argue that because of the important nature of teaching, teachers should not be allowed to strike. Others, however, assert that in some situations a strike provides the best chance for positive change.

Strikes can include anything from outright picketing, where teachers march in a line in front of schools and carry signs expressing their grievances with the district, to more subtle actions. For example, courts have held behaviors such as teachers refusing to sponsor extracurricular activities or attend certain meetings to be strikes. Teachers in Washington, D.C., staged a "sickout" in which hundreds of them called in sick because of their anger over three years without pay raises and 12 days of furlough for which they would not be paid. In one interesting example of strikes that occurred in the private arena, in 1995, graduate students who worked as teaching assistants for professors at Yale University refused to hand in grades for approximately 100 undergraduate students in an effort to force the university to raise their salaries and improve their benefits. The university refused to budge, however, and the Graduate Employees and Students Organization voted in favor of handing over the grades rather than suffering the consequences threatened by a number of professors.

Many states have made strikes by public school teachers, who are generally regarded as government employees, illegal, and many courts have upheld these laws as constitutional. Even so, teachers sometimes strike even when that action is prohibited.

Perhaps the best-known case regarding teacher strikes occurred in a state where such strikes are illegal. In *Hortonville Joint School District No. 1 v. Hortonville Education Association* [426 U.S. 482 (1976)], teachers in a Wisconsin school district went on strike after their union and the district were unable to reach agreement on a new contract for the teachers. Wisconsin law prohibits teacher strikes, and the district superintendent sent letters to the strikers reminding them of this fact and asking them to go back to work. When the teachers refused to comply, the school board informed them that a disciplinary hearing would be held. The board held the hearing and voted to fire the teachers. The teachers filed suit against the school district, claiming that the hearings did not meet the requirements of **due process.** The trial court held in favor of the school district, but the Wisconsin Supreme Court reversed the decision on the grounds that the board was not impartial and was, therefore, not the proper decision maker. The U.S. Supreme Court, however, disagreed and reversed this decision. The Court held that, in the first place, the teachers had failed to show that the board members were personally involved with the dismissal decision so as to require their disqualification. Furthermore, the school board had been given the power by the state to preside over decisions such as these, and according to the Court the striking teachers had no right to have the decision on whether or not they should be fired reviewed by any other authority.

TEN COMMANDMENTS Kentucky passed a law in 1978 that required all public school classrooms in the state to have a copy of the Ten Commandments posted on their walls. In an effort to avoid problems with the separation of state and religion, the drafters of the statute included the requirements that the posters be bought with private donations and that they bear the following notation: "The secular application of the Ten Commandments is clearly seen in its adoption as the fundamental legal code of Western Civilization and the Common Law of the United States." Despite these safeguards, the statute was challenged in *Stone v. Graham* [449 U.S. 39 (1980)]

When the Kentucky Supreme Court heard the case, it affirmed a lower court's ruling that the statute was valid because it had a secular, or nonreligious, purpose. Such a purpose is the first requirement of the three-prong *Lemon* test, which takes its name from the U.S. Supreme Court case ***Lemon v. Kurtzman.*** The *Lemon* test requires that in order for a law or state activity to comply with the **establishment and free exercise clauses** of the First Amendment, the law or activity must (1) have a secular purpose; (2) neither advance nor inhibit religion; and (3) not involve excessive entanglement of the government and religion.

Stone v. Graham eventually reached the U.S. Supreme Court, which held in 1980 that the statute failed the first prong of the *Lemon* test. The Court pointed out the sacred nature of the Ten Commandments for the Jewish and Christian religions. Although some of the commandments do deal with secular matters that are mirrored in the laws of the country and states, such as the prohibitions against murder and stealing, others have a plainly religious purpose, such as the commands to observe the Sabbath and worship the Lord God alone. Adding the notation of the posters' supposed secular purpose was simply not enough to get around the religious nature of the text.

The Court was also unimpressed with the legislature's attempt to avoid government entanglement with religion by funding the posters with private donations. The mere fact that the posters were hung under the authority of the state provided the "official support of the State Government that the establishment clause prohibits." Additionally, the Court pointed out in a footnote, the state did in fact spend money on the project by using public funds to administer statute, such as the requirement that the state treasurer collect the contributions.

The Court observed that the commandments could be included in the **curriculum** of public schools in an objective study of history or religion. Simply posting them on the walls, however, had a religious purpose rather than an educational one.

TENURE Expectation of continued employment conferred on a teacher after he or she works for a certain number of years on probationary status.

A probationary teacher has an expectation of continued employment for only the term of his or her contract. In order to dismiss such a teacher during the school year, a school board would have to provide the teacher with certain elements of **due process,** such as notice and a hearing.

At the end of the contract term, however, the school board has discretion over whether or not to renew a probationary teacher's contract without any particular process beyond notifying the teacher that his or her contract will or will not be extended. No state may choose not to renew a probationary teacher's contract for a reason such as race or gender, which would be prohibited by federal law as well as the constitutions of many states. Other than this restriction, states are free to set their own standards for when to let a probationary teacher go at the end of the school year. While statutes vary, many states simply require that the decision not be arbitrary or capricious. For example, while failure to abide by school rules or using excessive discipline might be legitimate reasons for nonrenewal, one court found in favor of a teacher whose contract had not been renewed due to prejudices against the teacher—she was overweight, did not go to church, and lived in a trailer. [*Johnson v. Dixon,* 501 S.W.2d 256 (Ky. 1973)]

Unlike a probationary teacher, one with tenure has a property interest in continued employment from year to year. Where tenure has been granted, a teacher may be removed only if the school board can establish good cause under the statutes of that particular state. For example, most states allow dismissal of tenured teachers where the school board can prove immorality (such as conducting a sexual relationship with a student), insubordination (such as blatantly disregarding school rules or legitimate administrative demands), or incompetence.

A number of courts have held that while tenure does confer an expectation of continued employment, that expectation does not extend to continued employment in a particular job. If a school board attempted to reassign a tenured teacher to a lower-level job, that would be considered a demotion and would raise issues of due process. If, however, the reassignment is a lateral move between two similar positions, such as switching a teacher who is certified to teach two different subjects from one subject to the other, the move would probably not offend the state's tenure statute. Furthermore, several courts have held that a grant of tenure applies only to an employee's primary role (e.g., teacher), and does not cover extracurricular or supplemental roles (e.g., football coach).

TINKER V. DES MOINES INDEPENDENT SCHOOL DISTRICT Landmark Supreme Court case establishing that students do not "shed their constitutional rights to freedom of speech or expression at the schoolhouse gate." [393 U.S. 503 (1969)] A group of students agreed to join a silent demonstration against the war in Vietnam by wearing black armbands during the 1965 holiday season. School administrators heard about the plan and, hoping to avoid controversy, adopted a policy that students who came to school wearing armbands would be asked to remove them or be suspended. Two high school students and one junior high student were punished accordingly, and they sued.

The trial court found in favor of the school authorities. According to the court, the action was necessary to maintain **discipline** in the school. The case eventually reached the U.S. Supreme Court, which reversed the lower court's decision. The Court held that the mere fear of a disturbance is not enough to warrant suppression of free speech [see **freedom of speech**]. Also, the Court was influenced by the fact that the regulation sought to squelch the expression of one particular opinion, while students were not forbidden to wear buttons from political campaigns and other symbols. The *Tinker* court did not go so far as to proclaim all speech by students to be beyond limitation, but speech that does not (1) materially disrupt class work or (2) violate the rights of others is protected under the ruling.

The test set out in *Tinker* is still used for deciding whether or not certain student expression may be limited. For example, students across the country participate in annual "See You at the Pole" rallies in which they meet at their school flagpoles to engage in voluntary prayer. Such assemblies most likely meet the requirements of *Tinker* because (1) they are held during nonclassroom hours and (2) no student is forced to participate. On the other hand, a federal trial court held in 1992 that students did not have a free speech-based right to wear shirts proclaiming "Drugs suck," because the school could legitimately foresee disruption occurring in classes as a result of the shirts. [*Broussard v. School Bd. of City of Norfolk*, 801 F. Supp. 1526 (E.D. Va. 1992)]

TRACKING The practice of dividing school children into groups supposedly based on their scholastic abilities. The intention is to provide each group with the types of educational opportunities its members need to succeed. Supporters claim that such systems allow each student to move at his or her own pace. However, controversies surrounding tracking often stem from the argument that this practice results in *de facto* segregation by placing a disproportionate number of minority students on the "slow track." In 1967, for example, in the first case based on this argument against tracking, a federal court invalidated a tracking scheme in the District of Columbia that was aimed at sidestepping a **desegregation** order and "designed to prepare some children for white-collar, and other children for blue-collar jobs." [*Hobson v. Henson*, 269 F. Supp. 401 (D.D.C. 1967)]

In 1975, the Fifth Circuit set out a standard in *McNeal v. Tate County School District* [508 F.2d 1017 (5th Cir. 1975)] that many other jurisdictions have adopted in considering such challenges:

> School districts ought to be, and are, free to use such grouping whenever it does not have a racially discriminatory effect. If it does cause segregation, whether in classrooms or in schools, ability grouping may nevertheless be permitted in an otherwise unitary system if the school district can demonstrate that its assignment method is not based on the present results of past segregation or will remedy such results through better educational opportunities.

In applying this standard, courts have upheld tracking systems in schools that can demonstrate that they have overcome any past history of racial segregation. For example, in 1989, the Fifth Circuit upheld a tracking system in a school district where "there was evidence that the achievement grouping system was educationally sound both in theory and practice, that students were not locked into place or tracked into a grouping system, and that there was an impressive degree of movement among achievement levels by blacks as well as white students." [*Quarles v. Oxford Mun. Separate Sch. Dist.*, 868 F.2d 750 (5th Cir. 1989)] Opponents of tracking, such as the **National Education Association (NEA),** maintain that regardless of a school system's past history with regard to segregation, tracking should be abolished across the board, since the means for separating students into their "tracks" (including **IQ tests,** which many believe to be biased in favor of middle-class white children) have the effect of creating racially separate classes from which it is difficult to escape.

TRUANCY Failure of a child to comply with **compulsory attendance** laws. Children with excessive unexcused absences may be considered truant, as well as children who do not attend school at all.

Truants face a variety of potential punishments. For instance, schools may adopt regulations requiring **academic sanctions,** such as the lowering of grades, in classes where a student has a certain number of unexcused classes. Habitual truants may find themselves referred to the courts, where a student who refuses to attend school might be held in contempt of court for disobeying a judge's order to attend school. At this point, he or she might be placed in a juvenile detention center or declared in need of judicial supervision and have a guardian appointed for him or her.

Courts also consider the parents' responsibility for a child's truancy. Parents who simply refuse to send their children to school can face criminal punishment. For example, a Colorado judge sentenced the parents of a 15-year-old girl who had missed 43 days of school to spend a month in jail and fined them $300.

Some states, frustrated with seemingly ineffective methods of compelling attendance, have shown ingenuity in dealing with the problem of truancy by sentencing the parents to attend school. In one case, a judge ordered the mother of a sixth grader who had missed 45 days to attend classes with her daughter for the remaining three months of the school year. In another, a judge in Chicago sentenced a mother to attend 30 days of high school classes with her 15-year-old daughter after the daughter missed classes despite a court order to attend school.

Such drastic measures, however, do not always work: one set of parents who had been sentenced to attend school with their truant son found themselves summoned to court to explain to the judge why they, too, had skipped classes. Also, critics such as the **American Civil Liberties Union (ACLU)** charge that it is unfair to punish one person for another person's crimes and that mothers are generally the parents on the receiving end of such sentences.

V

VACCINATIONS In 1894, the U.S. Supreme Court stated that the police power of the states includes the power to institute compulsory vaccination laws. [*Lawton v. Steele,* 152 U.S. 133 (1894)] By the turn of the century, many cities and towns regularly required vaccination of children before they could be admitted to a public or private school. Today all states have some form of vaccination law directed at school students, but not all students are vaccinated.

Generally, a child may be exempted from complying with the vaccination requirement if he or she has a physical condition that makes vaccination unsafe. For example, some physical conditions, such as acquired immune deficiency syndrome, allergies, or certain types of cancers, suppress the immune system and therefore make vaccination inadvisable. These unvaccinated children are usually still allowed to attend school, but in the event of an outbreak of disease they may be forced to remain at home for their own protection.

Also, all states but West Virginia and Mississippi allow exemptions to compulsory vaccination requirements where it conflicts with the principles of the parents' religion. Each state has its own unique test for determining if the child is eligible for a waiver due to religion, but states must be careful, in deciding eligibility, not to go against the establishment clause [see **establishment and free exercise clauses**] of the Constitution by giving greater respect to the religious beliefs of some citizens than to the beliefs of others.

Even in a private school setting, the state may exercise its right to protect children over the wishes of their parents and order children to be vaccinated in the face of an epidemic. For example, in 1991, a measles epidemic swept through a Philadelphia private school and killed five of its 350 unvaccinated children. The city went to family court to get an order to vaccinate certain children deemed to be at risk of contracting the illness. The judge issued the order and the children received the vaccinations the next day.

VIOLENCE Violence in U.S. schools has received a great deal of attention in recent years. Violent incidents are no longer restricted to the occasional fistfight in the hallway; dangerous weapons such as guns and knives appear in schools with alarming frequency. Some students are also victims of **sexual harassment,** either by school employees or other students.

Common sense dictates that it is more desirable to prevent violence in the first place than to address the problem after the fact by punishing the perpetrator and compensating the victim. Indeed, Goal Number 7 of **Goals 2000** calls for an end to violence in U.S. schools. First, it requires states receiving Goals 2000 money (which is just about every state) to implement a policy of expelling [see **suspension and expulsion**] for one year any student who brings a weapon to school. Second, it provides additional grants to cover the cost of security personnel, conflict resolution courses, **metal detectors,** and programs designed to prevent acts of violence.

States and local school districts have experimented recently with other ways of reducing violence. In addition to using traditional methods of **discipline** on students, such as suspension, expulsion, and—where allowed—**corporal punishment,** some jurisdictions have begun to send repeat trouble makers to special **alternative schools.** Still others, faced with the realization that some students were beaten up and sometimes even killed for their designer clothing and sneakers, have begun encouraging (and in some places requiring) students to wear **school uniforms** instead. Other schools have implemented strict **dress codes** restricting the wearing of **gang clothing.**

In spite of the recent wave of public concern over school violence, it is not always easy for schools to deal with student perpetrators. For example, the **Individuals with Disabilities Education Act (IDEA)** requires that a disabled student not be removed from his or her designated educational plan until certain elements of **due process** are met. If the student's parents disagree with the proposed change in the plan, a hearing must be held. If the parents disagree with the outcome of the hearing, they then have the right to appeal the decision through the court system. Indeed, when the parents of two California students accused of stealing money and choking a fellow classmate objected to the school's proposal to suspend their children for the duration of the hearings, the controversy went all the way to the U.S. Supreme Court. The Court, in ***Honig v. Doe,*** held in favor of the parents, since the "stay-put" provision of the statute does not contain an exception for dangerous students.

Besides the provisions in the Goals 2000 legislation, Congress has also passed another law in response to the school violence problem. The **Gun-Free School Zones Act,** passed in 1990, made it a federal crime to carry a gun within 1,000 feet of a school. Five years after the act's passage, however, the Supreme Court declared it an unconstitutional use of Congress's power under the commerce clause to intervene in what would otherwise be strictly a state concern. The Court was unimpressed by the argument that guns in school lead to a hostile learning environment, which in turn leads to a poorly educated work force, which in turn has a negative impact on interstate commerce.

Sometimes students who have been victimized at their schools sue. One theory under which a student (or his or her parents) might choose to bring an action is negligent supervision, which means that the school failed to live up to its duty to exercise the same care as a parent would in the protection and guidance of its students. In order to recover under such a theory, the plaintiff would have to show that the school had or should have had knowledge of the risk to the student. For example, when a school installs a metal detector but a student gets in with a weapon anyway and injures another student, the presence of the metal detector might serve as evidence that the school doubted the safety of its students. In such a case, the plaintiff could argue that the school had knowledge of the danger and took some steps to protect against it, but that these were insufficient. Another avenue that an injured student might consider pursuing would be a civil suit [see **civil suits**] for a constitutional tort under 42 U.S.C. § 1983, although the success of such an action would vary from jurisdiction to jurisdiction.

VOUCHERS

"Coupons" that states give to parents to redeem for tuition at the schools of their choice. Some states, such as Vermont and New Hampshire, have used voucher systems for many years to avoid having to build schools in sparsely populated areas. Instead, the state gives some of the money it would have spent on those students (had public schools been available in their districts) directly to the parents, who use the funds to cover the cost of sending their children to the public or private school they choose.

In most other states, however, vouchers are a relatively new idea spurred on by the increasing popularity of **school choice.** In 1990, Wisconsin enacted the first voucher plan that would open up the choices offered to parents to include some private schools. The program, which applies only to Milwaukee students and schools, offers approximately $2,500 per student to families earning no more than 175 percent of the poverty level so their children may attend participating private schools.

Voucher proposals often lead to arguments over whether or not state-funded vouchers should be allowed to be spent at religious schools. While some claim that such action violates the establishment clause [see **establishment and free exercise clauses**] of the U.S. Constitution, others maintain that as long as the program (1) has a secular intent—in this case, advancing education; (2) neither advances nor inhibits religion; and (3) does not excessively entangle the state with religion, it passes the test set out in ***Lemon v. Kurtzman*** and is, therefore, constitutional. Milwaukee's program avoids this controversy by restricting voucher usage to nonsectarian, or nonreligious, schools.

Voucher programs like the one established in Wisconsin have not been enthusiastically embraced in other states. Since 1990, Oregon, Colorado, New Mexico, and California have rejected voucher legislation. The vote in California was the 19th time in 20 ballot initiatives since 1966 that voters have rejected the idea. Some legislative analysts believe that the reason the California voucher referendum failed in 1993 was passage of two school choice laws providing for open enrollment within school districts and a pilot program allowing local districts to accept a certain number of interdistrict transfers. Both options are seen by many as a more moderate solution than the funneling of state money into private institutions.

W

WELFARE Government money that is given to poor people to help them make ends meet. Traditionally, many welfare programs have offered funds to whoever met the financial requirements. Recently, however, some states have begun considering tying receipt of welfare money to some sort of action on behalf of the recipient, such as getting treatment for a drug problem or refraining from having additional children while on welfare.

In 1987, Wisconsin became the first state to tie welfare receipt to children's school attendance. Through a program called "Learnfare," the state began monitoring the attendance of children whose families receive Aid to Families with Dependent Children (AFDC). When a child has two or more unexcused absences in a month, his or her family's AFDC payment for the next month is reduced by the amount allocated to that child. Supporters of the Learnfare program claim that it encourages parents to become involved in their children's education, which in turn could help break the cycle of poverty. Critics, however, point to studies showing that Learnfare has not had as much of an impact on attendance rates as hoped.

Regardless of how effective the program may or may not be, a number of other states have watched closely with an eye toward implementing programs similar to Learnfare. By 1996, nearly half of the states had some variation of this program in place. The federal government has also at times considered passing such measures. In 1995, a member of Congress from Wisconsin introduced a plan before the House of Representatives that would require parents in the District of Columbia who receive AFDC to attend quarterly parent-teacher conferences. Parents who fail to appear at the meetings would have their AFDC benefits discontinued.

Another welfare program that has an impact on education is Supplemental Security Income (SSI), a federal program administered by the Social Security Administration (SSA). The money, which usually amounts to several hundred dollars a month for each recipient, is given to disabled children and adults.

Prior to 1990, the SSA used "listings"—inventories of nearly 60 impairments—to determine whether or not a child qualified for SSI benefits. As a result, the applications of many children whose disabilities did not fall neatly into one of the listings were denied. In 1990, however, the Supreme Court declared that the SSA should not automatically disqualify any child who failed to fit into a listing. [*Sullivan v. Zebley,* 493 U.S. 521 (1990)] Instead, the SSA should give great weight to the consideration of whether the child's impairments kept him or her from performing at his or her age level. In the new regulations put out in the wake of the *Zebley* opinion, the SSI also specifically included new conditions, such as drug and alcohol abuse disorders and hyperactivity.

Over the next four years, the number of children receiving the SSI payments more than doubled. While the majority of parents use this money to provide for their children's special needs, such as by building wheelchair ramps or paying for special private schools, others have blatantly abused the system. Some of these parents take money that is sent to benefit children with legitimate disabilities and put it to other uses. Still others encourage children who are not disabled to "act crazy" in order to meet the standard of not performing at the appropriate age level in order to get on the SSI rolls.

Critics of the program argue that it invites abuse by handing out "free money" to anyone who qualifies and by putting no restrictions on how the money is to be spent. After all, they point out, SSI recipients qualify for Medicaid, a government health insurance program for the poor, which should take care of medical treatment. Furthermore, a disabled child is already entitled under the **Individuals with Disabilities Education Act (IDEA)** to all kinds of **special education** programs, from occasional speech therapy to sign language interpreters to nursing services like catheterization—whatever related services might be necessary for the child to benefit from his or her **Individualized Educational Program (IEP).**

West Virginia Board of Education v. Barnette

Supreme Court decision holding that students may refuse to take part in a state-mandated flag salute and recitation of the **Pledge of Allegiance** if such activities violate their religious beliefs. [319 U.S. 624 (1943)]

In 1941, West Virginia enacted a statute that required all teachers and students in the state's public schools to take part in a daily flag salute and recitation of the Pledge of Allegiance. The purpose of this statute was to promote national unity, and students who refused to abide by it were punished for insubordination and expelled until they would comply with the law [see **suspension and expulsion**]. During the time they were out of school, they and their parents could be criminally prosecuted for **truancy.**

A group of Jehovah's Witnesses sued to enjoin, or stop, the state from enforcing this law because of the effect it had on the exercise of their religion. Jehovah's Witnesses take quite seriously biblical prohibitions against worshiping secular images. Because they consider flags to be such images, their children refused to take part in the salute and were punished accordingly.

The trial court held in favor of the Jehovah's Witnesses, and the state Board of Education appealed to the U.S. Supreme Court. The Supreme Court affirmed the decision of the lower court and held that by requiring participation in the salute and pledge, the state government overstepped the boundaries that the U.S. Constitution places on government power and violated the First Amendment rights of its people.

The state argued that legislatures are charged with guarding the liberties and freedoms of the people and that, therefore, controversies over whether or not they are using their power wisely should be decided "in the forum of public opinion and before legislative assemblies rather than to transfer the contest to the judicial arena." The Court disregarded this argument and stated that:

> The very purpose of a Bill of Rights was to withdraw certain subjects from the vicissitudes of political controversy, to place them beyond the reach of majorities and officials and to establish them as legal principles to be applied by the courts. One's right to life, liberty, and property, to free speech, a free press, freedom of worship and assembly, and other fundamental rights may not be submitted to vote; they depend on the outcome of no elections.

This language is often quoted to reaffirm the idea that civil rights are civil rights for the specific reason that they may not be voted away by the majority.

Wisconsin v. Yoder Supreme Court decision holding that parents have a right to bring their children up according to their religious faith and that this right sometimes restricts the right of the state to require **compulsory attendance** of its children in schools. [406 U.S. 205 (1972)]

A group of Old Order Amish parents in Wisconsin refused to send their children to school past the eighth grade, violating the state's compulsory attendance law requiring children to attend school until the age of 16. The parents did not object to formal education through the eighth grade, because it provided the fundamentals their children needed in order to read the Bible and lead productive lives as Amish farmers and housewives. After that point, however, the parents viewed formal education as a threat to their religion.

During the high school years, rather than send their children to school, the Amish parents trained their children in the vocational aspects of Amish life and tended to the children's spiritual development in preparation for adult baptism, at which time the young people would officially join the Amish church community. The parents worried that sending the children to high school, which they believe stresses competition and intellectual pursuits, would contradict their religious teachings (based on a simple lifestyle and cooperation) and so violate their right to free exercise of their religion as guaranteed by the free exercise clause [see **establishment and free exercise clauses**] in the U.S. Constitution's First Amendment.

The state, on the other hand, claimed that its interest in compulsory education was great enough to override the parents' right to choose the path of training for their children. The state based this claim on two arguments: that (1) citizens need education if they are to be effective participants in the political system and that (2) people need education in order to be "self-reliant and self-sufficient participants in society."

When the case ultimately reached the U.S. Supreme Court in 1972, the Court pointed out that although the state's fundamental arguments were true as applied to most people, one of the main tenets of the Amish religion and lifestyle is to be a part of neither the mainstream political nor social systems. Also, the Amish tend to be extremely self-reliant and self-sufficient people, as required by their faith. Not only do the Amish shun **welfare,** but Congress even enacted legislation exempting them from paying social security taxes, since they reject receiving social security benefits. The Court also cited expert testimony given at the trial that forcing the Amish children to attend high school "could not only result in great psychological harm to Amish children, because of the conflicts it would produce, but would also . . . ultimately result in the destruction of the Old Order Amish church community as it exists in the United States today."

The Court decided in favor of the parents and declared that the First Amendment did, in fact, prevent the state from requiring formal education of the Amish children past the eighth grade. The Court found that the Amish had made a showing that few other religious groups could make in demonstrating the sincerity of their religious beliefs and the extent to which these beliefs molded their lifestyle. The state, on the other hand, had failed to show a compelling interest that would justify abridging the parents' right to free exercise of their religion.

Wisconsin v. Yoder opened the door for other religion-based objections to the compulsory attendance laws. However, courts tend to look strictly at such claims, and the parents must convincingly demonstrate that their objections to the law stem from religious convictions—not merely from their culture or lifestyle.

WORKERS' COMPENSATION Insurance money paid to a worker who suffers a work-related injury. Most workers' compensation statutes require a showing of a clear relationship between the employment and the injury. Where the injury is sudden and physical, this is generally not a problem. For example, when a house painter falls off his ladder and breaks his leg the causal relationship between his job and his injury is readily apparent.

In the case of teachers, however, sometimes cases arise in which the teacher claims that work-related mental stress caused his or her injury. In these cases, the necessary relationship is easier to show where the mental stress is sudden. For example, a teacher who is attacked in the hallway and suffers a heart attack brought on by fright would probably not have a difficult time establishing his or her case. It might be more difficult, on the other hand, to establish that chronic, ongoing stress ultimately caused a heart attack or ulcer, but all states recognize that a job-related mental stimulus can cause a compensable physical injury. For instance, a data processing instructor at an Oklahoma university was able to recover workers' compensation for a heart attack caused by chronic anxiety over a conflict with his manager, a poor evaluation, and fear of losing his job. [*Decker v. Oklahoms State Tech. Univ.*, 766 P.2d 1371 (Okla. 1988)]

Cases in which the injury is caused by a mental stimulus, such as stress, and is mental in nature are touchier. Not all states accept such claims. Of those states that do recognize these claims, some require that the mental stimulus be sudden. Others, such as New York, require that the mental stimulus be unusual.

In one particularly interesting New York case, a former vocational high school cosmetology instructor with a long history of mental illness appealed for many years the decision to deny his claim for mental injury caused by unspecified types of job-related stress. He suffered a mental breakdown during the 1967–1968 school year; in 1970, he shot his supervisor to death and was acquitted by reason of insanity. In 1989, a court reversed the decision to deny his workers' compensation claim. This surprised his attorney from the manslaughter case, who was quoted as saying, "In the trial, we proved he was crazy way before that. . . ."

Y

YEAR-ROUND SCHOOLS A number of schools have begun experimenting in recent years with year-round schedules for two reasons. First, many see it as an improvement over the traditional 180-day schedule, which many argue allows students to backslide over the long summer vacation and potentially require remediation each fall. Second, many see a year-round schedule as a means for keeping up with the number of new students pouring into public schools each year and the inability of school budgets to provide for a sufficient number of new schools to accommodate the growth. By staying open all year and dividing the student body into "tracks," one of which is always on vacation, a school can serve a greater number of students. Whatever the reason, more and more schools are adopting such a schedule; 42 percent of students in the public schools of Los Angeles were enrolled in year-round programs as of 1994.

Proponents of year-round schooling point out that the traditional nine-month school year developed in response to the needs of agricultural families for the help of their children during the summer months. It found support during World War II, when psychologists declared that vacations would increase the productivity of factory workers. These vacations were usually scheduled during the summer, when teachers would be available as short-term replacement labor. The nine-month school year does not work as well, however, with today's families, many of which do not have a parent at home during the day.

While students, parents, and teachers are usually resistant to the idea of losing the long summer vacation, many eventually decide the new system is better. Some, however, do not, which can lead to problems. Some parents, for example, do not like having children assigned to different tracks, which can make it difficult to coordinate family vacations. School systems that adopt year-round schedules for some of their schools must decide how to handle such complaints. Will the rules allow parents to request waivers so their children will be sent to schools with traditional schedules? If so, will the district provide transportation to the new schools?

Some teachers like the idea of working in the schools all year and feel that the year-round schedule enhances the professionalism of teaching. Others, however, count on lengthy summer vacations for respite or for supplemental employment. Switching schools to a year-round schedule inevitably raises issues with teachers' unions. The **National Education Association (NEA),** for example, stated this position on the matter in 1987:

> The [NEA] believes that local affiliates must participate fully in the design, authorization, implementation, evaluation, and continuation of year-round schools. . . . Employment in these programs must be on a voluntary basis.

The law in California reflects this position, requiring that school districts implementing year-round schedules in some schools "make every reasonable effort to assign certificated employees who prefer the regular school schedule to schools of the same level retaining the regular school schedule."

For Further Reading

Alexander, Kern, and M. David Alexander. *The Law of Schools, Students, and Teachers in a Nut Shell.* St. Paul, MN: West Publishing Co. 1984.

This book is now fairly out of date. Even so, it provides an excellent overview of the history of education law up to the date of publication.

Bartlett, Larry D. and Lelia B. Helms. *Recent Developments in Public Education Law.* Topeka: National Organization on Legal Problems of Education. 1994.

This booklet is a re-print of a 1993 report of the American Bar Association's Committee on Public Education. It touches on a variety of topics, from student constitutional rights to special education to issues in higher education, but it does not provide comprehensive coverage of any particular area.

Bosmajian, Haig A., ed. The First Amendment in the Classroom Series. New York: Neal-Schuman Publishers, Inc.

Each book in this series—*The Freedom to Read Books, Films and Plays* (1987); *Freedom of Religion* (1987); *Freedom of Expression* (1988); and *Academic Freedom* (1989)—provides synopses and the actual opinions of various court cases pertaining to education.

Hudgins, H. C., Jr., and Richard S. Vacca. *Law and Education: Contemporary Issues and Court Decisions.* Charlottesville, VA: The Michie Company. 1991.

Besides providing in-depth coverage of the many facets of public education law, this book also provides two helpful chapters that give an overview of the American legal system and that explain how to use the tools of legal research to do independent research in law libraries.

Journal of Law & Education. Cincinnati, OH: Jefferson Law Book Company.

Quarterly publication edited at the South Carolina Law Center and the University of Louisville School of Law. Each issue contains several in-depth articles regarding emerging issues in school law, as well as abstracts of recent cases concerning education law and of recent related articles in other law reviews.

Levin, Michael I. *United States School Laws and Rules.* St. Paul, MN: West Publishing Co. 1995.

Compilation of federal statutes and regulations affecting education law, such as Goals 2000 and the Individuals with Disabilities Education Act. The 1995 edition was the second annual edition published, and the publisher hopes to recompile and republish annually.

McCarthy, Martha M., and Nelda H. Cambron. *Public School Law: Teachers' and Students' Rights.* Boston: Allyn and Bacon, Inc. 1981.

Divided into two sections, one devoted to teachers and the law and the other to students and the law, this book provides a good foundation in the area of public education law as well as a glossary of basic legal terms.

Mawdsley, Ralph D. *Legal Problems of Religious and Private Schools.* Topeka, KS: National Organization on Legal Problems of Education. 1995.

While most sources on education law concentrate on the arena of public education, this book concentrates on the private arena and covers topics such as tort liability, contractual considerations, and the application of federal anti-discrimination legislation.

Price, Janet R., Alan H. Levine, and Eve Cary. *The Rights of Students.* Carbondale and Edwardsville: Southern Illinois University Press. 1988.

Part of a series of books published by the American Civil Liberties Union concerning the rights of certain individuals, such as employees, prisoners, and young people. Written in a question-and-answer format, this book is easily understood by laypeople.

Reutter, E. Edmund, Jr. *Schools and the Law.* Dobbs Ferry, NY: Oceana Publications, Inc. 1981.

A brief overview of school law published by the National Association of Secondary School Principals.

Rubin, David, with Steven Greenhouse. *The Rights of Teachers.* Toronto: Bantam Books. 1983.

Another volume in the American Civil Liberties Union series concerning individual rights. Although it is over 15 years old now, it is still useful as a starting point for teachers interested in learning more about their rights.

School Law Bulletin. Chapel Hill: Institute of Government, University of North Carolina at Chapel Hill.

Periodical published quarterly with a focus on North Carolina legislation pertaining to higher education as well as to elementary and secondary education. Despite the focus on North Carolina law, many of the articles provide a national overview of the topics covered.

Tyack, David, Thomas James, and Aaron Benavot. *Law and the Shaping of Public Education: 1785–1954*. Madison: University of Wisconsin Press. 1987.

An excellent overview of the historical development of the American education system, this book recognizes the highly political nature of public education.

Van Geel, Tyll. *The Courts and American Education Law*. Buffalo, NY: Prometheus Books. 1987.

A lengthy and well-indexed volume providing in-depth coverage of trends in school law issues through the mid-1980s.

Yearbook of Education Law. Topeka, KS: National Organization on Legal Problems of Education.

Comprehensive collection of abstracts of cases affecting education law published annually since 1933.

Table of Cases

Haug v. Franklin, 690 S.W.2d 646 (Tex. Ct. App. 1985), 92
Hazelwood School District v. Kuhlmeier, 484 U.S. 260 (1988), 63, 120, 138–139, 180–181
Healy v. Independent School District No. 625, 962 F.2d 1304 (8th Cir. 1992), 197
Hedges v. Wauconda Community United School District, 9 F.3d 1295 (7th Cir. 1993), 95
Helbig v. City of New York, 597 N.Y.S.2d 585 (N.Y. Sup. 1993), 105
Hendrick Hudson Board of Education v. Rowley, 458 U.S. 176 (1982), 141–142, 156–157, 170
Hobson v. Henson, 269 F. Supp. 401 (D.D.C. 1967), 243
Hoffman v. Board of Education of the City of New York, 400 N.E.2d 317 (N.Y. 1979), 107
Honig v. Doe, 484 U.S. 305 (1988), 148–149, 157, 248
Hortonville Joint School District No. 1 v. Hortonville Education Association, 426 U.S. 482 (1976), 239
Hunter v. Carbondale Area School District, 829 F. Supp. 714 (M.D. Pa. 1993), 67
Immediato v. Rye Neck School District, 873 F. Supp. 846 (S.D.N.Y. 1995), 69
In re Isiah B., 500 N.W.2d 637 (Wis. 1993), 166
In re Jackson, 352 S.E.2d 449 (N.C. Ct. App. 1987), 35
In re Joseph G., 38 Cal. Rptr. 2d 902 (Cal. Ct. App. 1995), 165
In re William G., 709 P.2d 1287 (Cal. 1985), 165
Ingebretsen v. Jackson Public School District, 864 F. Supp. 1473 (S.D. Miss. 1994), 190
Ingraham v. Wright, 430 U.S. 651 (1977), 80
IOTA XI Chapter v. George Mason University, 993 F.2d 386 (4th Cir. 1993), 119
Israel v. West Virginia Secondary Schools Activities Commission, 388 S.E.2d 480 (W. Va. 1989), 44
Jeffries v. Harleston, 21 F.3d 1238 (2d Cir. 1994), 120
Jeglin v. San Jacinto Unified School District, 827 F. Supp. 1459 (C.D. Cal. 1993), 124
Johnson v. Dixon, 501 S.W.2d 256 (Ky. 1973), 241
Johnson v. Lincoln Christian College, 501 N.E.2d 1380 (Ill. Ct. App. 1986), 93
Joki v. Board of Education of Schuylerville Central School District, 745 F. Supp. 823 (N.D.N.Y. 1990), 206
Jones v. Clear Creek Independent School District, 977 F.2d 963 (5th Cir. 1992), 161–162, 189

Jones v. Latexo Independent School District, 499 F. Supp. 223 (E.D. Tex. 1980), 231
Kadrmas v. Dickinson Public Schools, 487 U.S. 450 (1988), 216
Kansas City Star Co. v. Fulson, 859 S.W.2d 934 (Mo. Ct. App. 1993), 184
Katzman v. Cumberland Valley School District, 479 A.2d 671 (Pa. Commw. Ct. 1988), 20
Keyishian v. Board of Regents, 385 U.S. 589 (1967), 17
Klein v. Smith, 635 F. Supp. 1440 (D. Me. 1986), 73
Lamb's Chapel v. Center Moriches Union Free School District, 113 S. Ct. 2141 (1993), 35, 111
Lamont v. Woods, 948 F.2d 825 (2d Cir. 1991), 116
Lander v. Seaver, 32 Vt. 114, 76 Am. Dec. 156 (1859), 73
Lanner v. Wimmer, 463 F. Supp. 867 (D. Utah 1978), 205
Larry P. v. Riles, 502 F.2d 963 (9th Cir. 1974), 160
Lau v. Nichols, 414 U.S. 563 (1974), 108–109
Lawton v. Steele, 152 U.S. 133 (1894), 247
Lee v. Weisman, 505 U.S. 577 (1992), 36, 161–162, 189
Lemon v. Kurtzman, 403 U.S. 602 (1971), 94, 121, 162–163, 189, 193, 206, 210, 240
Lenzer v. Shawano-Gresham School District, 458 N.W.2d 388 (Wis. Ct. App. 1990), 234
Levin v. Harleston, 770 F. Supp. 895 (S.D.N.Y. 1991), 120
Lexington Theological Seminary v. Vance 596 S.W.2d 11 (Ky. Ct. App. 1979), 93
Lynch v. Donnely, 465 U.S. 668 (1984), 210
McCollum v. Board of Education, 333 U.S. 203 (1948), 204
McGlothin v. Jackson Municipal Separate School District, 829 F. Supp. 853 (S.D. Miss. 1992), 209
McIntire v. Bethel School, 804 F. Supp. 1415 (W.D. Okla. 1992), 98
McNeal v. Tate County School District, 508 F.2d 1017 (5th Cir. 1975), 243
McWright v. Alexander, 771 F. Supp. 256 (N.D. Ill. 1991), 203
Martinez v. School District No. 60, 852 P.2d 1275 (Colo. Ct. App. 1992), 33
Massachusetts Board of Retirement v. Murgia, 427 U.S. 307 (1976), 28
Maynard v. Greater Hoyt School District, 876 F. Supp. 1104 (D.S.D. 1995), 57
Means v. Sidiropolis, 401 S.E.2d 447 (W. Va. 1990), 99
Melton v. Young, 465 F.2d 1332 (6th Cir. 1972), 75
Merriken v. Cressman, 364 F. Supp. 913 (E.D. Pa. 1973), 55
Meyer v. Nebraska, 262 U.S. 390 (1923), 10, 17, 102, 172–173
Mills v. Board of Education of the District of Columbia, 318 F. Supp. 866 (D.D.C. 1972), 1, 173, 232

Minarcini v. Strongsville City School District, 541 F.2d 577 (6th Cir. 1976), 164
Minersville v. Gobitis, 310 U.S. 586 (1940), 188
Mississippi Employment Security Commission v. McGlothin, 556 So. 2d 324 (Miss. 1990), 209
Mississippi University for Women v. Hogan, 458 U.S. 718 (1982), 224
Missouri v. Jenkins, 115 S. Ct. 2038 (1995), 169
Moody v. Cronin, 484 F. Supp. 270 (C.D. Ill. 1979), 84
Morris v. Clarksville-Montgomery County Consolidated Board of Education, 867 S.W.2d 324 (Tenn. Ct. App. 1993), 75
Morrison v. Board of Education, 461 P.2d 375 (Cal. 1969), 75
Mozert v. Hawkins County Board of Education, 827 F.2d 1058 (6th Cir. 1987), 85
Napolitano v. Princeton University, 453 A.2d 263 (N.J. Ct. App. 1982), 187
NCAA v. Board of Regents, 468 U.S. 85 (1984), 39
Nelson v. Board of Education, 587 A.2d 1327 (N.J. Sup. Ct. 1991), 196
New Jersey v. T.L.O., 469 U.S. 325 (1985), 33, 101, 165, 179–180, 231, 232–233
NLRB v. Jones & Laughlin Steel Corp., 301 U.S. 1 (1937), 129
Nola M. v. University of Southern California, 20 Cal. Rptr. 2d 97 (Cal. Ct. App. 1993), 61
North Carolina v. Whittle Communications, 402 S.E.2d 556 (N.C. 1991), 24
Novak v. Revere Local School District, 583 N.E.2d 1358 (Ohio Ct. App. 1989), 196
Ordway v. Hargraves, 323 F. Supp. 1155 (D. Mass. 1971), 191
Palmer v. Ticcione, 576 F.2d 459 (2d Cir. 1978), 28
Pandazides v. Virginia Board of Education, 804 F. Supp. 794 (E.D. Va. 1992), 204
P.A.R.C. v. Commonwealth of Pennsylvania, 334 F. Supp. 1257 (E.D. Pa. 1971), 1, 173, 185–186, 232
Parducci v. Rutland, 316 F. Supp. 352 (M.D. Ala. 1970), 18
Parents United for Better Schools v. School District of Philadelphia Board of Education, 646 A.2d 689 (Pa. Commw. Ct. 1994), 71
Peloza v. Capistrano Unified School District, 37 F.3d 517 (9th Cir. 1994), 82
People ex rel. O'Sullivan v. New York Law School, 22 N.Y.S. 663 (1893), 92
People v. DeJonge, 449 N.W.2d 899 (Mich. 1989), 238
People v. Dukes, 580 N.Y.S.2d 850 (N.Y. City Crim. Ct. 1992), 171
Perry Education Association v. Perry Local Educators' Association, 460 U.S. 37 (1983), 63

School District of Abington Township v. Schempp, 374 U.S. 203 (1963), 48–49, 161, 190, 215
Scopes v. State, 289 S.W. 363 (Tenn. 1927), 36, 82, 222
Searcy v. Harris, 888 F. Supp. 1314 (11th Cir. 1989), 139
Sherman v. Community Consolidated School District, 8 F.3d 1160 (7th Cir. 1993), 95
Sherman v. Community Consolidated School District, 980 F.2d 437 (7th Cir. 1992), 188
Shuman v. Cumberland Valley School District Board of Directors, 536 A.2d 490 (Pa. Commw. Ct. 1988), 91
Silva v. University of New Hampshire, 888 F. Supp. 293 (D.N.H. 1994), 19
Slocum v. Holton Board of Education, 429 N.W.2d 607 (1988), 20
Slotterback v. Interboro School District, 766 F. Supp. 280 (E.D. Pa. 1991), 94
Smith v. Regents of University of California, 844 P.2d 500 (Cal. 1993), 217
Smith v. St. Tammany Parish School Board, 316 F. Supp. 1174 (E.D. La. 1970), 75
Snow v. State, 485 N.Y.S.2d 987 (N.Y. 1984), 107
Snyder v. Charlotte Public School District, 333 N.W.2d 542 (Mich. Ct. App. 1983), 228
Springdale School District v. Grace, 693 F.2d 41 (8th Cir. 1982), 171
State v. Board of School Directors, 111 N.W.2d 198 (Wis. 1961), 18
State v. Mark Anthony B., 433 S.E.2d 41 (W. Va. 1993), 233
State v. School Board of Sarasota County, 561 So.2d 549 (Fla. 1990), 52
Steffan v. Perry, 41 F.3d 677 (D.C. Cir. 1994), 147
Steirer v. Bethlehem Area School District, 987 F.2d 989 (3d Cir. 1993), 68
Stone v. Graham, 449 U.S. 39 (1980), 240
Student Press Law Center v. Alexander, 778 F. Supp. 1227 (D.D.C. 1991), 57
Sturrup v. Mahan, 305 N.E.2d 877 (Ind. 1974), 42
Sullivan v. Zebley, 493 U.S. 521 (1990), 252
Sunshine Books, Ltd. v. Temple University, 697 F.2d 90 (3d Cir. 1980), 38
Swann v. Charlotte-Mecklenburg Board of Education, 402 U.S. 1 (1971), 57–58
Tinker v. Des Moines Independent School District, 393 U.S. 503 (1969), 2, 47–48, 63, 76, 94, 97, 119, 123, 133, 139, 242–243
Tobias v. University of Texas, 824 S.W.2d 201 (Tex. Ct. App. 1991), 128
Toungate v. Bastrop Independent School District, 842 S.W.2d 823 (Tex. Ct. App. 1992), 224
United States v. Board of Education for the School District of Philadelphia, 911 F.2d 882 (3d Cir. 1990), 209
United States v. Board of Education, 832 F. Supp 836 (D. N.J. 1993), 25, 203

Index

LaVergne, TN USA
22 May 2010
183543LV00002B/49/P

9 780874 368130